The Signature of Power

The Signature of Power

SOVEREIGNTY, GOVERNMENTALITY AND BIOPOLITICS

MITCHELL DEAN

Los Angeles | London | New Delhi
Singapore | Washington DC

Los Angeles | London | New Delhi
Singapore | Washington DC

SAGE Publications Ltd
1 Oliver's Yard
55 City Road
London EC1Y 1SP

SAGE Publications Inc.
2455 Teller Road
Thousand Oaks, California 91320

SAGE Publications India Pvt Ltd
B 1/I 1 Mohan Cooperative Industrial Area
Mathura Road
New Delhi 110 044

SAGE Publications Asia-Pacific Pte Ltd
3 Church Street
#10-04 Samsung Hub
Singapore 049483

Editor: Chris Rojek
Editorial assistant: Martine Jonsrud
Production editor: Katherine Haw
Copyeditor: Kate Harrison
Proofreader: Mary Dalton
Marketing manager: Michael Ainsley
Cover design: Lisa Harper
Typeset by: C&M Digitals (P) Ltd, Chennai, India
Printed and bound by
CPI Group (UK) Ltd, Croydon, CR0 4YY

© Mitchell Dean 2013

First published 2013

Library of Congress Control Number: 2012953382

British Library Cataloguing in Publication data

A catalogue record for this book is available from
the British Library

ISBN 978-1-4462-5699-2
ISBN 978-1-4462-5700-5 (pbk)

CONTENTS

ABOUT THE AUTHOR

Mitchell Dean is author of *Governmentality: Power and Rule in Modern Society* (1999, revised second edition, Sage, 2010), Professor of Public Governance, Copenhagen Business School, Denmark, and Professor of Sociology at the University of Newcastle, Australia. His previous books include *The Constitution of Poverty: Toward a Genealogy of Liberal Governance* (Routledge, 1991/2012), *Critical and Effective Histories: Foucault's Methods and Historical Sociology* (Routledge, 1994), and *Governing Societies: Political Perspectives on Domestic and International Rule* (Open University Press, 2007). He co-edited with Barry Hindess, the first national application of governmentality studies, *Governing Australia: Studies in Contemporary Rationalities of Government* (Cambridge University Press, 1998). He has previously held the positions of Professor of Sociology and Dean of the Division of Society, Culture, Media and Philosophy at Macquarie University, Sydney. His publications range across a large number of fields focusing on problems of government, sovereignty and power, liberalism and neo-liberalism, political and social thought, historical sociology, and social and public policy. However he has also published on topics as diverse as risk management, e-government, political mythology, ancient societies, war and peace, contemporary art, cinema and fashion. Among his current projects are ones on the political morphology of the event and the reconfiguration of the social domain.

ACKNOWLEDGEMENTS

I warmly thank Chris Rojek for his suggestion that I might write a book bringing the concept of power up to date, although he of course cannot be held responsible for the outcome; John Potts for providing an excellent sounding board for many of the ideas found here; and Jeni Porter for her continued support, love and care. I have benefited from the many individual responses I received at two public lectures which introduced the thesis of the book in the autumn of 2012: at the Centre for Advanced International Theory at the University of Sussex, and at the Security and Publics workshop at Carleton University, Ottawa. I am grateful to Hans-Martin Jaeger for providing me with a very thoughtful critique and appraisal of my presentation of the argument at the latter event, and to Angie Bletsas for her attempts to integrate my 'theoretical' work into the concerns of her workshop on Public Governance at the Intersection of Welfare and Work at the University of South Australia. I must also thank my colleagues at the University of Newcastle, particularly John Germov, for providing me with the time and the intellectual space to write this book, and to all those colleagues there who patiently listened and politely questioned me on the several occasions I presented what must have seemed strange lines of inquiry.

The introduction to this book has drawn upon a paper originally published as 'The Signature of Power' in the *Journal of Political Power* (2012), volume 5, number 1, pages 101–17, www.tandfonline.com.

1

INTRODUCING THE SIGNATURE OF POWER

1.1 The concept of power has long been central not only to the social and political sciences but also in everyday language and discussion. We often assume that we know what we mean when we use the term and that it helps us describe the world in which we live. Yet, today there are some influential thinkers who will claim that 'power' cannot explain anything and that therefore it is a relatively useless concept. In doing so, they reject a longstanding reason for the study of power: to offer a critique of society, its institutions and practices and even its ways of reasoning and forms of knowledge. Explicitly or implicitly, such critique implies that there are alternative ways of doing things. Perhaps this involves overcoming or overturning power, or more simply, particularly in the case of the complex history of liberalism, making sure its exercise is legitimate. This means asking certain types of question. How can power be made accountable and transparent? How can power be made safe from its inherent dangers? How can we guard against the corruption inherent in it, for as Lord Action wrote in 1887, and every schoolchild now learns: '[p]ower tends to corrupt and absolute power corrupts absolutely' (Dalberg-Acton, 1907: 504). These kinds of question about the appropriate, safe and legitimate use of power are normative ones. They concern the 'ought' of power, rather than power as an actuality or operation.

Our starting point is more analytical than normative. An analytics of power is less interested in the normative questions of how power should be exercised than the establishment of perspectives and concepts that help us understand how power relations operate. This distinction, of course, is far from clear-cut and every description of power implies an ethos or orientation. Looked at in a certain way, every analytical, descriptive or diagnostic statement about power contains within it a normative evaluation of the phenomenon under discussion. If we say, for example, that in contemporary liberal-democracies, 'sovereign forms of power have been replaced by complex networks of governance', or that 'a biopolitics of the population has been replaced by a more grassroots vital politics', we appear to be offering an analysis. Yet each of these contains a normative element that could endorse current social and political arrangements over past ones. However, that does not mean that we should refrain from attempting to develop an analytically oriented set of concepts.

This book seeks to combine that rigorous approach to concept and method with an ethos that might appear contrary to it. It wants to maintain a sense of the essential mystery of power as a set of concepts and practices, that power is not as obvious as we think it or as passé as some contemporary thinkers maintain. It asks the reader to journey into some obscure and arcane topics and stories in the service of understanding this term.

But first, what is power? In many languages there is more than one term for what is meant by the English word 'power'. Thus in German *Kraft* and *Macht*, and in French, *puissance* and *pouvoir*, broadly contrast the force of something with the capacity to do something. In this sense they allow us to distinguish between the power of the President's speech, that is, of its rhetoric, logic, and arguments, and his power as Commander-in-Chief of the United States' military. Despite this situation, each of these languages has a key equivalent in the scientific discussion of power: *Macht* in German, *pouvoir* in French and *potere* in Italian. In the romance languages, these same words serve as a noun for power and a verb for 'can', thus underlying the closeness of the relationship between power and capacity, ability or potentiality. Centrally, in these three languages, *Macht*, *pouvoir* and *potere*, are the terms one uses to express the case when someone has power over someone else.

This is a commonplace observation but it allows us to make a point that is far from trivial: the concept of power is located in a dense field of distinctions and relations with many other terms. In English, there is authority, domination, legitimacy, jurisdiction, violence, government, coercion, control, capability, capacity, ability, force, and so on. In this respect, we can agree with a point made by Mark Haugaard (2010) that it is not enough to recognize, as we have since at least Steven Lukes (1974), that power is 'an essentially contested concept' (Gallie, 1956). We must also accept that there is no essence to the concept of power beyond its contested uses. Haugaard instead, following Wittgenstein, permits only a set of 'family resemblances' between uses and concepts of the term.

This view provides us with two starting points. The first is the simple one that the study of power should be broad in its themes, its topics and its perspectives, and be prepared to accept that the exploration of the concept of power might lead us to the most unexpected of places. This book takes up that challenge in its approach and its structure. The second is that to propose that there is no essence of power is not to say that there is no discernable structure or architecture to these 'family relations' that obtain between concepts of power. So we start from the presupposition that it is possible to chart, to map, or to make a diagram of, the ways in which various senses, concepts, ideas and even theories of power exist in relation to one another. This, as the reader will discover, is captured by the idea of 'signature' in this book's title.

The initial horizon for the present investigation of concepts of power was to contribute to an understanding of its conceptualization and ultimately to both its 'genealogy' (the study of the conditions of emergence of organized practices and ways of thinking), and its 'analytics' (the key questions that might be asked of how power operates in any given situation). By the end of this book, this starting point will lead us not only to endorse the genealogy of the arts of government and an analytics of power, as Michel Foucault called them, but to a number of other projects: a political archaeology of glory, a historical sociology of sovereignty and an analytics of sovereign practices, a political morphology of the event and an analytics of publicity. These projects are a part of a research program about power that emerges when one considers not only the work of Foucault, which we will do, but that of two other thinkers, both controversial to different degrees – Carl Schmitt and Giorgio Agamben. In addition, many other thinkers are considered here, often with lines of descent from Max Weber, and the book will address themes and areas not usually found in books on the concept of power. These include Christian theological arguments about the Trinitarian 'economy', order and providence and the study of religious and political rituals and symbols. They also include organizing terms and debates, such as secularization, rationalization, and legitimation, that address the novelty or otherwise of the present, including its forms of power, in relation to the past. Importantly the book focuses on three concepts that have occupied much of the recent discussion about different forms, types, zones, or clusters of relations of power: sovereignty, government (or governmentality), and biopolitics. Rather than seek to define them at the outset, or how we might approach them, we shall let them emerge from the work under discussion.

The investigation proper begins with the next chapter. The main point of this introductory chapter is to provide and illustrate the key that will help us explore this mysterious terrain and that will allow us to begin to examine the structure of these 'family resemblances'. We will call this the signature of power, notwithstanding that the use of the term 'signature' here is far more limited than that of its most renowned recent exponent, Agamben. This introductory chapter is a preparation for a journey, not the journey itself. It situates the journey in the much wider geography and identifies the 'signature' as a kind of passport that allows us to move freely from one territory to another. Just as getting one's passport is not as exciting as the places it allows you to visit, but is essential if you wish to do so, the demonstration and definition of the signature of power is nowhere near as interesting as the exploration it allows.

Concepts of power

1.2 For the lay person, it is hardly necessary to pause and consider the notion of power. Power is quite self-evidently the preserve of the powerful, is exercised over those with less power or the powerless, and ensures that those who hold it get their way in most situations and typically gain substantial material or other rewards. This definition of course is tautological and would please neither logicians nor social and political scientists. Yet when the most famous of sociologists, Max Weber, formulated a definition of power in the early years of the twentieth century he did so with something similar to this view of power in mind:

> 'Power' is the probability that one actor within a social relationship will be in a position to carry out his own will despite resistance, regardless of the basis on which that probability rests. (1968: 53)

Since then this definition of the form of power has been repeated and refined many times, most eminently by Robert Dahl and Steven Lukes. Dahl, writing in McCarthyite America, translated something like this into the alphabetical terms that would kick off 'the community power debate' with what he saw as a 'bedrock idea of power':

> A has power over B to the extent that he can get B to do something B would not otherwise do. (1957: 202–3)

Continuing in the same vein, Steven Lukes, in a discussion which both completed that debate and inaugurated much of the recent discussion of power, stated:

> The absolutely basic common core to, or primitive notion lying behind, all talk of power is the notion that A in some way affects B ... in a non-trivial or significant manner. (1974: 24)

In recent years, these definitions of power are less the building blocks of a theory of power than the point from which that theory departs. While all three suggest a situation of two or more actors in which one realizes its aims or will at the expense of others, we see a shift from Weber's notion of power as probability, and hence as a capacity or even potentiality, to Dahl's concept of power as something possessed, although his own formulae are expressed as probabilities. This idea of power as possessed has been called into question, most famously by Foucault (1979: 94), and all three quotes could be read as implying a 'zero-sum' conception of power in which the exercise of power by one actor subtracts from the power, or even the freedom, of other actors.

In so far as all three imply an asymmetrical relationship between more than one actor, they could be viewed as instances of power as 'power over', itself occasionally identified with domination. However, Weber's definition of power also contains the fundamental notion of the capacity of an actor to carry out his own will. In this sense, Weber's definition encompasses an even more basic sense of the word power as capacity. This idea of power as 'power to', or the capacity of actors to achieve their purposes, can be found in the canonical figure of the English state-theorist of the seventeenth century, Thomas Hobbes: 'The Power of a Man is his present means to obtain some future apparent Good' (1996: 62). We have already, then, departed from the everyday view of power with which we started. Power is not simply the power of one actor (individual, institution, etc.) over another or others, but, even more fundamentally, the capacity to achieve some desired end. We can thus distinguish between power into 'power over' and 'power to'.

Barry Hindess (1996) has argued that 'power to' and 'power over' are each variants of a notion of power as a kind of quantitative capacity to realize an actor's will, and so part of a single conception of power. This conception, he insists, can be contrasted with the other major conception or discourse of power in the West, power as right, or legitimate power. This conception of power usually appears in relation to what Hindess calls sovereign power, 'the power that is thought to be exercised by the rule of the state or by its (central) government' (1996: 12). This kind of power for Hindess is most clearly exemplified in the work of a later English political theorist, John Locke, with his notion of political power both as the right to make laws and the capacity to enforce them (Hindess, 1996: 52). Power as right is hence a concern with the legitimacy of political power, which Locke and the framers of the American Declaration of Independence viewed as residing in the decision of the people themselves (p. 53). In Locke's case, the crucial question, 'Who decides?', is answered with the 'people'. However, as John Dunn and Quentin Skinner have both pointed out, Locke provided an account of the origins of legitimate government, not every occasion of the exercise of political power by it (Dunn, 1969: 141–7; Skinner, 1998: 27, n. 84).

With Max Weber, this question of power as right, or what he calls legitimate domination is less a feature which may or may not reside in the relationship of people to their government, and more the sociologically specifiable conditions which secure the compliance of subjects to most, if not all, the commands of the ruler. Unlike Locke, legitimacy is secured on different grounds, including legal, charismatic and traditional ones (Weber, 1968: 215). However, in modern types of administration, legitimacy for Weber bears a striking similarity to Locke's notion of political power as the right to make and enforce laws in that it is based on rational grounds 'resting on a belief in the legality of enacted rule and the rules of those elevated to authority under such rules to issue commands'. In many twentieth-century variants of liberalism and in notions of 'good governance', the domination of the state is held to be legitimate to the extent to which it corresponds to the 'rule of law'.

Another antinomy thus displaces that between 'power to' and 'power over'. This is power as capacity (including power to and power over) and power as right or legitimate power (itself including the effective capacity of law enforcement). Even those who start from 'power over' find themselves drawn to the problem of legitimacy of power. Thus Lukes famously asks, in relation to what he calls the 'third dimension of power':

> Is not the supreme and most insidious example of power to prevent people, to whatever degree, from having grievances by shaping their perceptions, cognitions and preferences in such a way that they accept their role in the existing order of things, either because they can see or imagine no alternative to it, or because they see it as natural and unchangeable, or because they see it as divinely ordained and beneficial? (1974: 24)

Lukes's third dimension of power clearly rests upon the idea of power as right. The idea that power so shapes people's consciousness that they are not in a position to know, let alone air, their grievances, implies a 'radical' view of power. Lukes thus presupposes an ideal of a community of morally autonomous individuals who would be capable of giving consent to the exercise of political and social power, had they not been prevented by its 'supreme and insidious' exercise. Lukes therefore holds not only a conception of power as 'power over' but as legitimate or illegitimate as the case may be. While power as the capacity to realize one's will is usually thought to imply an analytical or empirical approach concerned to describe how power is exercised, power as right implies an ideal of how power ought to be exercised, and is thus at the basis of many normative conceptions of power.

The idea of a community of morally autonomous subjects who freely consent to the binding commands of sovereign political authority runs through much moral and political philosophy with Locke as a key exemplar. It is found in twentieth-century critical theory, such as that of Herbert Marcuse's critique of one-dimensional man and Jürgen Habermas's specification of the conditions for an ideal speech situation, and in the Italian Marxist, Antonio Gramsci's view of hegemony. In the latter, the rule of the bourgeoisie in advanced capitalist societies is based on both coercion and consent, but consent is given by those who do not know it is in their interests to overthrow the system of capitalist production. This is of course very similar to Lukes's view. Alongside the distinction between power over and power to, and between power as capacity and power as right, we have empirical (or analytical) and normative conceptions of power. The defining characteristic of critical theory, and most of what is called political theory, may be that, however it is analysed, power is approached from such a normative point of view.

We are beginning to get a sense of where the signature of power might lie but we shall first explore two or three more instances of this phenomenon.

1.3 Another distinction is often drawn between conflictual and consensual views of power. The former emphasizes the sense in which power is exercised at the expense of or in relation to another party and focuses on power over or domination. The latter, by contrast, emphasizes what might be called 'power with', a kind of collective version of power to. In the case of the ancient distinction between *potentia* and *potestas*, as taken up by Spinoza, the former represents an original constitutive force. The formation of the state is no longer a foregoing of certain aspects of humans' power in the constitution of the sovereign but remains grounded in the collective power of the multitude (Saar, 2010). Michael Hardt and Antonio Negri (2000) have recently invoked the multitude as a kind of constitutive power that is created by and acts as a counterforce to the forms of power characteristic of the global Empire. While there are a large number of twentieth-century thinkers, including Talcott Parsons, who adopt a consensual view of power, it is Hannah Arendt who most clearly states that:

> Power is always, as we would say, a power potential and not an unchangeable, measurable and reliable entity like force or strength. While strength is the natural quality of an individual seen in isolation, power springs up between men when they act together and vanishes the moment they disperse. (1998: 200)

Unlike recent social scientists who have stressed the dependence of the exercise of power on assemblages made up of technical, material and inhuman elements (Latour, 2005), Arendt strikingly argued that 'the only indispensable material factor in the generation of power is the living together of people' (1998: 201). In this sense, power then concerns plurality. It can be divided without its decrease, *contra* the zero-sum notion of power as domination, and the checks and balances upon power do not repress but facilitate it and generate more power.

Arendt's notion of power opposes power not only to domination, but also to strength, force and to violence. Rather than existing on a continuum of forms of power, it is violence that destroys it, undermining the sense of humans acting in concert. Rule that relies on violence is known as tyranny: 'the time-honored fear of this government is not exclusively inspired by its cruelty...but by the impotence and futility to which it condemns the rulers as well as the ruled' (1998: 202). For Arendt then, we could also oppose a productive conception of power to one of repression. A similar sentiment is found in Foucault for whom neither consent nor violence 'constitute the basic principle or basic nature of power' and whose definition of power as a 'way of acting upon one or more subjects by virtue of their acting or being capable of action' implies something akin to this notion of potential or capacity of all human individuals and collectives (2001: 341).

The attempt to define and characterize power leads us down the path of a multiplying and cross-cutting set of distinctions. The distinctions between productive and repressive, consensus and conflict, 'power with' and domination, power and violence, can be read as versions of 'power to' and 'power over', although they also clearly bring into play conceptions of power as right and normative views of power. A further distinction can be made between what might be called episodic conceptions of power implied in the alphabetical scenarios of the initial definitions and 'economic' conceptions of power.

Foucault's most famous and widely cited work, *Discipline and Punish* (1977) uses the term 'economy of power' surprisingly often. He writes of an 'internal economy of a penalty' (p. 18), imagines situating systems of punishment in a 'certain "political economy" of the body' (p. 25), views the true objective of the eighteenth-century penal reform movement 'as to set up a new "economy" of the power to punish' (p. 82), adopts the 'standpoint of the economy of the power to punish' (p. 99), analyses a 'whole learned economy of publicity' (pp. 109–12), describes the relationship of the new disciplines to the body as one of 'the economy, the efficiency of movements, their internal organization' (p. 137), and shows how the examination 'transformed the economy of visibility into the exercise of power' (p. 187). It is, we might venture, not simply a matter of a metaphor, whether in quotation marks or not, but an indication of an approach to the analysis of power that has become, since his initial contribution, increasingly influential.

One theorist of organizational power, Stewart Clegg (1989), amplified our vocabulary of power when he added two other 'circuits of power' to the episodic exercise of power captured in our initial definitions. They were 'dispositional power', which for him sets up the rules of the game and 'facilitative power' that, like Foucault's notion of 'positive power', establishes the game itself, and forms the actors and agents that enter into episodic interactions. Clegg himself also speaks of an 'economy of power' to capture this sense that practices, such as disciplinary techniques, and forces, coalesce to create the conditions under which actors are shaped and power in its episodic sense might be exercised (p. 18).

This notion of an 'economy of power' is extremely intriguing and has come to occupy a central place in recent discussions of and indeed suspicions of power. Here, economy suggests an ordering, or form of management, of power relations and thus recalls the earliest etymology of economy (or *oikonomia*) as the management of the household (*oikos*) in Ancient Greece. This idea of power as a kind of self-managing order was proposed, without the word economy, in one of the first attempts by Foucault to understand power.

> It seems to me that power must be understood in the first instance as the multiplicity of force relations immanent in the sphere in which they operate and which constitute their own organization ... (1979: 92)

Power comes to be viewed as strategic in this regard and often it is Machiavelli who is invoked as the admittedly scandalous godfather of this conception (by both Clegg and Foucault, for instance). Another contrast thus opens up between the causal, mechanical, episodic view of power, which Clegg regards as Hobbesian, and a strategic, fluid, 'economic' or dispositional view of power, which is Machiavellian.

Clegg presciently drew upon the early work of two French thinkers, Michel Callon and Bruno Latour, who have subsequently made influential interventions in science and technology studies and the study of economics. Their approach, sometimes termed actor-network theory or ANT, has more recently led Latour to the conclusion that:

> 'Drunk with power' is not an expression fit only for generals, presidents, CEOs, mad scientists, and bosses. It can also be used for those sociologists who confuse the expansion of powerful explanations with the composition of the collective. This is why the ANT slogan has always been: 'Be sober with power', that is, abstain as much as possible from using the notion of power in

case it backfires and hits your explanations instead of the target you are aiming for. There should be no powerful explanation without checks and balances. (2005: 260–1)

This conclusion thus juxtaposes the structural analysis of social scientists which presupposes some form of class, gender, racial, or economic, power structure, and the view that power is the outcome of a set of relations of forces, of different actors, technologies, materiality, forms of knowledge and so on. From this perspective, power takes the form of the resultant association and the concept cannot be used to explain anything.

> Once again, we don't want to confuse cause and effect, the *explanandum* with the *explanans*. This is why it's so important to maintain that power, like society, is the final result of a process and not a reservoir, a stock, or a capital that will automatically provide an explanation. Power and domination have to be produced, made up, composed. (Latour, 2005: 63–4)

There have come to exist a plethora of terms, with their own nuances of course that describe this self-organizing 'economic' conception of power. The economy of power was inaugurated with Foucault in recent times but has a long history beginning with the notion of *oikonomia* as the management of the household, found in Aristotle and Xenophon. Foucault used the term *dispositif*, often translated into English as apparatus; it is, however, derived from the Latin *dispositio*, one translation of *oikonomia*. Latour and Callon, following Gilles Deleuze, use the term *agencement* or assemblage. These terms have been applied to science and technology, to law, and as if at last making a rendezvous with their own implicit destiny, to the work of economists in the production, or 'performation', of markets themselves (Callon, 2006).

   All of this suggests how far we have come, just by following recent definitions and uses of the term power, by no means exhaustive but at least illustrative of a vast and rich literature, from the commonsense view of power and the 'power over' definitions we started with. Indeed, it is very hard to generalize about the study of power in the social and political sciences today if we take into account the extraordinary array of disciplines, debates, theories and approaches to the concept, from sociology, political science, anthropology, gender and cultural studies, to fields of management and organization studies.

But all these examples tell us something about the signature of power or at least where we might look to locate it.

Signature of power

1.4 At this point, you, as the reader, should be given thanks for your patience, and we can now state our initial hypothesis, which will be essayed in relation to the key texts and authors this book will address (especially those of Michel Foucault, Carl Schmitt and Giorgio Agamben). This hypothesis is that the concept of power is marked by a kind of permanent movement or reversibility between two poles, themselves changing as a consequence of this movement. The concept of power is only possible as a result of a series of binary distinctions, some of which we have touched on here. We have witnessed this in 'power over' and 'power to', power as capacity and power as right, the consensual and conflictual, and the episodic and economic. There are many more we haven't précised: hard and soft power in Joseph Nye comes immediately to mind. Even when these poles are recognized as instances of something more fundamental, as when 'power to' and 'power over' are revealed as instances of power as capacity, this new concept exists only in opposition to something else, in this case power as right. Similarly, power as capacity and power as right are viewed as elements of juridical theory of sovereign power that is now opposed to the economic, dispositional and facilitative conception of power as an immanent domain of self-organizing forces.

What is distinctive about the concept of power is the way the notion refers us to a set of oppositions that in turn can become unities in relation to other oppositions. What the discussions of the concept of power thereby illustrate is that there is an 'excess' in the concept of power beyond what it might signify or mean, which marks it and forces this movement towards oppositions, their unification and further opposition. In the sense that 'power' is marked by this recurrent bipolarity, it is, to borrow and adapt a term from Agamben, less a concept and more a 'signature' attached to the concept of power (2009: 33–80).

We should, however, distinguish our use of the term from that of Agamben. Quite simply for our purposes the signature of the concept of power entails only three things:

1 That the concept of power is marked by a determinate but historically changing field of interpretative and pragmatic relations, which is very difficult, if not impossible, to evade or escape.

2 That to engage with and use the concept of 'power', we need to recognize its signature, understand how it operates and the different forms it takes, and mobilize it in our analyses.

3 That an analytics of power, the project initiated but not fulfilled by Foucault, cannot be accomplished without this because the signature of power is integral to how we think about, exercise and experience power relations in our societies.

It is too early to make further claims than these about the signature of power. We will be careful not to place the signature of power in a specific 'discursive formation', 'episteme', 'paradigm', or 'rationality', that is, in any framing that denotes a particular temporal or spatial ordering of knowledge or discourse. Neither do we propose the signature as a general interpretative concept, make any claim about concepts in general, nor make any claim about the ineluctable movement of concepts from one domain to another, such as from the sacred to the profane, or the theological to the political, unlike many of the thinkers we shall discuss.

We simply observe that the signature is present in much European-derived political thought since at least the 'early-modern' period of the seventeenth century, if not before, and can be found in most, if not all, contemporary academic discussions in disciplines such as political science, sociology and jurisprudence. Rather than proposing a general account of the source of the concept of power in Christian theology, our central concern is the way this signature places power (which in its most basic semantics is nothing more than capacity or potentiality in the sense of the word 'can') into a political domain, both in the narrow sense of the government of the state, including its law-making and law-enforcing activities, and in the broader sense of the antagonistic relations between groups internally characterized by a degree of unanimity. Our central concern is thus with the renovation of the concept of power through an understanding of its signature and how its works.

The concern here, as we put it before, is with the architecture or structure of family relations of concepts of power. While we are interested in the claims of those thinkers who link political concepts, particularly power, to a theological inheritance, we make no general claims that the signature of power explains its inheritance from theology, or that its signature necessarily refers power back to these theological origins, or that the signature substitutes for the empirical analysis of the transfers among theological, political and economic domains. Indeed we do not invoke a general theory of signatures but start with the observation and the demonstration, undoubtedly located in time and place, that the concepts of power widely in use today in both expert and everyday language bear this signature. We are thus interested in claims for the theological eminence of concepts and practices of power, advanced in different ways by Schmitt, Weber, Agamben and even Foucault, to the extent that we find in these claims the possibility of a broadening and deepening, elaborating and rectifying, of existing assumptions or accounts concerning the concept of power. For these thinkers, and indeed for most discussions of the recent social and political sciences, the key form of the signature can be broadly expressed as the relationship between sovereignty and reign, on the one hand, and economic management and government, or governance, on the other.

Indeed, if there is anything that unites our three principal characters here, it is their common recognition of the appearance of similar signatures of power in their own work and the three different ways in which they seek to escape them. Perhaps the most contentious of our propositions is that all three can be viewed as failing not in their attempts to escape them but because they think it is necessary to make such an attempt.

We are not in a position to say whether the signature of power is a universal feature of all concepts and practices of power. It is, however, certainly very widespread and, as such, provides us with a perspective that will allow us to examine the intellectual struggles of important and influential thinkers and, with their help, to open up and envisage the various fields of investigation their work portends.

About this book

1.5 It is customary to add a small guide at this point to allow the reader to navigate through the book. But the form that this book takes is not so much a rational or pedagogical order as an unfolding of an engagement with something of a mystery. The book looks for stories, clues and exemplars, and searches for notions of power in the studies of symbols and rituals, and in obscure debates. The reader should be warned that they will find discussion of diverse topics such as the 'savage life', angels, and secrets. They will find the passage that links the ancient oral rites of the Arunta people in central Australia to Agamben's most recent conception of power. The book refuses to reduce the mystery of this basic concept and, like every good mystery, it begins with a murder. This one unfortunately is real and still, tragically, unsolved. It ends with a ceremony of state. At many points, the reader will find we return to an epigram that acts as a touchstone for our investigation: 'the King reigns, but he does not govern'.

The next three chapters (Chapters 2, 3 and 4), 'The Shadow of the Sovereign', 'Economies of Power' and 'The Prince and the Population', start with Foucault and trace his own difficult and ambiguous legacy. This allows us to introduce the three key concepts of sovereignty, governmentality and biopolitics, and the program of a genealogy of the arts of government. Foucault's discussions of liberalism and neo-liberalism are important signposts, and we return to these rationalities of power during the book. If there is an overall theme to Foucault's thinking on power it is the recurrent search for a new form of power, or a new critique or concept of power, which will allow him, and us, to escape the shadow of sovereignty. Chapter 4 uses recent scholarship on Machiavelli and Malthus to question Foucault's narrative of a governmental shift from sovereignty and territory to security and population. In its final sections, we begin to grasp Foucault's legacy and see our own intellectual physiognomy in his.

The next two chapters (Chapters 5 and 6), 'Enemy Secrets' and 'Secular Orders', introduce our second principal character, Carl Schmitt, but keep what we have learnt from Foucault in play. We thus approach Schmitt through what we have discovered in Foucault, and Schmitt's thought provides another perspective on Foucault. We compare them on a range of themes, including the political, legitimacy, sovereignty, government and international law. We will find Schmitt's relationship with his teacher, Max Weber, exceptionally important, and follow Schmitt into the core of his political theology and the debate on secularization of the 1960s, which engaged Karl Löwith and Hans Blumenberg, among others. This is a debate that casts Foucault's search for a new, non-sovereign power in a different light and so too his claims about pastoral power. Schmitt certainly makes a central contribution to our theme of sovereignty, particularly in its restriction to a set of competences rather than an image of omniscience and omnipotence. Yet 'order' (in the form of *nomos* and concrete order) also starts to become significant, and refers us back to the sources of 'neoliberalism' in the German 'Ordoliberals', who are analysed by Foucault and interlocutors of Schmitt. Between Foucault's governmental atheism and Schmitt's political theology it is, tellingly, the Ordoliberals who, drawing on medieval thought, seek an 'economic theology'.

The final two chapters (Chapter 7 and 8), 'Reign and Government' and 'Glorious Acclaim', are extended meditations that use Giorgio Agamben's most recent work as their source. Again, Foucault and Schmitt are kept in play. Given what we have learnt in the previous chapters, we will primarily be concerned with Agamben's economic theology or what he calls a 'theological genealogy of the economy and government'. We shall follow some of the common references and sources that link Agamben to Foucault or to Schmitt, such as theologians from Gregory of Nazianus to Erik Peterson, political theorists and economists such as Rousseau, Adam Smith and the Physiocrats, or the dense strands and knots that bind much of twentieth-century German sociology, economics and jurisprudence to Weber. The question of order, inherited from medieval cosmology, becomes even more central, but so too do the miracle and the event, and splendour and publicity in the form of the glorification and acclamation of divine and worldly sovereign rule. We shall offer a diagnosis of Agamben's political anthropology of 'sabbatism' and 'inoperativity'.

The reader should be aware that none of our main characters will be spared strong criticism when it is warranted, even if they have built a platform that allows us to begin to glimpse something of the new continent to which our voyage has taken us. The reader will find, at the end of Chapter 8, an outline of the features of the rich fields of study this discussion helps us envisage, and some conclusions concerning the three concepts of fields of power: sovereignty, governmentality and biopolitics.

Each chapter is divided into a number of small sections. Each section was a kind of exercise that allowed the author the freedom to pursue the by-ways, clues and little stories that edged his understanding forward or perhaps simply increased the pleasure of the journey, often by allowing him to keep good or even bad company. Hopefully the sections are coherent in themselves but the reader should understand they are part of a much more intricate puzzle whose pieces include not only our three thinkers, but other major figures, intellectual and political movements, concepts and debates. The argument emerges at times through this discontinuous investigation. It takes place, as Foucault once said of his own work, 'between unfinished abutments and anticipatory strings of dots' (2001: 223). To remedy this, at the end of each chapter, there is a section (in one case, two) that summarizes and signposts what has been discovered and prepares for the next stage of the journey. In any case, this has been a most enjoyable book to write and hopefully it will also be enjoyable to read.

2

THE SHADOW OF THE SOVEREIGN

2.1 Let us begin our investigation into recent conceptions of power with the work of Michel Foucault. The influence of his approach to power and his conceptions of its various forms is beyond doubt. While he would reject the idea that he offered a 'theory' of power, he nevertheless has come closest to providing a general framework for critical thought and action since the crisis and decline of Marxism from the 1970s. While he was careful not to locate himself on the conventional political spectrum, his reception has been largely as a radical thinker aligned with struggle, contestation and, as he would put it, 'resistance'.

It is possible that the very concept of power might be thought to be a term of those committed to struggle and resistance. If so, it would be the domain of those discontented with the existing social and political order, that is, those who want, through reform or revolution, agitation or activism, to change or, at least, call into question, aspects of it. Socialists, feminists, anarchists, anti-racists, identity activists, environmentalists and anti-colonialists, have all sought to name and to decide the best ways to contest and combat different kinds of power.

Yet this is not to say that the concept of power belongs exclusively to 'the Left'. Conservatives might assert the necessity of power or of certain types or power to a good and stable society and extol the virtues of traditional, monarchical, religious or hierarchical ordering of societies. For them, power is often associated with authority and tradition, which are held to be its deep source of legitimacy even when it must take decisive action in the face of pressing threats. By contrast, those who might be called liberals are generally concerned with the procedures that confer the legitimacy of power, that is, of making its exercise accountable and transparent and distinguishing it from the violence or coercion they hold to be characteristic of tyranny and dictatorship. For them, power will operate in a way that is consistent with individual freedoms.

Michel Foucault's thought on power has something to say to each of these traditions. He indicates the subtle mechanisms of a liberal art and rationality of governing that no longer presumes to be able to guarantee its own effects and that finally models government 'on the rational behavior of those who are governed' (2008: 312). He thus adds to our knowledge of economic liberalism and its search for an economic government. In perhaps his most famous book (1977), he reveals the pervasiveness of discipline and its centrality to modern institutions of education, punishment and production, and could thus be said to inadvertently confirm a conservative thesis. In his lectures, he would famously castigate socialism as lacking an 'autonomous rationality of government' that he found in liberalism.

Nevertheless, his work appears to address itself most to those who oppose themselves to existing forms of social and political order, established practices and hegemonic 'regimes' of truth and knowledge and forms of subjectivity and identity. Whether this will always be the case, it is not possible to say. However, we can say that his conceptualization of power defined, more broadly and more thoroughly than any other, the analysis that characterized those decades when the Marxist conception of power based on production and the class struggle could no longer command its former authority. It is this sense of a critical engagement with power relations that makes Foucault the starting point for our current investigation and a continuing exemplar or paradigm with whom we might compare others.

Foucault can be regarded as inaugurating a new conception of power or a new approach to power that was productive of certain key concepts such as biopolitics, governmentality, pastoral power, discipline, and so forth. In a brief period of little more than half a decade, 1974–79, in which he really concentrated on this problem, his conception of power took many twists and turns. However, whichever way it changed, his thought stood resolutely against one based on the theory of sovereignty and its key concepts such as law, legitimacy and right. Despite his repeated desire to cut off the King's head in political thought and analysis (e.g. 1979: 89; 1980: 121), the ghost of the sovereign, like Hamlet's father, keeps reappearing in his work.

A murder and Maoism

2.2 Let us invoke one event or moment purely as a signal for the birth of this new 'conceptualization', rather than 'theory', of power, as he would put it many years later (2001: 329). It is the meeting in a vacant lot between two men in the provincial northern French town of Bruay-en-Artois in June 1972. This event is a small moment in a much larger *Affaire Bruay* that revolves around the still unsolved murder of a teenaged daughter of a local mining family and the role of the Maoist group Gauche Prolétarienne (or GP) in using the event to agitate the miners and their community. The vacant lot was where children playing there had found Brigitte Dewèvre's body in early April 1972. A placard had been placed there, bearing the legend: 'On this spot, Brigitte Dewèvre, the daughter of a miner, was murdered by the bourgeoise of Bruay' (Macey, 1993: 302).

A local lawyer, Pierre Leroy, connected with the region's major mining company, and his lover, were each in turn held and questioned by the police, concerning the killing. Leroy would be jailed for three months before being released.

The younger man at that meeting in the vacant lot was François Ewald, who taught philosophy at the local *lycée*, but was also the point man of the GP on the spot. He had agitated within and participated with the local community in demonstrations calling for justice in the case, and invited the older man to the meeting to publicise the case. The latter was the already famous philosopher, Michel Foucault, who had recently taken up his Chair of the History of Systems of Thought at the Collège de France. Foucault approved the Maoist mobilization in Bruay, saying that 'without these interventions, Leroy would have been freed' (Behrent, 2010: 593). The two men in the vacant lot would continue a relationship that for Ewald would continue long past Foucault's death in 1984.

The meeting between Ewald and Foucault could stand as something of a hinge in radical theories of power. The purpose of Ewald's presence there, as the young Maoist, was not only to demand justice in a system imagined to be invariably class-based, and hence dedicated to the protection of a local 'bourgeois' lawyer, but also to educate the masses on the impossibility of justice under a capitalist order. The individual killing, and the fact of the class affiliation of the suspect, were, for the militants, exemplary of a second and wider point. Not only were the legal system, the courts and the police, systematically enforcing a class justice but also the rule of the bourgeoisie was, to put it simply, systematic murder. The brutal murder of the young girl was linked with the number of deaths per year that occurred in mining. Only a couple of years before, after 16 miners were killed in an explosion at Lens, several Maoists attacked the company offices with Molotov cocktails and were arrested. In response, the Maoists established a 'democratic tribunal' to judge the crimes of the coal-pits, that is, to prosecute the mining company for responsibility for the death of the miners. The individual who acted as prosecuting attorney in this court was none other than France's most famous living philosopher, Jean-Paul Sartre, who had devoted much of his later years to working with the Maoist militants. Despite their intellectual differences, and previous polemics, Foucault and Sartre cooperated in public demonstrations and other political activities during these years.

The French Maoists argued that the system of capitalist pro-duction resulted in any number of deaths 'by accident' every year. Taking the view that all actions entail responsibility, which can be traced to Sartre's existentialism, they viewed the bourgeoisie as the authors of the actions that resulted in these deaths. Thus, at the heart of power was capitalist production. At the heart of this produc-tion was the exploitation of the proletariat. And, at the heart of this exploitation, was intentional and systematic murder. In this respect, for these Maoists, contemporary liberal capitalism was no different from fascism and Nazism. All of this was expressed in incendiary language in the reporting in the GP's paper, *La Cause du peuple*, which called for justice to be done against the suspect in the Bruay case. Under the headline, 'And now they massacre our children', it demanded, in no uncertain terms, the torture and castration of Leroy (Behrent, 2010: 290). According to Foucault's biographer, David Macey, Ewald, along with two local workers, was 'at least in part responsible for the notorious 1 May number of *La Cause du peuple*' (1993: 303).

In an interview in Foucault's archives, discovered by the American historian Michael Behrent, his response was far from the one endorsed by the Maoists. For Foucault, the case reveals the possi-bility of the 'reversal of the punitive apparatus' in that people were trying to bring the magistrate over to their side. Foucault uses the terminology to be found in his writings some years later to argue that far from having class power inevitably inscribed within them, the local and capillary sites of power were ones of possible contestation and reversibility (2010: 593). However, Foucault defended the tactics of the GP on the grounds that Leroy would have otherwise been freed. 'This is the first time that the bourgeoisie of the Nord, which has always been protected, has ceased to be protected, and that is why what has happened in Bruay-en-Artois is so important' (cited in Macey, 1993: 303).

Only a year earlier, and with the people's tribunal at Lens in the background, Foucault had taken a rather different view of the institutions of the court in a rather combative and terse discussion with Maoists:

> In my view one shouldn't start with the court as a particular form, and then go on to ask how and on what conditions there could be a people's court; one should start with popular justice, with acts of justice by the people, and go on to ask what place a court can have within this. We must ask whether such acts of popular justice can or cannot be organized in the form of a court. Now my hypothesis is not so much that the court is the natural expression of popular justice, but rather that its historical function is to ensnare it, to control it and to strangle it, by re-inscribing it with institutions which are typical of a state apparatus. (Foucault, 1980: 1)

For Foucault, the Lens counter-court was 'no real exercise of alternative judicial power' but a breaking of the monopoly of information held by the bourgeoisie and a dissemination of alternative views. Foucault argues that two important kinds of power were in operation, 'the power of knowledge of the truth and the power to disseminate this knowledge' (1980: 34).

Here Foucault enunciates a political view antipathetic to the idea of the state and the principles that are held to be embodied in the court system: the idea of neutrality, of impartial, disinterested justice, and of the appeal to justice as a universal norm. Foucault displays a preference for acts of popular justice over this court system and directs attention to the politics of information. While there are nascent themes for which he will later become famous, such as that of the relationship between power and knowledge, and power and truth, at this point he does not see the courts as a potential space for the reversibility of power. Rather the court is the space for the strangulation and control of popular action and struggle. Foucault's thought will remain until the last one that asserts the primacy of the relation of forces over the institution (e.g. 2001: 343)

This figure of the privilege of the extra-juridical over the juridical, the singular over the universal, action and activity over norms, popular struggle over state apparatus, of relations of power over the institution, appears again and again in Foucault's thinking about power, and indeed his ethics, and with very different effects depending on the occasion. In this case, it is an argument for acts of popular justice over judicial procedures. (One could only hope those acts are not the ones recommended by *La Cause du peuple*.) By the end of the 1970s, however, it will be an argument for the primacy of the arts of government over the exercise of sovereignty; a little later, for the practice of ethics over the codes of morality. In arguments for a productive conception of power over a repressive one, for starting at its local, capillary forms rather than its centralized point, for the recession of the law in the face of proliferating norms, for a government through civil society, for the constitution rather than deformation of the subject in power-knowledge, for governmentality over institution, this figure of the Sovereign, Law and Right, and its state apparatuses and institutions will loom large as the negative foil. The paradox of Foucault's thought on power is that while he (sometimes radically) changes his account of the new non-juridical conception of power, and even rejects a substantive theory of power, he remains haunted by the headless sovereign.

But all this is still some way off. Nevertheless, in the meeting on that tragic bit of ground, in the dust and smoke of these old ideological battles, in their intense and combative debates, however, a new figure of the radical analysis of power was being born. In the discussion over the affair of Bruay, Foucault enunciates the first principle of this view of power: the essential reversibility of power relations particularly at their local, capillary point of exercise. That principle would be the first of many, as Foucault would develop a view of the new form of power that would be sketched against the theory, imagery and practice of sovereignty.

2.3 The emergence of this new non-juridical conception of power would affect both parties to that conversation in June 1972 in Bruay. For Foucault, the next decade would entail an intense reflection on concepts of power in relation to historical analyses of prisons, sexuality, abnormality, and later liberalism and neoliberalism. It would be conceptually very fertile. Different concepts and forms of power would be tried, discarded, modified and developed. Disciplinary power, biopower, pastoral power and governmentality would be advanced, modified, abandoned or advanced once more. For Ewald, the Bruay affair would lead to his break with Maoism, although it was left to other militants to object to the tone and content of the May issue (Macey, 1993: 304). However, he would later join Foucault's seminars, and complete a thesis on the welfare state under his direction and go on, among other things, to edit Foucault's shorter works, interviews and papers and become the general editor of Foucault's lectures some years later. In all these respects, Ewald would prove to be one of Foucault's most exemplary and sensitive students.

In the decade that followed Foucault's death, François Ewald would offer an evaluation of his supervisor's *actualité*. Of the four points of the latter's continuing relevance, it is only the first that need detain us here. As early as the late 1970s, Ewald tells us, 'Foucault posited that our current situation [*actualité*] is very fundamentally post-revolutionary: if there was an event in the 1970s, it was the disappearance of revolution' (1999a: 85). Ewald's logic is proleptic. By this anti-revolutionary gesture, Foucault had anticipated a 'world that would be our own' including the fall of the Berlin Wall. Moreover, the end of revolution was related to another notorious ending: 'It is clear that the end of revolution and the end of History represent the same event: it is an event in our consciousness of time.' The consequence is that temporal consciousness leads away from the caesura of past and future and towards an 'eternal present' which 'leads toward an activity only of the order of administration, of management' (Ewald, 1999a: 86). Thus:

> Foucault explained that there are not any events to be anticipated with respect to the state: the state, in a certain manner, is no longer a philosophical concern ... The stakes are with respect to power, and this a totally different location, a totally different zone, a totally different type of reality. (Ewald, 1999a: 86–7)

In a few words, Ewald has moved Foucault's *actualité* from that of the state and sovereign, and its contestation in the figure of the revolution, to that of the order of management and administration, and a new kind of power. We shall demonstrate the importance of this

double figure of power throughout the present book. Most commentators have stressed the renewed potential for political struggle
in Foucault's expansion of the concept of power outside traditional
revolutionary and party politics. However, it is the abandonment of
the latter, not the embrace of the former, which is stressed by Ewald.

This abandonment of the revolution would come to embody
a more positive sense in Ewald's own trajectory. This would take
Ewald from writing about *L'État Providence* (1986) or the welfare
state, and the history of risk and insurance (1991, 1999b), to working for the insurance industry and finally to being the highest profile
intellectual voice of *Medef*, a peak employers' and business association (Behrent, 2010: 585–6). There he would become the advocate
of the *refondation sociale* (social reconstruction) or what in English
would be called 'welfare reform' and 'labour-market reform'.
Through him, as Maurizio Lazzarato has remarked, 'what Foucault
had revealed about neoliberalism has played a part in its implementation as social policy' so that the very tools fabricated from Foucault's
lectures on governmentality were used to reconstitute French society
(2009: 110).

The analysis of sovereignty

2.4 Michel Foucault's apparent antipathy towards an analysis
in terms of sovereignty did not prevent him from fashioning
some of his most striking images from the practices and mythologies
of sovereign power, of its ceremonies of punishment, and of its language and symbols.

One thinks of the first few pages of *Discipline and Punish* (1977),
where he describes the execution of the regicide, Damiens, in 1757,
and the scenes of the 'tortured, dismembered, amputated body, sym-
bolically branded on face or shoulder, exposed alive or dead to public
view' (1977: 8). In the following chapter, the 'spectacle of the scaffold'
is described 'not only as a judicial, but a political ritual' (p. 47). In a
citation from Muyart de Vouglans that would attain an emblematic
status in Foucault's characterization of sovereign power, the right to
punish belongs to 'that absolute power of life and death which Roman
law calls *merum imperium*, a right by virtue of which the prince
sees that his law is respected by ordering the punishment of crime'
(p. 48). For Foucault, *la supplice*, the ritual of public torture and

execution, is a way for the sovereign to exact retribution and for the momentarily injured sovereign to be reconstituted. It is an exercise and policy of 'terror', a 'liturgy' of torture and execution, in which the justice of the King was shown to be an armed justice, and the sword of execution was the same sword that pursued the king's enemies. 'The ceremony' of *la supplice* 'displayed for all to see the power relation that gave force to the law'(p. 50).

At other times, Foucault stresses less the ceremonial and ritual aspects of the practice of sovereignty than its symbolic dimension. Thus in the first volume of the *History of Sexuality* (1979), sovereignty operates through a 'symbolics of blood'. While it claims 'a right to decide life and death' descended from the Roman *patria potestas*, which granted the father the right to 'dispose' of members of his household as he saw fit, its symbol is the sword, and 'blood constituted one of its fundamental values' (1979: 135, 147). Blood was '*a reality with a symbolic function*' (original italics). It owed 'its high value at the same time to its instrumental role (the ability to shed blood), to the way it functioned in the order of signs (to have a certain blood, to be of the same blood, to be prepared to risk one's blood) and also to its precariousness (easily spilled, subject to drying up, too readily mixed, capable of being quickly corrupted)' (p. 147). A society of blood is ruled by sovereign power, characterized by systems of alliance, and organized into orders and castes. The 'value of descent lines were predominant'.

There is vividness in Foucault's discussion of sovereign power, its rituals, language and symbols. But, in a lecture delivered between the publication of the two books we have mentioned, Foucault states that it is necessary to bid 'farewell to the theory of sovereignty insofar as it could – and can – be described as a method for analyzing power relations. I would like to show you that the juridical model of sovereignty was not, I believe, able to provide a concrete analysis of the multiplicity of power relations' (2003: 43).

Why should this be case? Certainly it is consistent with his discussion with the Maoists, in which he prefers the acts of popular justice over the ensnaring institution of the court. To get to the heart of Foucault's new conception of power – or concept of the new power – we need first to understand what he thinks is the old conception and practice of power he is replacing. For while there are certain ambiguities over the status of the concept of sovereignty in Foucault as either a theory or an empirical reality, as imagery or practice, the new can only be defined against the old, and that interweaving of the definition of new and old is of mutually exclusive categories. This new conception of power can only be defined, as Jeffrey Minson understood earlier than anyone else commenting on Foucault's writings on power, within a necessary and somewhat inflexible 'bi-polar structure' (1980: 18).

2.5 It is in his 1976 lectures at the Collège de France, 'Society Must be Defended', that Foucault explains why he must reject the theory of sovereignty in his analytical approach to power.

Sovereignty, he argues, cannot account for the concrete multiplicity of powers and the element of domination found within them in modern societies. It assumes first a 'subject-to-subject' relationship or cycle and thus an individual with natural rights (Foucault, 2003: 43). Second, it supposes that the multiplicity of powers, capacities and potentials refer back to a 'fundamental and foundational unity' (p. 44). Finally, the problematic of sovereignty is one concerned with the legitimacy of power; a legitimacy 'more basic than any law and that allows laws to function as such'. Each of these points would undermine an analysis for Foucault that must start from the relations of power, and the 'operators of domination' within them (p. 45). This analysis of domination should not be grounded in natural individual rights but in a concrete analysis that reveals how 'relations of subjugation manufacture subjects'. Such an analysis would need to start not from the problem of the unity of sovereignty in the state, and its legitimacy, but to examine the 'real relations of domination, and to allow them to assert themselves in their multiplicity, their differences, their specificity, or their reversibility'. To be sure, global strategies can be constructed on the basis of these singular powers and multiple forms of domination and subjugation. However 'all these mechanisms and operators of domination are the actual plinth of the global apparatus' (pp. 45–6).

If we turn our attention a few pages before these passages to the end of the second of these lectures, it is clear that it is the material techniques of domination, associated with disciplinary mechanisms of power, which hold the key to this explanation of the insufficiency of the theory of sovereignty. Here sovereignty is both practice and theory. It referred 'to the actual power mechanism: that of the feudal monarchy' (Foucault, 2003: 34). It was an instrument that helped constitute the 'great monarchical institutions' of Absolutism. It was a weapon of struggles that sought to limit or enforce royal power in the sixteenth and seventeenth centuries; and it was used to 'construct an alternative model to authoritarian or absolute monarchical administrations: that of parliamentary democracies' (p. 35). But while the theory of sovereignty actually described the operations of power in the feudal type of society, a new mechanism of power appeared in the seventeenth and eighteenth century that was 'absolutely incompatible with relations of sovereignty':

> This new mechanism of power applies primarily to bodies and what they do rather than to the land and what it produces. It was a mechanism of power that made it possible to extract time and labor, rather than commodities and wealth, from bodies. It was a type of power that was exercised through constant surveillance and not in discontinuous fashion through chronologically defined systems of taxation and obligation. It was a type of power that presupposed a closely meshed grid of material coercions rather than the physical existence of a sovereign, and it therefore defined a new economy of power... (Foucault, 2003: 35–6)

Further on, he will reveal that this non-sovereign form of power, so alien to sovereignty, is disciplinary power. We could go on with the contrasts, but even Foucault admits that 'this type of power is the exact, point-for-point opposite of the mechanics of power that the theory of sovereignty described' (p. 36). By the end of this second lecture in 1976 Foucault had, in any case, clearly sketched a bipolar conception of power between a now archaic, but lingering sovereignty, and a modern form of discipline.

But why should we remain so bedazzled by the theory of sovereignty when the transformation of power is not something concealed but visible within many of our major institutions such as factories, schools, prison and hospitals, as Foucault himself admits? Moreover, rather than existing in the obscurity of 'the silent basement of the great mechanics of power' the 'disciplines in fact have their own discourse' (p. 38). The answer is simple. The theory 'made it possible to superimpose on the mechanism of discipline a system of right that concealed its mechanism and erased the element of domination and techniques of domination involved in discipline' (p. 37). Foucault comes uncomfortably close to a theory of law as ideology, in which our experience of rights and individual sovereignty conceals the insidious spread of techniques of domination, and which deflects politics onto a neutralizing, juridical ground.

Point by point, as Foucault said, each of these thoroughly heterogeneous forms and discourses of power are opposed to and cannot be reduced to one another (p. 37). Thus the oppositions multiply: a public right versus a polymorphous set of mechanisms, a juridical rule versus the society of norms and normalization, the edifice of law versus the human sciences, and jurisprudence versus clinical knowledge (p. 38).

The brilliance of Foucault lies in his lucidity, both in his books and in his lectures. One feature of his lucidity is his facility for juxtaposition. But this facility can lead to problems. In a moment, we shall discuss its implications for law. But it is enough to note here that by the end of these very same lectures, Foucault had modified his juxtaposition. Within the new power of discipline he will discern the emergence of another kind, biopower, which will no longer be an individualizing power attached to human bodies but a collective power working through the human species. Foucault will juxtapose, in the final lecture of this series, biopower to discipline. But this method, or should we say this proclivity, of Foucault's thought, which accounts both for its lucidity and for its weakness, finds it hard to allow for anything more than two, inter-defined and opposed terms. Sure, there will be attempts to turn sovereignty, discipline and biopower into a historical series and thereby to radically delimit the claims for discipline as the modern form of power he had made only two months before. But ultimately, the three terms must become two. Given that the principal pole of opposition to the modern conception of power is and will remain sovereignty, discipline will eventually be subsumed under the more general term of 'biopower', which, again, can be opposed to a theory of sovereignty that could never hope to render it intelligible.

Law

2.6 Minson directs our attention to the work of the legal historian, John H. Langbein – *Torture and the Law of Proof*. Originally published in 1977, it would be republished almost 30 years later. The original work addressed torture and its abolition in Europe and England at the end of the Middle Ages. In the introduction to the later edition (2006), its author would also examine the limitation of the use of torture as an investigatory tool in the interrogation of prisoners held by the United States and Britain in the contemporary wars in Afghanistan and Iraq.

In outline, Langbein rejects as a 'fairy tale' the view that the abolition of judicial torture in Europe was the result of the 'forceful writings' of publicists such as Beccaria and Voltaire and enlightened rulers like Frederick the Great and the Emperor Joseph II. Rather, he argues, it came about through changes within the legal system itself. He notes firstly, the entry of a subsidiary system of proof alongside the 'Roman-Canon' law of proof, found in documents such as the Ordinance of 1670, by Colbert, which Foucault also draws upon. He then considers the effects of the development of alternative penalties other than the death penalty or 'blood sanctions', such as involuntary servitude on galley ships. The latter, under the Ordinance, could be imposed 'on the same quantum of circumstantial evidence for which medieval law permitted only investigation under torture to obtain full proof' (Langbein, 1977: 59). Given the possibility of jurists imposing penalties of less than death for even capital crimes, the old, higher-level requirement of proof was no longer necessary. In such a situation, torture was no longer required for conviction and punishment. Langbein concludes:

> Of course, judicial torture continued to be permitted and employed in the ancien régime. But the revolution in the law of proof destroyed the raison d'être of the law of torture. When full proof was no longer the exclusive prerequisite for punishment, the law of proof was liberated from its dependence on confession evidence. Judicial torture was at last vulnerable to the ancient abolitionist critique. (1977: 59–60)

For Foucault, the presence of torture among the penalties of the 1670 Ordinance demonstrates the persistence of the spectacular order of sovereign power, which still awaited the historical effectivity of the reformers' criticism. However, if we follow Langbein's argument, the very act of classification of torture as one punishment among others might well signal its imminent fall into disuse and be, as Minson puts it, 'a tacit invitation to the courts not to use it (1980: 22). Accordingly, 'Foucault misses this transformation in the law of evidence' and as a result 'only reinforces the customary historical overestimation of the reformers' role in securing the abolition of torture...'.

The validity of Langbein's argument is a matter for historical investigation and evidence. However, the view of law as the symbolic expression of the sovereign does not allow the possibility of an analysis of the internal practices of the law such as these changes in the rules of evidence or to the range of penalties available in respect to specific crimes. Nor does it allow us to consider the possible efficacy of such changes. Such assumptions would be, it must be said, extremely disabling for historians of medieval and absolutist law. Yet, from our point of view, this is not the most serious problem with Foucault's view of law. If sovereignty is to be displaced by a modern conception of power (whether discipline, biopower, or governmentality), then law itself will be regarded as increasingly residual. This residual character of law occurs throughout Foucault's disquisitions on different kinds of power.

2.7 In *Discipline and Punish* Foucault discusses the relationship between law and discipline. Again, the bipolar structure of sovereignty and discipline is maintained so that although the parliamentary system makes it possible 'for the will of all to form the fundamental authority of sovereignty, the disciplines provide, at the base, a guarantee of the submission of forces and bodies' (1977: 222). It is the disciplines that constitute the foundation of formal juridical rights and liberties. While the disciplines appear as an 'infra-law' extending law to infinitesimal details, they actually form a 'counter-law' that makes it possible to 'distort the contractual link systematically from the moment it has as its content a mechanism of discipline' (p. 223). And while law seems to present limits to power, on the underside of law there appears 'a machinery that is both immense and minute, which supports, reinforces, multiplies the asymmetry of power and undermines the limits that are traced around the law'. If law is the expression of an archaic sovereignty, heterogeneous to the actuality of disciplinary powers, then at best law disguises, enables, and inverts, the actual operation of this new power. In short, law takes on an increasingly hollow and residual role in modern society.

Haven't we seen, however, the empirical expansion of constitutions and laws, and their enforcement by courts and tribunals? Foucault considers this objection and replies that 'we should not be deceived by all the Constitutions framed throughout the world since the French Revolution, the Codes written and revised, a whole continual and clamorous legislative activity: these were the forms that made an essentially normalizing power acceptable' (Foucault, 1979: 144). This is from the famous last chapter of the *History of Sexuality I*, and by then, the content of the modern conception of power, this normalizing power, will be somewhat different. Here, law does not merely disguise the operations of this normalizing power; 'the law operates more and more as a norm' and 'the juridical institution is increasingly incorporated into a continuum of apparatuses (medical, administrative, and so on) whose functions are for the most part regulatory' (p. 144).

For Foucault, law is anything but the explicit discourse of justice, right, and impartiality that is attached to it, which he had viewed as untenable for a conception of popular justice in his discussion with the Maoists. In a third move, it is no longer simply a disguise for modern power, or even simply integrated into its apparatuses. It becomes, in his lectures on governmentality, a technology of government. In the Course Summary of his 1979 lectures he sums up his final statement about law (2008: 321). The juridical form, he argues, was more effective as a technology of regulation than the 'wisdom and moderation of the governors'. Far from a natural affinity of liberalism with the law, 'law defines forms of general intervention excluding particular, individual, or exceptional measures' and the parliamentary participation of the governed in law-making is 'the most effective system of governmental economy'. The rule of law and the representative system might have been bound up with early liberalism but 'democracy and the Rule of Law have not necessarily been liberal, nor has liberalism been necessarily democratic or bound to the forms of law'.

Now Foucault argues an extension of the argument of *History of Sexuality*. Law is not simply more like the norm and a part of the continuum of the regulatory apparatus. It also becomes a privileged instrument of liberal governing in that it entails general interventions consistent with the regulation of an economy and allows a participation of the governed in the framing of such regulation. Just as before, it could no longer be characterized in terms of the disciplines it disguised and allowed to function, or the norm it would become like and the apparatuses within which it would be integrated. It now receives its character from the technical requirements of a liberal art of governing.

Law is again placed under the sign and logic of what is considered to be the new non-juridical power. This gives, in passing, different ways of approaching the law and legal institutions but they all, nonetheless, confirm its residual status and that we 'have entered into a phase of juridical regression in comparison with the pre-seventeenth-century-societies we are acquainted with' (Foucault, 1979: 144).

We shall see that the notion of the norm changes between the focus on disciplinary power and those of biopower and governmentality. It changes further and more radically in the work of his exemplary student, Ewald (1990; see Dean 2010a: 141–2). Nevertheless, every time Foucault attempts to specify what is new about power, and strives to produce a conceptualization of power adequate to that newness, he finds a shadow and an outline from which he must distinguish it. It is of a power found behind law, which is the expression or command of the sovereign, and of its constitutional and institutional manifestation, the state and its institutions. It is the same shadow that threatened to ensnare the acts of popular justice he extolled in conversation with the Maoists. But, by 1979, seven years after that discussion, this idea of law is no longer one that could have any appeal to the Gauche Prolétarienne (as did the earlier one, see Macey, 1993: 304). For the idea of law, and the ideal of the Rule of Law, that permits the formulation of general measures, which allows no rectifications after its effects are produced, which binds the state as much as others, and which is suitable to governing economic activities of individuals, comes not from the old proletarian left but from what some, at that time, called the New Right, and later, neoliberalism. It is the view of law, as Foucault demonstrates in a few deft passages in his 1979 lectures (2008: 172–4), which Friedrich Hayek first laid out in his *Road to Serfdom* (2001).

New powers

2.8 Foucault's 1976 lectures at the Collège de France are, it is well known, interesting in that they mark a transition in his thought about the nature of this new, modern, conception of power. In the last lecture, delivered on 17 March 1976, the modern conception of power is no longer discipline, but biopower. This will be one of only a handful of places in which he would turn his attention to the question of biopower. Another is the final chapter of the first volume of the *History of Sexuality*. After that, apart from a few brief apologetic references three years later, and its preservation as the title of a lecture series, the term will simply vanish from his thought.

In this final lecture of 1976, Foucault's first move is to distinguish 'power's hold on life' from the 'right of life and death', which was a basic attribute of sovereignty (2003: 239–40). The right to take life or let live, characteristic of sovereign power's effect on life, is penetrated and permeated by 'rather precisely the opposite right', 'the power to "make live" and "let die"' (p. 241). Again, however, this is not a 'transformation at the level of political theory but rather at the level of the mechanism, techniques, and technologies of power' (p. 241).

This, of course, is all very familiar, and while it took some two decades for this lecture to be published, the same contrast is found in the final chapter, called 'The Right of Death and the Power over Life'. Yet it is not the familiarity of the territory that should concern us here but the secret problem Foucault immediately faces. What is the relationship of this new power over life to disciplinary power, which even at the beginning of the same lecture series was still, as in the pages of *Discipline and Punish*, published only the previous year – the characteristic form of the modern anti-juridical power?

To answer this question, the bipolar machinery of Foucault's conceptual apparatus starts up again to address this distinction between a disciplinary and a 'new nondisciplinary power', between a power addressed to man-as-body and one to the living man or man-as-species, the former 'individualizing', the other 'massifying' (2003: 242–3). 'After the anatomo-politics established in the course of the eighteenth century we have, at the end of the [eighteenth] century, the emergence of ... a "biopolitics" of the human race' (p. 243).

Now, while this new non-disciplinary power is not exclusive of discipline, it does modify, infiltrate and embed itself within disciplinary techniques. Clearly there are all sorts of salient differences here. As we have just shown, the first is the level at which it works: the species rather than the body. There are also its sites: those of public hygiene and health, of social welfare and insurance mechanisms, and of the urban problem. And it will find a new object: the population. But what is most interesting about it is the way in which it will change the very nature of the term 'norm'.

In disciplinary power, the norm is intrinsic to the conduct required in various practices, such as work, schooling, and military training; or it is defined in terms of the ends of discipline, such as optimizing efficiency and increasing docility; or it is something which is specified by the newly emergent human sciences, especially the 'psy-' disciplines. For example, the norm places judgment as to the proof of guilt, to the sentence and punishment, within 'a scientifico-juridical complex' (Foucault, 1977: 19). Nevertheless, in all these ways the norm is something that is imposed on individuals, used to assess them as normal or abnormal, or locate them on a continuum of normality, and is linked to a 'technical prescription for a possible normalization' (p. 21).

In the new non-disciplinary power, the norm will be defined in statistical terms. It will take into account 'phenomena that are aleatory and unpredictable when taken in themselves or individually' but which collectively form certain patterns which can be known and acted upon. The mechanisms of this biopower are hence 'forecasts, statistical estimates, and overall measures' (Foucault, 2003: 246). Their purpose is not to modify the behaviour of any given individual but to intervene at the level of the generality of a population so that one, for example, can act to lower the mortality rate, try to change the birth rate, improve life expectancy and so on. 'In a word', Foucault says, and this word will be extremely important in his future attempts to specify this non-sovereign, non-juridical power, 'security mechanisms have to be installed around the random element inherent in a population of living beings so as to optimize a state of life' (p. 246). The norm is thus not something applied to an individual or their body but found within the regularities that occur within the population. Security is not about the protection of the sovereign and their subjects but optimizing the regularities of the population.

In doing so, Foucault appears to have introduced two forms of modern power, which can be distinguished and indeed juxtaposed. Yet, no sooner does he do this, than the shadow that haunts his whole analysis falls over his new non-disciplinary power. This is the ever-presence of sovereignty as theory and practice and the need to distinguish the new from the old. It is becoming clear that Foucault's problem is not the sociological one of the classification of different forms of power, but the philosophical one of capturing a new presence that releases us from the phantom that continues to haunt us. As such, he must remain strictly committed to the bipolarity of power concepts and structures.

There are a number of ways of getting around this problem, but they all have a cost. One is to limit disciplinary power to a particular period of emergence: 'It was established at the end of the seventeenth century, and in the course of the eighteenth' (Foucault, 2003: 242). But this is to jettison the claims made for disciplinary power at the end of *Discipline and Punish*: that its study would be the historical background to analyses 'of the power of normalization and the formation of knowledge in modern society' (Foucault, 1977: 308). It would also be to end the lectures at a completely different point from that at which they began. Nevertheless, the limitation of disciplinary power to an intermediary state would seem a satisfactory historical revision, a mere admitting and rectification of a previous hasty over-generalization.

Yet this is not satisfactory for Foucault because it fails to meet the philosophical ambition to demonstrate the archaism of sovereign power, its ineffectivity in respect of our analyses of power in the present, and its dangers of ensnaring and capturing our actions. While Foucault is concerned with the multiple and local sites of power, he is concerned *not* to multiply the forms of non-sovereign power. To do so is to risk leaving sovereignty in place among these forms and for what is especially new to lose its newness. So a second resolution of the problem is required – to find a link between disciplinary and biopower. Foucault finds this in the notion of the norm.

It is the norm that links 'the disciplinary and the regulatory, which will also be applied to the body and population alike, which will make it possible to control both the disciplinary order of the body and the aleatory events that occur in the biological multiplicity' (Foucault, 2003: 252). The normalizing society is not 'a sort of generalized disciplinary society', that is 'no more than a first and inadequate interpretation of a normalizing society' (p. 253). This is a stunning admission. And it has a cost. 'To say that power took possession of life in the nineteenth century ... is to say that it has, thanks to the play of technologies of discipline on the one hand and technologies of regulation on the other, succeeded in covering the whole surface that lies between the organic and the biological, between body and population'(p. 253).

The cost, then, is to produce a view of power as total, as complete, with parts as functionally interdependent, as anything that might have been imagined to stem from the theory of the state, and as rationalizing as any form of instrumental domination ever postulated by the Frankfurt School after Weber. The totalitarian power of biopower is confirmed when, in a final formulation, discipline is subsumed under biopower as merely one of the two basic forms of the 'power over life' and one of its two 'poles of development' (Foucault, 1979: 139). 'The old power of death that symbolized sovereign power was now carefully supplanted by the administration of bodies and the calculated management of life ... Hence there was an explosion of numerous and diverse techniques for achieving the subjugation of bodies and the control of populations, marking the beginning of an era of "bio-power"' (pp. 140–1). There is thus a 'systematicity, functional coherence, and totalizing reach' of forms of power, which is assumed here (Collier, 2009: 79).

Discipline and biopower can only be defined in relationship to one another. A bipolar figure emerges again. However, when they are inserted in the central bipolar narrative that will enable the characterization of modern power, they must somehow be forced into a unity. After toying with a historical periodization, Foucault needs to collapse discipline and biopower into one form that can be contrasted with sovereignty. Biopower subsumes both itself and discipline.

It is often said that due to his untimely death, Foucault left various aspects of his work incomplete. That may be the case, although there must be some doubt that he would ever have really returned to this problem of biopower. He lived and worked productively for over seven years after he asserted, in a finished book, that we live in 'an era of biopower'. There are seven full and long lecture series in which he could have taken up the problem again. (It does not even appear in the indexes to the final three lecture series (Foucault, 2005, 2010, 2011)). On the one occasion on which he has the opportunity afforded by their advertised title, he apologizes for not being able to get around to it, as we shall now see. For Foucault, the moment of the signalling of an era of biopower is not the moment of its centrality in his thought but that of the effective abandonment of the concept.

2.9 Foucault mentions the concept of biopolitics only three times in the lecture series entitled *The Birth of Biopolitics* delivered in 1979. He first assures his audience of his intention to do a course on biopolitics, as indicated by his focus on the problem of population, but contends that 'only when we know what this governmental regime called liberalism was, will we be able to grasp what biopolitics is' (2008: 22). Later on, he promises to address three themes: law and order, state and civil society, and biopolitics and life (p. 78). However, only the first two will be addressed in the rest of this series. Finally, he reassures his audience that he 'really did intend to talk about biopolitics' but that he changed his direction and had began trying out the notion of governmentality 'that is to say, the way in which one conducts the conduct of men', which 'is no more than a proposed analytical grid of these relations of power' (p. 186).

The relationship of biopolitics to these new themes of liberalism and governmentality is destined to remain somewhat obscure, at least in Foucault's work. There are, however, two more clues, but not strictly from the lectures. In an undelivered part of the manuscript of these lectures he says that biopolitics 'is only part of something much larger ... this new governmental reason', and that he would study 'liberalism as the general framework for biopolitics' (2008: 22, footnote). Foucault had subsumed disciplinary power into something larger and newer – biopower or the power over life. This note, no more than a half-realized idea, indicates a temptation now to subsume the power over life into a larger entity. The larger entity is not the 'new nondisciplinary power' called 'biopower' but 'this new governmental reason'.

In the Course Summary, from the reflective distance of some months after the lectures, we discover another, more complex relationship between the governmental reason of liberalism and biopolitics. Writing of the biopolitical problems 'characteristic of a set of living beings forming a population', Foucault suggests they were 'inseparable from the framework of political rationality within which they appeared and took on their intensity'. He continues: 'This means "liberalism" since it was in relationship to liberalism that they assumed the form of a challenge' (2008: 317). So rather than just being a part of a larger set, these biopolitical problems were placed in an antagonism with liberalism; a liberalism 'imbued with the principle "One always governs too much" – or at least, one should always suspect that one governs too much' (p. 319). In this case, biopolitics as a kind of totalizing imperative to optimize life and its forces meets a rationality of government concerned with the best and least costly means to achieve its ends. The problem is how to manage the imperative of optimization contained within biopolitics by limiting it in two different ways: one by the rights of the legal subject, a path we know Foucault has severe reservations about; but secondly, by the existence of 'individual free enterprise', something he found in his analysis of neoliberalism (p. 317). 'Governmentality should not be exercised without a "critique" far more radical than a test of optimization.'

From these clues, which are no more than indications and hesitations, the structure of the bipolar character of Foucault's thought on power re-emerges. Forms of power cannot be distinguished: they are either opposed to one another and, in particular, to the shadow of the sovereign, or subsumed under a unity. Yet the subsumption in this case is all the more complex. Biopower is subsumed not merely within a new form of power but by a new critique of power, and a new grid for the analysis of power, governmentality. Liberalism is the 'problem-space' for dealing with biopolitics; it is not warranted, in terms of Foucault's own text, to describe biopolitics as a 'problem space' (cf. Collier, 2009: 80, 90)

For all the promises regarding the concept of biopower, Foucault does not develop it. After his failure to do so in *The Birth of Biopolitics*, there were five more full lecture courses that followed. Although dedicated to themes and practices of antiquity, they do occasionally link these themes to governmentality, as we shall see, but, on currently published evidence, not to the notion of biopolitics. In his last interviews, it is governmentality that appears in the discussions of power and domination, not biopolitics (e.g. 1988a). If not the exigency of limited time, then what is the explanation for the dropping of biopower? There are certainly methodological problems associated with the term: its epochal character and its embeddedness in functionalist explanation. There is perhaps intellectual embarrassment: its totalizing character would rival any monster created by sovereigntist accounts of power. Maybe, too, there is political embarrassment: the potential for its analysis to lapse into a denunciatory mode. These are all possible explanations.

Governmentality and its synonyms, governmental reason or governmental rationality, and the art of government, certainly take the place of biopower as the marked term in the account of modern conceptions of power. But as all these and related terms indicate, it is not simply governmentality as a form of power but as a new space of critical thought about power, that takes on this value. The concrete intellectual-political formations against which this 'new governmental reason' will take shape for Foucault are many: Machiavelli's *The Prince*; the Christian pastorate with its Judaic sources; the Cameralist manuals of *Polizeiwissenschaft* (police science); and the doctrines and practices of *raison d'État* or reason of state. But over and above these shapes looms the much larger shadow of the juridical logic of sovereignty, still transcendent and capable of blocking the flowering of the arts of government.

The attraction of liberalism as a 'governmental reason' for Foucault is that he no longer needs to encase his own claim for the archaism of sovereignty as model and exemplar of power in a bipolar narrative. It is liberalism's art of government that will try to govern not through sovereign power but through the rationality of the governed, not by defending and advancing the interests of the state but by securing the processes and regularities that appear within the non-state domains of civil society, population and above all, economy, and not through a freedom that is the natural right of a juridical subject but first by the intrinsic interests of *homo œconomicus* and later by the shaping of choice as a technical artefact for the achievement of its ends. It is liberalism, or rather a particular type of liberalism, which would be an economic liberalism rather than a political liberalism, a liberal art of government rather than a liberal philosophy, that Foucault hopes will banish this ghost he has been fighting all these years.

Initial points

2.10
We have established a number of initial points regarding Michel Foucault's characterization of forms of power.

1 Prior to his lectures of 1978 and 1979, his conceptions of power partake a bipolar structure that posits a distinction between a now past juridical conception, in which the key terms are Sovereignty–Law–State, and his own present conception of a positive and productive power.

2 His conception of modern power relations produces another distinction between a form of power that focuses on the individual, their body and capacities, and one that acts upon the regularities observable in populations, that is, disciplinary power and biopolitics.

3 These two forms of modern power are ultimately collapsed as mutually supporting poles of a single power over life (or biopower) in order to mark the displacement of the archaism of the juridical form of sovereignty by modern power, its practice and its analysis.

4 Such a conception proves disabling for the historical investigation of law, which becomes a residual category in this account, variously reduced to the norm, to the continuum of normalizing apparatuses, and later to a technology of government amenable to liberalism.

5 Foucault is caught in the movement that characterizes concepts of power, what we have called its signature. This is its propensity to generate binary oppositions, which are in turn collapsed into a unity to be distinguished from a new, or more fundamental, term.

6 When Foucault drops the concept of biopolitics for a new conception of power – governmentality – he appears to have become aware of the way this signature repeatedly marks his concept of power.

7 This new conceptualization of power as governmentality, as both form of power and as critical reflection on the exercise of power, is thus an attempt to escape this signature and to continue the quest to defeat the shadow of the sovereign.

Perhaps the key discovery of this initial exegesis of Foucault's writings and lectures on power can be expressed in the following way: his central concern is not the identification and characterization of different kinds, styles or relations of power but the pinpointing of a new power that, in the radicality of its newness, effects a displacement of the hold of the juridical-political theory and practice of sovereignty on our political imaginations. This philosophical objective takes three different forms: the political form of the demand for the minimization of domination and the maximization of self-government in games of power; the epistemological form of breaking the link between identity and truth; and the ethical form of a self-conduct that challenges existing ontologies of the self. Foucault's analysis of power is not placed on the conventional terrain of inequality, legitimacy and social transformation, but on identity, technique and what he will call the government of self and others.

3

ECONOMIES OF POWER

3.1 In a career of famous lectures, the one Michel Foucault delivered at the Collège de France on 1 February 1978 is perhaps the most famous. While it has had a long bibliographic history in Italian and in English, it was only published as part of a lecture series in French in 2004 (Foucault, 2004b). It was the fourth lecture to be delivered that winter. Foucault had returned from a sabbatical year, so the series of which this one was a part was the first after those that had introduced the term 'biopolitics'. The context of this lecture series includes Foucault's active participation in discussions on the imminence of a Socialist government in France and in the promotion of Soviet dissidence (Sennelart, 2007: 371–7). More proximately, there are political events, including one, the 'Kroissant Affair', which raised both legal-political and intellectual issues in France concerning European terrorism; led to Foucault's personal injury during a demonstration; and introduced new lines of intellectual and political fracture that can also be useful as a point of reflection on context. However, here we shall remain solely with his text of these lectures, and those he gave in the following year.

The first and third terms of the trinity of the title of the 1978 lectures, *Security, Territory, Population*, are familiar from our discussion of biopower and indeed, at their beginning, these lectures appear to continue from where the previous lecture had left off (Foucault, 2007: 1). But apart from a second mention at the end of same lecture (p. 22), the notion of 'biopower' will not be addressed here. It is at the end of the fourth lecture that their main problematic will be introduced.

> Basically if I had wanted to give the lectures I am giving this year a more exact title, I certainly would not have chosen 'security, territory, population'. What I would really like to undertake is something that I could call a history of 'governmentality'. (p. 108)

This term means three things. Governmentality is a kind of power or at least 'the institutions, procedures, analyses and reflections, calculations, and tactics that allow the exercise of this very specific, albeit very complex, power that has population as its target, political economy as its major form of knowledge, and apparatuses of security as its essential technical instrument' (p. 108). Secondly, it is a line of force 'towards the pre-eminence over all other types of power – sovereignty, discipline, and so on – of the type of power we can call government'. But there is an ambiguity here, which it is necessary to grasp. For, although pre-eminent, government does not replace discipline or sovereignty; rather it is best to see these forms of power as a '... triangle: sovereignty, discipline, governmental management which has population as its main target and apparatuses of security as its essential mechanism' (pp. 107–8). The idea of biopower remains conspicuous here only by its absence.

The final characteristic of 'governmentality' is 'the process, or rather, the result of the process by which the state of justice of the Middle Ages became the administrative state in the fifteenth and sixteenth centuries and was gradually "governmentalized"' (pp. 108–9). Or, again, the major 'economies of power', as Foucault calls them, are, chronologically, the 'state of justice', the 'administrative state' and the 'state of government', corresponding, respectively, to a society of law, a society of regulation and discipline, and a society 'controlled by apparatuses of security' (p. 110). The state of government is no longer 'essentially defined by its territoriality' but by the 'mass of the population'.

Here, Foucault defines the three 'economies of power' in terms of the apparatuses, or, to be more precise, *dispositifs*, of law, discipline and security he had analysed in the first three lectures of *Security, Territory, Population*. These notions of an 'economy of power', and of the *dispositif*, require closer analysis. Nonetheless, in these dense few, canonical statements, Foucault draws them together to define government as type of power and governmentality as the conditions that allow this power to operate both as a pre-eminent power and one power among others, and to arrange the three *dispositifs* in sequence across a temporal schema.

The delineation of a new power; its equal presence and its juxtaposition among other powers; and its reworking of the chronological scheme, are all moves which are the same as Foucault's earlier discovery of biopower, which, it must be emphasized, has now been entirely dropped from the scheme. And again, it is precisely the same enemy, which is sometimes theoretical, sometimes historical and practical, and sometimes methodological, which necessitates the prevarications, revisions and ultimate collapse of the new power into a unity strong enough to fight its antithesis. Here the shadow of the enemy, sovereignty, is manifested in the two forms of an affective and an analytic over-investment in the state. The affective over-investment that takes a 'tragic form is the lyricism of the cold monster confronting us' (p. 109). The analytic over-investment takes the form of a functionalism of the state, and a reduction often to the productive forces and relations. The state, he concludes, does not have this unity, individuality, functionality, or importance, and is perhaps only a 'composite reality and mythicized abstraction'. 'What is important for our modernity, and that is to say, for our present, is not the state's takeover of society, so much as what I would call the "governmentalization" of the state' (p. 109).

Never does Foucault become so expressive as when he turns away from the 'new power' to the archaism that it is his quest to defeat. But here it is not the ensnaring and codifying state he discussed with the Maoists, or the spectacle that gave rise to the tortures and punishment of 'atrocity', or the symbolics of sword and blood behind a right to death, but the Nietzschean monster and the functionary of Marxist dialectics looming over society. From his *History of Madness* to the first volume of the *History of Sexuality*, Foucault had displayed an acute deployment of the analysis of art, architecture, ritual and literature, and of mythology, symbology, and epigraphy, in service of his study of power relations and their domains. With the rejection of the purely impressionistic, nineteenth-century image of the *monstre froid*, he seems to close the door to what would otherwise have been a fruitful discussion of the interweaving of political mythology and governmental rationality.

Undoubtedly there are subtleties to be appreciated here. This 'governmentalization of the state' is not a smooth and monotonous process. For Foucault had already observed that with the emergence of a new art of government the 'problem of sovereignty is more acute than ever' and 'discipline was never more important or valued than when the attempt was made to manage the population...' (p. 107). Yet somehow the distinctions, multiplicities and types of power must assemble themselves into a unity strong enough to oppose the hold that the domain of sovereignty, state and law has over our analytics and our politics. By 1978, we are no longer in the society of normalization discovered in 1975, or the era of biopower of 1976 – 'We live in the era of a governmentality discovered in the eighteenth century.'

If we live in an era of governmentality, or of governmental reason, or of a liberal art of government, which is as much a critique and grid of power as a form of power, then the language of state, sovereignty and law, would be inadequate to the analysis of government, the pre-eminent form of power in this era. In doing so, have we not rejoined with liberalism, or at least a kind of economic liberalism, in the desire to find another grid of analysis outside that of the state and to limit and restrict powers that would be sovereign? In the following year, and indeed through these lectures, Foucault tries to settle accounts with this issue. For most commentators, like Thomas Lemke, Foucault's analysis of contemporary governmental reason 'will enable us to shed sharper light on the effects of neo-liberal governmentality ... [which are] the product of a re-coding of social mechanisms of exploitation and domination' (Lemke, 2001: 203). But a provocative revisionism is also present in recent commentaries. Andrew Dilts has described Foucault's position toward neoliberalism as one of 'sympathetic critique and indebtedness' (2011: 133, n. 11). Michael Behrent has gone so far as to say he 'strategically endorsed it' (2009: 539).

Before we are in a position to evaluate these claims, however, we must examine another ace up Foucault's sleeve in his efforts to reconceptualize power, the notion of the *dispositif*, the sketching of which takes up most of his first three lectures in *Security, Territory, Population*. Just as Foucault would close the door on the study of political mythology and symbols, he would invoke this, the most 'economic' of methodological images.

Dispositif

3.2 The complexity of Foucault's thought on power appears in the first three lectures of *Security, Territory, Population*. For some, they are something of the curate's egg: parts of them allusive and very disconnected, others brilliant (Tribe, 2009); to others, they are a kind of master-key unlocking Foucault's new analytical approach and method (Collier, 2009). They discuss three *dispositifs*, of law, discipline and security and show their operations and interconnections in three examples of town planning and the organization of urban space, of the scarcity of grain and of epidemic and endemic disease. The emergence of the new *dispositif* of security in these sectors is marked by exemplary texts: Vigny's plan for the city of Nantes of 1755, Abeille's 1762 letter containing proposals for the regulation of grain, and Duvillard's 1806 presentation of the analysis and tables of the effect of smallpox on mortality at each age, and the efficacy of preventive vaccine (Foucault, 2007: 18–20, 35–40, 61–2). Foucault distinguishes and summarizes the legal, disciplinary and security *dispositifs* in relation to the simple example of the penalty (pp. 4–6), to urban space and the town (pp. 20–1), to scarcity (pp. 31–2), and finally to urban planning, scarcity and disease patterns as manifestations of the general phenomenon of the town itself (pp. 63–7). Further, he broadly distinguishes discipline and security in relation to scarcity (pp. 44–7) and to the norm and normalization (pp. 56–7). He ends the three lectures by asserting and analysing the remarkable entrance of a new personage, the population, which finally appears as an 'operator' of transformation in the sciences of life, labour and production, that is, the domains of his much earlier study, *The Order of Things* (1970).

It would no doubt be fruitful to follow the analytical decomposition of these *dispositifs* here. But that is not our point. *Dispositif* analysis, if we could call it that, is more complex, less functionalist, and certainly less epochal than other of Foucault's formulations, including the ones in the following lecture on governmentality that we have just analysed. After disavowing the idea of 'a series of successive elements', he suggests a model of 'a series of complex edifices ... in which what changes above all is the dominant characteristic, or more exactly, the system of correlations between juridico-legal mechanisms, disciplinary mechanisms, and mechanisms of security' (2007: 8).

There is a language or metaphorics of complication, of complexity, of fuzziness ('a much more fuzzy history'). What changes is not the form of power but the system of correlation within the *dispositif* so that the 'technology of security will be set up, taking up again and sometimes even multiplying juridical and disciplinary elements and redeploying them within its specific tactic' (p. 9). There is more contingency and less necessity in the relations between the technologies. There is redeployment, recombination, re-orderings and re-inscriptions. The notion of the *dispositif* brings Foucault close to the visions of complexity and systems that also inspired certain of the neoliberals he was studying (Hayek, 1967b).

Just before these lectures, a conversation with Foucault was published when he is asked directly the meaning and function of the term *dispositif*. The *dispositif*, he replies, is 'a system of relations between elements', which include 'discourses, institutions, architectural forms, regulatory decisions, laws, administrative measures, scientific statements, philosophical, moral and philanthropic propositions' and which form a 'heterogeneous ensemble ... the said as much as the unsaid' (1980: 194). What he is trying to do is precisely identify the 'nature of the connection ... the interplay of shifts of position and modifications of functions which can also vary very widely'. The *dispositif* has a 'dominant strategic function' that corresponds to 'an urgent need', and its strategic character means 'a certain manipulation of relations of forces, either developing them in a particular direction, blocking them, stabilizing them, utilizing them' (pp. 195–6).

A *dispositif* is something like a network of relations between elements that responds to an emergency and that organizes, enables, orients, fixes and blocks relations of force. It is simply an immanent ordering of a field of force according to a strategic function. While all of these terms are very abstract, they do indicate an attempt to detach the analysis from the epochal, functionalist and totalizing ones we have witnessed recurring in Foucault's thought. It would be a mistake to imagine that this is the true or authentic version of his thought, or the other is entirely without value. For even here, at the minor level of debates about the shape of Foucault's critical thought, method and analysis, we have yet another series of polarities, just as we have observed in his major categories of power: contingency and necessity, multiplicity and unity, heterogeneity and homogeneity, with the first term in each pair positively marked. If the epochal version of Foucault's analytics of power gave the bipolarity of power a grand narrative, the *dispositif* version equally reproduces that bipolarity, but this time in a series of methodological choices.

It would be a mistake, however, to view Foucault's lecture on the *dispositifs* of security, law and discipline as marking a new methodological orientation (Collier, 2009). This lecture is almost completely consistent with the chapter 'On Method' in *History of Sexuality I* (1979), which investigates the *dispositif* of sexuality. After proposing a number of theses appropriate to the study of power as 'the multiplicity of force relations immanent in the sphere in which they operate and which constitute their own organization' (1979: 92), that is, as *dispositifs*, Foucault provides his reason for doing so:

> In this way we will escape from the system of Law-and-Sovereign which has captivated political thought for such a long time. And if it is true that Machiavelli was among the few ... who conceived the power of the Prince in terms of force relationships, perhaps we need to go one step further, do without the persona of the Prince, and decipher power mechanisms on the basis of a strategy that is immanent in force relations. (1979: 97)

Perhaps we might like to say that Foucault abandoned this position on law and sovereignty, or, at least, that it begins to lose its axiomatic character, in *Security, Territory, Population*. Here, Foucault returns to a metaphor, no doubt with a different nuance, which he had used previously, to describe this strategic ordering of relations of forces. He speaks, in each lecture, of each of these *dispositifs* – of security, discipline and law – in terms of a distinctive 'economy of power'. He wishes to ask whether security forms a 'general economy of power' (p. 11). He insists on the need to identify whether the 'general economy of power' involves marking a territory, disciplining subjects, or constituting a population (p. 30). And he concludes that the examples of town, scarcity and epidemics have demonstrated the existence of a 'completely different economy of power' (p. 67).

While Foucault, on many occasions, takes pains to insist that he offers not a theory of power but a conceptualization of relations of power, his thought had to address the signature of power we observed in theories of power of the twentieth century, that is, this tendency to define power through ever new binaries. By 1977–78, he had to face this problem of the binary he had constructed between a juridical conception of sovereignty and a modern, non-juridical power, first of discipline and then of biopower. In his 1978 lectures, he responds in two ways: first, by inserting the element of critique, of critical thought, of the ethos of criticism, into the very genealogy of these relations of power. Thus governmentality or governmental reason, in particular liberalism, is a critique of power as much as a form of power. By this move he hopes to maintain his basic presupposition of the archaism of a conception of power in terms of sovereignty, law and state. This time, he will do this not via the axial and epochal bipolarity of forms of power, but by the emergence of a liberal art of government itself.

The second move is to elaborate the methodological notion of the *dispositif* so that rather than a simple epochal shift from one form of power to another there are different systems of correlations between multiple concrete ensembles that are contingent and empirically analysable rather than taking a necessary shape answering to functional imperatives. But this too remains a way of defeating the theory of sovereignty for the sovereign, rather than the supreme power within a domain, must become, as state institution, law, or executive decision, one or several of the elements, entering into widely varying relations, having different and modifiable functions, and occupying shifting positions within a complex network or ensemble. Questions of executive decision and exception, of law, legality and legitimacy, of supreme power and state, can all be tamed and domesticated, brought down from the heights of their claimed transcendence, by being repositioned within this eminently immanent and 'economic' analysis, that the *dispositif* makes possible. As we shall see (in §7.7), this word *dispositif* comes from the Latin *dispositio*, which Cicero has used in his study of rhetoric to translate the Greek word, *oikonomia*, or economy. In this strictly philological sense, then, it is correct to describe a *dispositif* as an economy of power.

For Foucault it is perhaps no longer quite a question of 'cutting off the king's head'. Rather it is one of replacing his Crown and royal regalia with a business suit, his Sword with a Master of Business Administration, and his Law with the myriad technical norms, standards, strategic plans and mission statements.

State-phobia

3.3 Foucault raises the problem of the different forms of overvaluation of the state, and of a fear of the state that gives rise to an anti-governmental eschatology several times during the course of his lectures in 1978 and 1979. It appears at the beginning of the fourth lecture in *The Birth of Biopolitics*. Citing a statement by the art historian, Berenson, that he feared the state more than the atomic bomb, Foucault interpolates the idea of 'state-phobia', its sources and themes, and its link to the twentieth-century history of political exile (2008: 75–6). It is a theme that appears to be at odds with his own theoretical anti-statism, which is perhaps why he describes this phobia about the state as 'ambiguous' (p. 76). However, he continues to insist 'I must do without a theory of the state, as one can forgo an indigestible meal' (pp. 76–7). To do so, means 'not starting with an analysis of the nature, structure, and functions of the state in and for itself' and 'not starting from the state considered as a sort of political universal' and not deducing the results of one's analysis from the state. Rather, Foucault insists that because 'the state does not have an essence' it should be approached as 'nothing else but the mobile effect of a regime of multiple governmentalities' (p. 77). This means going outside the problem of the state and investigating it on the basis of these practices of governmentality.

The discussion of state-phobia is not an aside. Rather, it is an introduction to what follows, which is 'to analyse, or rather to take up and test this anxiety about the state' (p. 77). The theme of state-phobia is then essayed or tested against the history of neoliberalism in its mid-century German form, and also its, slightly later, American one. In a sense, this is a genealogy of contemporary state-phobia, for both these formations 'share the same objects of repulsion, namely the state-controlled economy, planning, and state interventionism' and have John Maynard Keynes as their 'main doctrinal adversary ... the common enemy' (p. 79).

Foucault undertakes such a test and, after four lectures of biographies, history and discussion of the theses of post-war German neoliberalism, or Ordoliberalism (after the journal, *Ordo*), he returns to this theme. Keith Tribe, the historian of economic thought who has usefully compared Foucault's account with that of his sources for these lectures, has praised his argument as 'quite brilliant, not least because he manages to make a sense of ordo liberalism that no one else has ever managed, not least the ordo-liberals themselves' (2009: 690). There is, indeed, enough in these four lectures to launch a thousand governmentality ships and more. German neoliberalism emerges, to put it briefly, in contrast to classical liberalism. Rather than limiting the state in a quasi-natural market economy, however, it founds the state's very legitimacy and justifies its every action and form of regulation on the market economy (Foucault, 2008: 116–17). However, this market economy, and the necessary market society that accompanies it and is its condition of existence, is one that requires detailed construction. The market itself is founded on the principle of competition, which has nothing to do with the 'naïve naturalism' of the classical liberals (here the

Ordoliberals betray a debt to Edmund Husserl, the founder of phenomenology), but is an essence or an *eidos*, that needs 'to be carefully and artificially constructed' (p. 120). As a consequence, the mission of basing the state and its legitimacy on economic freedom presupposes an active policy and realm of interventions that seek to construct the very conditions of the market (pp. 86–7). While such policies must take the form, as Wilhelm Röpke puts it, following Walter Euken, of 'conformable actions' to the idea of the market, such as achieving price stability by appropriate monetary, taxation and trade policies, and making social policies consistent with the individualization of risks and economic growth, this will leave enormous scope for governmental innovation (pp. 137ff.).

These governmental innovations will include the *Gesellschaftspolitik* (the policy of society), a term Alfred Müller-Armack gave to Ludwig Erhard (p. 146). They will also include the space for the 'Rule of Law' and juridical institutions that would create the conditions for the game of market competition, as in the work of the Austrian, Friedrich Hayek, although not strictly part of this group (pp. 171–4). They will further encompass a *Vitalpolitik*, or a 'politics of life', advanced by Alexander von Rüstow, in which the enterprise form is generalized across the whole of society but provides also 'the moral and cultural values' that can compensate for the negative effects of the market (pp. 148–50). Finally, they include the 'social market economy', which Müller-Armack, as Secretary of State to Erhard's Minister of the Economy, would bring to the Treaty of Rome (pp. 103–4). The idea of the building of a 'common market' and the construction of the legitimacy and actions of a newly constructed political entity upon it would, as we know, have a fundamental, if not exclusive, role in the imagination which would shape modern Europe (Walters and Haahr, 2005).

For Foucault, the analysis of the productivity of this neoliberal rationality of government can be contrasted with socialism, which lacks 'not so much a theory of the state as a governmental reason' (2008: 91). With one eye on the two Germanies, East and West, and one on the possibility of a Socialist government in France, Foucault asserts that there is 'no governmental rationality of socialism'. Reflecting on the role of the social democrats in the development of post-war West Germany, and on the state socialism of the East, he argues that socialism is only ever connected up to forms of governmentality, whether of the liberal governmentalities he has been analysing or those 'governmentalities that would no doubt fall more under ... the police state' (p. 92).

When, after this vivid analysis, Foucault returns to the theme of state-phobia it seeks to test, it is to identify the elements that are constant in this 'critique of the state' (p. 187). The two elements he identifies are, first, the intrinsic power of the state in relationship to its target and object, civil society, and, second, the kinship it supposes between 'the administrative state, the welfare state, the bureaucratic state, the fascist state, and the totalitarian state' (p. 187). These two elements contribute to the 'inflationary critical currency', which manifests itself in a 'general disqualification by the worst'. This means that analysis loses its specificity and that any attempt to analyse specific practices, such as that of social security, will find its way towards a discussion of 'the concentration camps'. Citing his young student assistant, Ewald, who, we have seen, clearly had had experience of such things, such a disqualification fails to analyse an actuality and is merely a practice of 'denunciation'.

Foucault's next move is to suggest some theses to counter this inflationary critique of the state (pp. 190–1). This first possibly arises from his conversations with Ewald, who had presented on social insurance and workplace accidents in the previous year's seminar (Foucault, 2007: 367). It is that the welfare state, *L'État Providence*, is not the same and does not have the same roots as the totalitarian state. The latter rather results from 'a limitation, a reduction, and a subordination of the autonomy of the state'. This occurred in relation to the 'governmentality of the party which appeared in Europe at the end of the nineteenth century' (Foucault, 2008: 191). This party governmentality is but one of the two forms of the reduction of the state. The other is the neoliberal governmentality he had been analysing in Germany, and which he now proposes to follow in its diffusion into France and the United States. Foucault would appear to be distancing himself from, rather than 'strategically endorsing', this neoliberal governmentality.

However, Foucault would not have missed a certain irony. This inflationary critique of the state in terms of the expansion of its totalitarian powers bears an uncanny resemblance to his own analysis of the concerted articulation of two fundamental forms of power, discipline and biopower, at the end of the 1976 lectures and in his *History of Sexuality I* (1979). Biopolitics, which had been instanced by the institutional sites of public health and hygiene, social welfare and insurance, and urban planning, was linked in those statements to the development of state racism, both in its state socialist and more particularly National Socialist forms. Foucault himself had indeed produced an analysis that found its way from the welfare state to Nazism, its concentration camps, and the exterminations which took place there. He could have indeed had himself in mind when he gave the example of how 'an analysis of social security and the administrative apparatus on which it rests ends up, via some slippages and thanks to some plays on words, referring us to the concentration camps' (pp. 187–8). One of his criticisms of state-phobia is its lack of critical self-reflection and it appears that he is undertaking such an exercise here in the hope of an exculpation of past sins.

These passages are something like a recognition and reflection of his own state-phobia, or at least of his earlier state-phobia, and they underlie the longer journey that he and his students have made if not from Maoism, at least from supporting Maoist tactics. The genealogy of state-phobia is in part one of an ultra-Leftism that would lead German terrorists, such as the Red Army Faction, as well as some of his own colleagues, to denounce the West German state as 'fascist'. But its more fundamental line of descent is in neoliberalism, especially German Ordoliberalism. This somewhat surprising genealogy of state-phobia leads Foucault to recognize and critically reflect upon his own affinity with neoliberalism and its critique of the state. In the end, however, despite this recognition, it would be a bridge too far to say that Foucault 'strategically endorses' neoliberalism. He stands in wonderment at the apparent affinities, and sources, of his mistrust of the state; and he allows himself to be perplexed by the strange affinities and odd resemblances between wildly different political and intellectual projects.

None of these local, genealogical insights, however, would lead Foucault finally to renounce his own *theoretical* anti-statism.

3.4 There are two further themes that highlight Foucault's examination of anti-statism. The first is that of the place of Nazism and fascism in his analysis. The second is the question of an anti-governmental eschatology. They each deserve a brief mention because they indicate that Foucault did not wish his theoretical opposition to a statist analysis to be confused with a liberal or neoliberal political critique of an excessive state. They suggest the taking of a measured distance from neoliberalism and liberalism respectively.

In his discussion of the Ordoliberals, Foucault seeks to demonstrate that they view the history of Germany not as one of market failure but of state failure in which the market has never really been tried. They find the sources and examples of this in Friedrich List's nineteenth-century 'national economy', Bismarckian state socialism, the planned economy, and Keynesian-style interventionism (Foucault, 2008: 107–9). These are all so many versions of the 'anti-liberal invariant' (p. 111), which, in what Foucault regards as an intellectual *coup de force*, they also find exemplified in the monstrosity of the economic policies of Nazism. For the Ordoliberals, Nazism linked all this together 'in a strict coalescence of the different elements' (p. 109); it 'is the revelation of the necessary system of relations between these different elements' (p. 110). In his examination of the Ordoliberals' view of Nazism as unlimited state power, Foucault considers how they rejected a possible alternative analysis of this regime, which would be that it initiated a 'withering away of the state' by placing the *Volk* above law and right, the *Führer* above authority and administrative hierarchy, and the party above the state (pp. 111–12). The Ordoliberals are exemplary of a kind of 'negative theology of the state as the absolute evil', that is, of a critique which sweeps together the Soviet Union and the USA, concentration camps and social security records (p. 116).

This diagnosis indicates a radical departure from his earlier claim, somewhat resonant with the view he finds in Ordoliberalism, that Nazism was the development of modern power mechanisms, discipline and biopower, and their articulation with the sovereign right to kill, 'inscribed in the workings of all [modern] States' (Foucault, 2003: 260). In this earlier formulation, Foucault thus found the state possessed powers with ever-present monstrous or, as he put it elsewhere, 'demonic' potential, which was seized upon and taken by the Nazis to a 'paroxysmal point' leading to the 'final solution for the other races, and the absolute suicide for the [German] race'. A slightly more refined version of this is found in *History of Sexuality I* (1979: 149–50) but Foucault undoubtedly views Nazism as continuous with the biopolitical racism inscribed in the modern state. By contrast, in his response to the Ordoliberals, we have both a reflection on the commonplace denunciation of the state as necessarily fascist and an implicit self-critique of his own previous characterization of the articulated powers of the modern state as leading to Nazism.

In this second reading, the full implications of which Foucault did not explore, Nazism is less a pathology of the state and its integral powers and more a pathology of the radical anti-statism found across the spectrum of Western political culture. It is to 'party governmentality', and the idea of a state subordinated to the will of the people or the nation, rather than to intrinsic state logics that we must look to begin an understanding of this monstrosity.

3.5 This 'negative theology' of the state, which Foucault no doubt would have admitted he practised at a certain point, is grounded in what he calls anti-state 'eschatology' (2008: 356). In his genealogy of governmentality, Foucault proposes that doctrines such as *raison d'État* (reason of state) put an end to the medieval Christian theological cosmology in which the Christian empire located its own existence in the interval between Christ founding his Kingdom on earth and his Second Coming, and is thus an Empire of the final days. With reason of state as a rational art of government concerned with the maintenance and expansion of the state, Foucault suggests, we leave a world governed under this inevitable ending (the *eschaton*) and enter a world that is now one of 'an open time and multiple spatiality' (2007: 290). In this sense, reason of state brings Christian eschatology to a close, at least politically. However, Foucault's narrative continues, this purely secular rationality of government will itself be the object of critique by emergent liberalism conducted in the name of that which lies outside the state, particularly the discovery of 'civil society'. This discovery of a natural-historical domain prior to the 'artifice' of the state by those such as Adam Ferguson makes possible a 'revolutionary eschatology' and a series of counter-conducts. These can ground themselves in the prevalence of civil society as a domain of virtue over the state and its despotism; in the right of the population to revolt; or in the very essence and truth of the nation (2007: 356–7; 2008: 309–11).

If we follow Foucault in this line of reasoning, modern political eschatology, then, can take a nationalist form, such as the pitting of the 'Third Estate' against the *ancien regime* (with Abbé Sieyès as exemplar), a revolutionary form of the 'withering away of the state' in Marxist-Leninism, or, more pervasively, a liberal or even republican form of the instructive virtue and intrinsic value of civil society, such as found in Thomas Paine. In this diagnosis, Nazism would find points of contact with political eschatology and appear less as the elements of the modern state taken to an extremity and more as a political movement that seeks to undermine its characteristic features by placing the people, leader and party (or movement) above law and right, bureaucratic administration and the state.

To summarize, it would be too much to say that there is a fundamental break between the Foucault of 1976 and the one of 1978. However there are important movements in his thought relevant to our understanding of power that should be underlined but which do not all point in the same direction. Firstly, there is the relatively superficial replacement of biopolitics by governmentality and the maintenance of epochal formulations. Secondly, there is the development of *dispositif* analysis that seeks to avoid the functionalism and super-determinism that characterizes earlier formulations of transitions in power, and which seeks a domestication and taming of the study of the state. Thirdly there is an installation of critical self-reflection in the form of liberal governmental reason or governmentality at the heart of the trajectories of relations of power. And finally there is a consideration of the politically and analytically disabling effects of anti-statism under such rubrics as 'state-phobia' and anti-state 'eschatology'. *Pace* recent revisionist accounts, Foucault does not appear to endorse neoliberalism, questioning both its positioning of Nazism as condensing the 'anti-liberal invariant' of the illegitimate extension of the state into civil society, and calling for an analysis of the specificity of the welfare state.

Perhaps these later moves form a series of 'mea culpas' for aspects of his biopolitical analysis. But the central question is not whether Foucault is a statist or anti-statist but whether an analysis that views the state as a resultant of rationalities, techniques and practices of governmentality is the best way to understand the historical-institutional reality of the state as a law-governed and law-organized form of political organization which claims supreme authority and a monopoly of legitimate force within a given domain. Or, to put it another way, is an analysis which would flatten everything onto the domain of immanence capable of grasping a power that establishes itself as standing over and above all other powers in the glorious transcendence of its sovereignty?

Exceptions

3.6 It would also be unfair to say that Foucault completely excised himself from the sovereignty tradition and its themes of exception and emergency in either his methodological indications or in his genealogies of government. Jeffrey Bussolini (2010b: 92; 98) has drawn our attention to two aspects of his work that continue to contribute to this tradition of political thought in terms of aspects of sovereignty.

The first of these is expressed in methodological statements concerning the *dispositif*. Generally, Foucault seeks to deprive terms such as sovereignty, law, and state of a universal or transcendental status and places them as elements within the set of complex relations that form various *dispositifs*. Yet, in keeping with the sovereignty tradition, he allows that the *dispositifs* themselves can be formed in relation to an emergency, e.g. the food shortages in the second half of the eighteenth century (2007: 30), or the assimilation of an excess floating population into a mercantilist economy in the seventeenth century (1980: 195). The idea of urgent necessity or emergency is central, for example, to Jean Bodin's definition of 'the true marks of sovereignty' and, in his case, limits the extent to which the sovereign is bound by law.

Bussolini also draws our attention to his discussion of the political theatricality of the *coup d'État* in *Security, Territory, Population*. Foucault regards the *coup d'État* 'as a suspension of, a temporary departure from, laws and legality [that] ... goes beyond ordinary law' (2007: 261). Foucault cites Le Bret in 1632 who states that the exception creates a necessity, a force so great that like a 'sovereign goddess, having nothing sacred in the world but the firmness of its irrevocable decrees, it ranks everything divine and human beneath its power' (p. 263). He argues, drawing on Naudé, Chemnitz, Charron and Le Bret, that the *coup d'État* responds to a necessity over and above the law. Its violence comes when 'necessity demands' that '*raison d'État* becomes *coup d'État*', is not opposed to reason (or *raison d'État*) and is 'committed by wise men in concert', and that it is necessarily theatrical in that it 'brings tragedy into play on the stage of reality itself' (pp. 262–6). The theatrical character of the *coup d'État*, Foucault argues, is in fact the 'irruptive assertion of *raison d'Etat*' (p. 264), and thus continuous with it, and must be viewed as 'a mode of manifestation of the state and of the sovereign as the holder of state power', thus complementing the traditional ceremonies of royalty, the anointments, coronations, appearances and funerals that articulated the sovereign's 'power with religious power and theology' (p. 265).

It could be argued that this example of the *coup* and its relationship to the state of exception tradition underlines Foucault's efforts to place sovereignty, its practices and rituals on the side of the archaic and external to the contemporary *dispositifs* of discipline, law, security, sexuality, and so forth. Indeed most followers of Foucault would not recognize a view of Foucault that placed the sovereignty and state-of-exception traditions at the centre of his deliberations of power. Nonetheless, it is precisely here that there is a possibility of a kind of tactical disloyalty drawing on its 'capacity for elaboration', Ludwig Feuerbach's *Entwicklungsfähigkeit*.

However, there is a further example that makes this latter suggestion much less implausible and places the exception closer to the heart of what Foucault regards as modern security apparatuses. In the *Birth of Biopolitics,* Foucault outlined a view of the economy as exception in relation to Adam Smith and the Physiocrats: 'There is no sovereign in economics. There is no economic sovereignty' (2008: 283). Faced with the incompatibility of *homo œconomicus* – economic man – with the juridical framework of sovereignty, political economy, Foucault argues that the sovereign will be able to intervene everywhere except in the market. The 'market will be, if you like, a sort of free port or free space in the general space of sovereignty' (p. 293). What we have at the heart of liberal governmental reason is the economy as a sovereign exception, that is, as an exception to the juridical-political order. By employing the term *'franc port'*, Foucault indicates a genealogy of the creation of economies and economic zones as spaces of exception from the very formation of classical liberalism (2004a: 297). In this respect, we can undertake a genealogy of the economy as exception from the free market, to the free port as a place without custom duties and so on, to special economic zones and zoning technologies (Ong, 2006) and even forms of international government (Best, 2007). Accordingly, it is not a matter of separating, chronologically or analytically, the juridical-political doctrine of the exception, on one side, and the liberal government of and through the economy on the other. Rather the economy as exception is at the very heart of liberal governing itself.

Today, when we have witnessed both the juridical exception in the war on terror and the economic exception in the years of financial crisis, Foucault's thought appears most relevant when it forsakes the quest to escape the juridical-political model of sovereignty and abandons a purely 'immanentist' conception of power.

The later Foucault

3.7 The concept of governmentality would prove pivotal in Foucault's thought, providing a passageway between these dense and difficult, ambiguous and complex, explorations of relations of power to his later concerns for the questions of ethics and the care of the self. The idea of freedom will prove crucial to this transition.

Governmentality is mentioned several times in these later lectures in 1982, 1983 and 1984 (*The Hermeneutics of the Subject*, 2005; *The Government of Self and Others*, 2010; and *The Courage of Truth*, 2011) Here, Foucault's topic is not modern power but ancient ethics and ascetics. In the earliest, he expands upon what might be called a 'relational' conception of governmentality, which is capable of linking and analysing power relations, governing the self and others, and the relation to oneself, as a chain that makes it possible to connect political government with ethical self-government, and politics to ethics (Foucault, 2005: 252). Later, he places the analysis of governmentality in relation to other dimensions of his work. His general approach is to uncover the conditions and practices through which apparently given, stable and universal entities emerge, including what he calls 'focal points of experience' such as madness, sexuality, disease and criminality. Here 'procedures of governmentality' move beyond the history of domination in the same way as 'regimes of veridiction' displace the history of knowledge and a 'pragmatics of the self' replaces the history of subjectivity (Foucault, 2010: 5).

These are indications that 'governmentality' remained a key grid for understanding power relations even when Foucault moved his discussion from forms of neoliberalism to questions more concerned with the relationship of self to self, and self to truth. Perhaps, however, the 'final Foucault' on the topic of power – a paradoxical label for a thought that always remained provisional – is summed up in some smaller texts and interviews.

3.8 'The Subject and Power' displays a reluctance toward and desire to be done with the very terminology of power. It avers that its author's main concern is the subject, not power (2001: 327), and asks whether we need a theory of power, rather than an ongoing conceptualization. Stalinism and fascism are described, in inverted commas, as 'pathological forms' or 'diseases of power', which begs the question of the norm they are being judged against. That seems to be answered later in the piece (which gives the appearance of loosely connected thought-fragments rather than a realized essay) in which neither consent nor violence 'constitute the principal or basic nature of power' (p. 341). The exercise of power instead is 'a set of actions upon other actions'. Indeed, the term 'conduct', with its double meaning of 'to lead' and 'behaviour', should be employed, argues Foucault, so that the 'exercise of power is a "conduct of conducts" and a management of possibilities'. Power is more a *game* of freedom: it is only exercised over free subjects and in so far as they are free. 'By this we mean individual or collective subjects who are faced with a field of possibilities in which several kinds of conduct, several ways of reacting and modes of behavior are available' (p. 342). The conclusion suggests that the notion of power has become somewhat exhausted in Foucault's vocabulary: 'Basically, power is less a confrontation between two adversaries or their mutual engagement than a question of "government"' (p. 341).

This term links us to the lectures of 1978 and 1979. It suggests a kind of elision of power and government, and a retirement of the former term. This would seem to substantiate Pasquale Pasquino's oft-cited claim that due to the threat that the study of the disciplines would lead to 'an extremist denunciation of power – according to a *repressive* model' it was replaced by '...the question of *government* – a term gradually substituted for what he saw as the more ambiguous word "power"' (1993: 79, original emphasis). This evaluation suggests Foucault sought to deactivate the signature of power he discovered by retreating to its immanent pole. It also provides a key link to his concerns for ethics.

In an interview only a few months before his death, Foucault not only explores this new language of 'relationships of power as strategic games between liberties' in which 'some people try to determine the conduct of others' but distinguishes these relations of power from 'states of domination, which are what we ordinarily call power' and governmental technologies, which lie between the two (1988a: 19). The primary sense of power here is of open and reversible relationships between different and unequal partners, while domination is an ossification and blocking of power relations, 'to render them impassive and invariable and to prevent all reversibility of movement' (p. 3). However, this 'agonistic' game of free subjects utilizes governmental technologies, or a governmentality which implies 'the relationship of self to self ... the totality of practices by which one can constitute, define, organize, instrumentalize the strategies which individuals in their liberty can have in regard to one another'. Given that this 'relationship of self with self' is central to the definition of ethics and the history of ethical problematizations (Foucault, 1985: 6), then questions of power are ultimately, or ultimately linked to, ethical ones.

However, like questions of power and governmentality, questions of ethics are, for Foucault, to be contrasted with the juridical perspective of law and prohibition. Thus, in the introduction to *The Use of Pleasure* (1985: 13), he proposes 'to substitute a history of ethical problematizations based on practices of the self, for a history of morality based, hypothetically, on interdiction'. In the 1984 interview, he similarly rejects the 'juridical notion of the subject' as simply one of the conferral or denial of rights by law and the state. In contrast, the notion of governmentality, playing off the freedom of the subject and the relationship to others, 'constitutes the very matter of ethics' (1988a: 20). The problem of power is thus an ethical one, neither to abolish relations of power nor dissolve them in a utopia of perfect communication, but 'to give one's self the rules of law, the techniques of management, and also the ethics, the *ethos*, the practice of the self, which would allow these games of power to be played with a minimum of domination' (p. 18).

The notion of governmentality is the bridge to Foucault's ethics. But the shadow of the sovereign casts itself even over them. And these ethics will lead him to a fairly commonplace normative commitment to minimize domination or what 'we normally call power'.

3.9 Foucault thus makes the link between his analyses of relations of power and those of ethical practices and 'problematizations'. This conception of power as a game between free individuals entails a 'thin' or even 'empty' subject as a locus of forces and capacities. This is the non-sovereign subject, devoid of anthropological and psychological predicates, which can act upon itself through 'practices of the self' or 'self-technologies' to enhance capacities and transform itself, and also be acted upon through technologies of government. It can thus both govern (itself and others) and be governed. The subject is, as Gilles Deleuze might have said in his book on Foucault, simply a 'folding' of relations of force upon themselves (1988).

This subject bears many similarities to the *homo œconomicus* Foucault first found in the American neoliberals of the Chicago School and its theory of human capital (Dilts, 2011). There the subject is one of choice, governable because it responds to each modification in its environment in a non-random way, as Gary Becker postulates (Foucault, 2008: 269), and that acts to invest in itself to augment its own human capital, which will provide satisfactions and earnings. For the American neoliberals, '*homo œconomicus* is an entrepreneur, an entrepreneur of himself', in which the key actions are investments in the self (p. 226). In contrast, for Foucault, *homo ethicus* is a free subject, in relation to self, in which the key actions are practices or technologies of the self. Just as *homo œconomicus* is made governable in relation to the field of economic knowledge, so too is *homo ethicus* made governable, but in relation to games of truth and regimes of veridiction, from those of ancient ascetics, economics, dietetics and erotics to modern therapy and self-help knowledge.

Andrew Dilts has argued that we should not push these analogies too far, for the neoliberals could neither imagine their project as an ethical one nor think self-critically about their own regime of truth, in the way that Foucault did (2011: 145). There is a certain process of discovery, and of 'sympathetic critique and indebtedness' here. But there is also a little more than this – an intuition that American neoliberalism has glimpsed something of the transformation of the relations of power which Foucault, throughout all these years, had, one way or another, been pursuing:

> what appears on the horizon of this kind of analysis is not at all the ideal or project of an exhaustively disciplinary society in which the legal network hemming in individuals is taken over and extended internally by, let's say, normative mechanisms. Nor is it a society in which a mechanism of general normalization and the exclusion of those who cannot be normalized is needed. (Foucault, 2008: 258)

To put it clearly, in American neoliberalism Foucault found a view of society in which neither legal, disciplinary, nor biopolitical mechanisms, constitute the basic forms of power. Instead, we see 'the image, idea, or theme-program':

> of a society in which there is an optimization of systems of difference, in which the field is left open to fluctuating processes, in which minority individuals and practices are tolerated, in which action is brought to bear on the rules of the game rather than on the players, and finally in which there is an environmental type of intervention instead of the internal subjugation of individuals. (Foucault, 2008: 259–60)

Foucault senses, in American neoliberalism, the existence of an exercise of power that is consistent with what has been called a 'minor' politics, or minority politics – a politics of identity, or a politics of difference. It is an exercise of power that utilizes, tolerates and facilitates difference, rather than proscribes and prohibits it. Rather than the exclusive logics of a prohibiting law, or a disciplinary norm and its forms of marginalization, or of a biopolitical normalization of populations, we have, with American neoliberalism, a diagram for governing and power which will be entirely immanent, non-sovereign, anti-authoritarian, inclusive, indirect and facilitative. In this respect, Foucault had already made the connection between neoliberalism and postmodern identity politics that would be observed, from different points of view, by Marxist critics of neoliberalism (Harvey, 2005) and theorists of Empire (Hardt and Negri, 2000).

We should note, however, that this bridge to ethics requires a power that does not need and should not be founded on law and 'the political institution' of the state (Foucault, 1988a: 20). It also relies on perhaps the simplest binary, an elementary instance of the signature of power, between a power to and a power over, between power as a capacity to achieve one's ends and power as a system of domination.

There is an underlying ambivalence in Foucault's relationship to liberalism and neoliberalism. He distances himself, as we have seen, from the Ordoliberal analysis of Nazism as a concatenation of historical elements in an 'anti-liberal invariant', and he calls for specificity in the analysis of the welfare state. However, there is a line that reaches from the critique of biopolitical and disciplinary mechanisms inscribed in all modern states (in 1976) to this search for a new form of power, which is non-statist and which allows the maximum of autonomous self-creation and difference, that bears uncanny resemblance to what he would find in the American neoliberalism he was studying.

Intermediate points

3.10 Foucault's production of concepts concerning and derivative of power has ensured his rightful place as the progenitor of much thinking about substantive kinds of power, such as discipline, biopolitics and government, and the development of methodological frameworks, such as an analytics of government, *dispostif* analysis, and genealogies of governmentality. While it was not his intention, he could rightly be regarded as the pre-eminent 'post-structuralist' theorist or philosopher of power.

In addition to the seven propositions of §2.10, we can now add the following intermediate conclusions to our investigations:

1 Foucault's concept of governmentality seeks to overcome the bipolar and axial narrative of power by three distinct but related moves: the assertion of a pre-eminence of government over discipline and sovereignty rather than a serial displacement; the development of the methodological approach of the *dispositif*; and making the critique of sovereignty and the state a feature of the art of government itself, that is, of liberalism.

2 The moves remain, however, within the shadow cast by the sovereign by seeking to deny its claims to 'transcendence' in the form of state and law. Thus the governmental ethos of critique is a critique of transcendence. Rather than a transcendent narrative of forms of power, this critique is immanent to the arc of modern power relations or liberal art of government and *dispositif* analysis seeks to tame and domesticate sovereignty within the immanence of the *dispositif* of law.

3 While Foucault's genealogy of state-phobia can be viewed as an instance of critical self-reflection, it does not amount to a rejection of analytical, methodological and theoretical anti-statism. The state is still a construction, resolvable into its techniques of governmentality.

4 Foucault's thought on power appears richest when he moves away from the bipolar and axial model to discover state-of-exception

exemplars in both early modern (the *coup d'État)* and modern (liberal notions of the economy and exceptional spaces in relation to law) power formations.

5   His analysis of governmentality, and its passageway to the discussion of ethics as an action of 'self on self', comes close to a retirement of conventional conceptions of power and replacing them with an ethical problematic of how to practise games between liberties with the minimum of domination.

6   Foucault learns from the forms of neoliberalism, particularly in respect to the political-ethical subject, even if his 'sympathetic critique' rejects their analysis of the welfare state and the denunciatory politics associated with it. American neoliberalism offers, at least in ideal form, a governmental problematic that no longer ties the individual to the commands of law, or 'subjectifies' through the hold on the body by discipline and regulates life by the production of biopolitical norms. It presents the image of a form of regulation that allows minority practices and individuality to flourish and works through the play of difference.

Whatever the advantages, which are considerable, of the path Foucault chose in his analysis of power, his approach cannot answer fundamental questions. Why the state? Why the law? If the state is nothing more than a composite of techniques of government or a complex set of correlations, combinations and inscriptions between heterogeneous *dispositifs*, and the law is either one of these *dispositifs* or has become a technology of government, then why does the local, immanent exercise of power keep referring to the state as a source of its authority and legitimacy, and why does it need to wrap itself in the symbols, traditions, hierarchies and topologies of the law? Can the state and law simply be historical residues masking the real operation of the new powers, archaic leftovers of feudalism and absolutism and the struggles around them, as Foucault once contended, or do they form an axis, a component, a set of elements in the field in which power is exercised in the present? Are they, indeed, essential to how power is exercised in the present?

Before moving to a summary of the overall physiognomy of Foucault's thought on power, we shall address one major example of the persistent presence of the bipolar narrative even in his work on the *dispositif* and governmentality, that of the claims he makes around the transition from the form, image and program of power relations organized around the Prince and his territory to one of the government of populations. It is the problem of Machiavelli and Malthus, if one likes, and it is simply too fundamental to be allowed to pass without what in this case must be called correction.

4

THE PRINCE AND THE POPULATION

4.1 During his lecture of 25 January 1978, Foucault argues that there is a 'very important change' in the eighteenth century, which leads away from 'Machiavelli's problem' which was 'precisely how to ensure that the sovereign's power is not endangered, or at any rate, how can it keep at bay, with full certainty, the threats hanging over it' (2007: 65). The change is to a 'completely different problem' that is no 'longer fixing and demarcating the territory, but of allowing circulations to take place, of controlling them, sifting the good and the bad, ensuring that things are always in movement, constantly moving around, continually going from one point to another, but in such a way that the inherent dangers of this circulation are canceled out'. In summary, he explains this shift, which is a key to understanding liberal governmentality: 'No longer the safety (*sûreté*) of the Prince and his territory, but the security (*sécurité*) of the population and, consequently, those who govern it.'

As if to underline the importance of this transformation from territory to population, at the beginning of his next lecture, there has been a replacement within the title, *Security, Territory, Population*. 'In short, in the last lectures we were concerned with the establishment of the series "security-population-government"' (Foucault, 2007: 88). The omission of territory from his account of 'governmentality', and its restriction to an archaic form, is a fundamental feature of Foucault's evolving thought on power which relies not on the complementarity, as one might imagine, of territory and population as elements within techniques of security, but the replacement of one with the other.

Unfortunately, there are questions as to whether Machiavelli's *The Prince*, at the beginning of the sixteenth century, and the concept of population at the end of the eighteenth century, can quite act as the epochal markers Foucault needs them to be in his characterization of the emergent liberal art of governing.

Lo stato and Machiavelli

4.2 For Foucault, Machiavelli 'marks ... the end of an age' (2007: 65). Such a position puts him at odds, as Keith Tribe notes (2009: 685), with his Anglophone contemporaries, J.G.A. Pocock and Quentin Skinner, who remain enormously influential figures in the study of the history of political thought. When Foucault made that statement, Pocock had already published his masterpiece, *The Machiavellian Moment* (1975), whose ambition is expressed in its subtitle, *Florentine Political Thought and the Atlantic Republican Tradition*. In it, Pocock locates Machiavelli as an exemplar of the 'civic humanism' of Florence, concerned with the 'presentation of the republic, and the citizen's participation in it, as constituting a problem in historical self-understanding' (1975: vii–viii). The Machiavellian moment is, for Pocock, one in which the republic confronts its own temporal finitude. It is a problem of moral and political stability in a stream of irrational events, of the relationship between virtue and fortune, *virtù* and *fortuna*. It uses the language of corruption to discuss the dissolution of virtue of rulers and ruled. But rather than the revival of classical themes and language being an anachronism, Pocock argues, it prospered and gained 'ascendancy' in eighteenth-century England and America until the American Revolution (p. ix).

As if to underline the continuing salience of Machiavelli's problem, Pocock draws the implication of his history for the present to show that Americans 'having made the republican commitment to the renovation of virtue, remained obsessively concerned by the threat of corruption – with it must be added, good and increasing reason' (p. 548). He makes this point after the then recent Watergate affair and goes on to name two of its principals, whose particular roles need not detain us. 'In the melodrama of 1973, the venality of [vice-president Spiro] Agnew makes this point in one way; and [presidential aide, John] Ehrlichman's more complex and disinterested misunderstanding of the relation between the reality and the morality of power makes it in another'. Even more striking is his diagnosis of the continued presence of the Florentine vocabulary of politics and government in the contemporary United States, which has the following effects:

> Hence the persistence in America of messianic and jeremiad attitudes towards history; hence also, in part, the curious extent to

which the most post-modern and post-industrial of societies continues to venerate pre-modern and anti-industrial values, symbols
and constitutional forms, and to suffer from its awareness of the
tensions between practice and morality. (Pocock, 1975: 549)

Here we have what Foucault would no doubt have called a 'history
of the present' with the Machiavellian moment as its fulcrum. While
not all his reviewers appreciated Pocock's Machiavelli, and its sweep-
ing historiographical ambitions (Whitfield, 1978; Vasoli, 1977), we
should note that his insistence on its enduring significance in the
shaping of America's civic culture leads him to pose, with respect
to that culture, a problem that Foucault cannot pose because of his
wish to be done with the juridical-political theory of sovereignty:
the co-presence and inter-relationship of the symbolic, spectacular
and the glorious with the rational and the instrumental, of the legal-
constitutional order with the economic-governmental one.

4.3 Quentin Skinner's two-volume work, *The Foundations of Modern Political Thought* (1978a, 1978b) and his essay on
'The state' (1989), allow us to consider the reading of Machiavelli's
The Prince that Foucault attributes, if not directly to Machiavelli,
then to an 'extensive body of anti-Machiavellian literature', whether
Catholic, Jesuit, or Protestant, 'overt or surreptitious' (2007: 90–1).
Foucault argues that 'the Prince exists in a relationship of singularity and externality, of transcendence, to his principality' (p. 91). This
means there is no essential, fundamental, natural or juridical connection, but rather a 'synthetic' one between the Prince and the principality. The major problem therefore is to maintain and protect the
relationship of the Prince to his principality, which is necessarily a
fragile one, and that the Prince must first identify dangers and work
out how 'to hold onto his principality' (p. 92).

Foucault makes Machiavelli stand for, whether himself or in the eyes of
his adversaries, the transcendent, unitary and external form he attributes
elsewhere to sovereignty. Machiavelli's problem, for Foucault, is the problem of holding onto the state over which one rules. However, the idea of a
state in the Renaissance is complex and ambiguous, as Skinner has shown,
and does not come to completion in the modern sense of the word until the
seventeenth century, after the writings of those such as Bodin and
Hobbes. For Skinner, the Italian republican thinkers of Renaissance
Italy had inherited the view from Aristotle's *Politics* that 'the sphere of

politics should be envisaged as a distinct branch of moral philosophy, a branch concerned with the art of government' (1978b: 34). In this sense they began, 'to develop a conception of the apparatus of government as a set of institutions independent of those who control them' (1989: 109). Machiavelli and his contemporaries had thus renewed the ancient problematic of an art of government, a task Foucault assigns to various 'anti-Machiavellians' in what was, in effect, a reactionary and religious response to what is characteristic in Machiavelli. In this respect, Foucault thus stands in direct contradiction to Skinner's thesis on the art of government.

Furthermore, the modern concept of the state 'has a doubly impersonal character', argues Skinner, in which we 'distinguish the state's authority from that of the ruler or magistrates entrusted with the exercise of its powers for the time being. But we also distinguish its authority from that of the whole society or community over which its powers are exercised' (1989: 112). While Machiavelli, particularly in the *Discourses*, gestures towards this concept of state, he 'continues largely to employ the term in the most traditional way', which assumes a personal, and therefore anything but synthetic relationship of the Prince to *lo stato*.

> Even in *The Prince*, however, it is generally clear that, when Machiavelli speaks of his desire to advise 'a prince wishing to maintain his state' (*uno principe volendo mantenere lo stato*), what he usually has in mind is the traditional idea of the prince maintaining his existing position and range of powers. (Skinner, 1978b: 354)

In other words, Foucault commits a common prolepsis when he attributes to Machiavelli and his associates a conception of the state as an impersonal entity, separate from the rulers, that is, to use his words, connected only by a synthetic and external link. Such a conception of the state would not be available for perhaps at least another century. The relationship of the prince to the state is a personal connection so that when the prince's rule ends, under whatever set of events, so too does the principality. *Lo stato* in this sense is derived from the Latin, *status*. This is far removed from the idea of an external and impersonal notion of state in which the office of prime minister or president endures the comings and goings of the various holders of the office. To maintain one's state, *mantenere lo stato*, is not to maintain and strengthen an external entity in order to hold office, but to maintain one's stateliness or status – to not allow it to be eroded in any way. Both Skinner (1978b: 354) and Pocock (1975: 175–6) confirm the findings of a classic paper by J.H. Hexter (1957), which examined every instance of the use of the term, *lo stato*, in *The Prince*.

To say the least, then, Foucault under-estimates the degree to which the notion of the state as a unified and impersonal body (or at least a claim to that status) separate from both rulers and ruled, comprising an articulated set of public offices separate from their incumbents, was a central governmental innovation from the seventeenth century, and which therefore could not have been present in the literature to which he attributes it. He also neglects the extent to which Machiavelli and his contemporaries continued to elucidate the ancient theme of the art of government.

4.4 The other dimension of Foucault's understanding of Machiavelli, or at least of the way he is portrayed in the literature that criticizes him, is the notion of territory. This is easier to deal with: Machiavelli and his contemporaries cannot have used the notion of territory as a marked concept because there was not at that time a fundamental conception of territorial sovereignty; that is, of a single ruler or administration governing the space of a unified jurisdiction. As Paul Hirst suggested, the Renaissance writers faced a complex late-medieval society in which 'political power was distributed differentially across it, creating multifaceted relations between space and politics' (2004: 33). It could be thought of as a patchwork of enclaves, often under multiple and competing jurisdictions, with large gaps between them, and multiple powers claiming various elements of what Jean Bodin would call the 'marks of sovereignty'. These 'powers competed to control the same spaces, claiming forms of territorial rule that were ill-defined in their scope and rights' (Hirst, 2004: 31). They included not only kings and nobles, but also the Pope and the Holy Roman Emperor, leagues of cities such as the Hanseatic League, monastic military orders, mercenary forces, principalities, municipalities, charities and city-states. While the latter were territorially coherent, they existed in a complex system of liberties, privileges and obligations with monarchs, empires and leagues, and presented an important limit to wider territorial forms of rule.

The notion of territorial sovereignty, in which a ruler exercises supreme power over a specific delimited domain, would develop only towards the end of the seventeenth century and take its national form in the nineteenth century. The relation of ruler and state, with its emphasis on territory, thus belongs to what we might regard as 'modern' forms of power, not to the archaic form of sovereignty Foucault attributes to Machiavelli's problem. On the other hand, Machiavelli's concern for the effects of disorder and threat are, argues Pasquale Pasquino (1993: 82), who here departs from his former teacher, indicative of 'the problematic of the government of others'. This underlines the possibility that the 'art of government', as the 'right disposition' of 'men and of things', is an ancient, not early modern, phenomenon, as Foucault contends.

In his treatment of Machiavelli Foucault appears to have inverted the sequence of the emergence of central concepts of political power and neglected the difficulty of the process of political innovation that brought about both the concept and institution of the state as the territorial sovereign. This leads one to conclude with Pasquino, but *contra* Foucault, 'that there are still good reasons for following the worn-out paths of juridicio-political theory – if one wishes to call it that – the paths of law, order, and peace' (1993: 84).

The Malthusian effect

4.5 The safety, or *sûreté*, of the Prince and his territory is contrasted with the security of the population. The formation of the population as a kind of subject-object of knowledge is crucial to Foucault's characterization of what is new or novel about the arts of government, which emerge from the end of the eighteenth century. The concept of population has already been central to his definition of the 'biopolitics of the population' and its distinction from the 'anatamo-politics' of the body. But it is equally important in his account of governmentality. The double entry of population as an object of knowledge and a target of government marks, for Foucault, both the 'threshold of modernity' of the West (1979: 143) and the 'era of governmentality' (2007: 109).

In respect to the earlier formulations of the population problem in *History of Sexuality I* and related lectures, it would be correct to find in Foucault a too unified conception of population and a lack of consideration of the arc of its development since the eighteenth century.

This is remedied by the third lecture of *Security, Territory, Population* (2007: 67–73). Here population is viewed through a complex trajectory that confirms Foucault as a specialist of what he often called the 'classical age'. He identifies population in turn: firstly, in relation to problems of the need for repopulation; secondly, as a sign of the sovereign's strength; thirdly, as a fundamental element and productive force in mercantilism and cameralism; and finally, with the Physiocrats and the *économistes* at the end of the eighteenth century, as a 'set of processes to be managed at the level and on the basis of what is natural in these processes' which forms a kind of non-voluntary and not negotiable limit to the sovereign (p. 70). This leads him to a fundamental contrast between the 'sovereign–subject relationship', in which the 'limit of the law is the subject's disobedience', or the 'no' of refusal, and the government–population relationship, in which the limit of the sovereign is something other than the people's refusal of its decision (p. 71).

In other words, at the level of the population, its processes, regularities, customs and history, we have a nature towards which the sovereign must apply reflected techniques of government, and which presents a kind of limit to its exercise of power. This notion of population for Foucault thus signifies something of a break with earlier ones found in mercantilism or cameralism, in which the question of population was still posed in relation to the will of the sovereign, or the will and rights of the people as subjects. It is in this context that Foucault mentions, for the only time in these lectures, the contribution of Thomas Robert Malthus in a contrast between 'the bio-economic problem' of population and Marx's postulate of the class struggle (Foucault 2007: 77). 'Malthusian' is used as an adjective twice in *History of Sexuality I*. His name does, however, appear in *The Order of Things* (Foucault, 1970: 257) where, as Foucault now indicates, Malthus's principle of population, will act as 'the operator of transformation for the transition ... from the analysis of wealth to political economy' (2007: 78).

Foucault's failure to address Malthus's contribution in any depth, and the way in which he acted as an 'operator of transformation', needs to be addressed. The present author has taken up the task of assessing what might be called the 'Malthusian effect', in relationship to the development of the government of poverty in England and the emergence of a science of economics (Dean, 1991). In that, he has joined with Giovanna Procacci (1978; 1993), who has addressed the relationship of Malthus to the techniques of governing the poor and pauperism in nineteenth-century France. Moreover, in a classic study,

Keith Tribe has followed the pathway of the 'formation of economic discourse' in classical political economy. He has shown the links (despite other disagreements) between Malthus's principle of population and the pedagogical narrative of the movement from better to worse soils under population pressure that underlies Ricardo's different theory of rent. This theory might be regarded as the first theoretical demonstration of the distribution mechanism of an 'economy' (Tribe, 1978: 120–6).

This Malthusian effect has a number of components. From the beginning, that is, from the first of its many editions, the *Essay on the Principle of Population* proposes a bio-economic necessity that will prove to be foundational for both the science of economics and the art of government. This necessity lies at the very centre of humans' ontological relationship with nature. Malthus posits an ontologically given disequilibrium between the rate of growth of the population and the rate of growth of its means of subsistence. For him, nature is not in itself niggardly; in fact there is no need to assume its absolute limits. Rather, it is because the 'power of population being a power of a superior order, the increase of the human species can only be kept commensurate to the increase of the means of subsistence by the constant operation of the strong law of necessity acting as a check upon the greater power' (Malthus, 1982: 76). For Malthus, the problem of scarcity is radically distinct from the one found in Foucault's rendering of the Physiocrats, which is a problem of letting supply and demand for grain be adjusted by the processes of the market. Malthus's problem, by contrast, is that of a fundamental, catastrophic conflict between humans and nature within a confined space that necessarily leads to war, epidemic and famine, or more broadly, 'vice and misery'. Economics, in this respect, has always been a science of human impact on the biosphere.

This has important implications for the notion of the 'event'.[1] The 'event' is not only, as in Foucault's lectures, an aleatory and contingent occurrence that can be dealt with at the level of the regulation of quasi-natural processes, e.g. the way that scarcity is dealt with by the fluctuation of the supply of grain according to price (2007: 41–2). The event, in a catastrophic form, is inscribed within, in the sense that it is literally written into the very premises of, Malthus's principle of population. This results in the 'hardships of savage life' (1804: 22 ff.)

---

1 I have not been able to incorporate fully the remarkable theses of Ute Tellmann (2013) on catastrophe, savage life and temporality in Malthus, due to the fact that her outstanding article was published while the present book was already in press.

of the Indigenous peoples of Australia, the Americas and the Pacific, which Malthus finds described in the writings of explorers and colonialists. This savage life is characterized by 'the idleness and indolence of the improvident savage' and 'the strange and barbarous customs' including the 'violent and cruel treatment of women', the infanticide of children, murderous war and cannibalism, and susceptibility to epidemics (1804: 15–36; Tellmann, 2013). A key cause of war here is the movement and appropriation of land and territory in a hunter-gatherer society. The other manifestation of the event at the heart of the principle of population is the condition of domestic poor, who would procreate without sufficient foresight as to the resources necessary to support their offspring, particularly when given to expect the certainty of public poor relief, and without sufficient regard to the 'industry' required to procure this subsistence.

The first component of the Malthusian effect is the intertwining of a general concept of the life of the human population with singular forms of life: the savage life of the native, the improvident life of the indigent poor, the industrious life of the civilized. We can note, too, that these singular forms of life are arranged on a temporal continuum so that while savage and civilized life co-exist in the same present they do so in different temporalities; and that indigent life, depending on poor relief, is one of the 'great causes which render a nation progressive, stationary, or declining', thus threatening its position on this temporal continuum (1804: 251).

The second is that the principle of population does not remain an ideal horizon or supposition, with Malthus a kind of jeremiad towards the poor and public relief, but enters into the constitution of political economy and of economic government. David Ricardo's theory of rent, starting with his 1815 *Essay on the Influence of a Low Price of Corn on the Profits of Stock* (1951), is based on a narrative of the differential productivity of decreasingly fertile lands brought into cultivation by virtue of the principle of population. It is thus driven by the Malthusian supposition. This means that this ontological scarcity enters the premises of classical political economy. It is thus a condition of possibility of economic knowledge, which, as Foucault argues, is the key form of knowledge of governmentality, or the emergent liberal art of government. But the notion of population and scarcity here is quite different from the ones found in the Physiocrats and stressed by Foucault. Quite inexplicably, Foucault, in his later lectures, seems to have forgotten his own findings in the *Order of Things*:

What makes economics possible, and necessary, then, is a perpetual and fundamental situation of scarcity.... It is no longer in the interplay of representation that economics finds its principle, but near that perilous region where life is confronted with death. And thus economics refers us ... to the biological properties of the human species, which, as Malthus showed in the same period as Ricardo, tends always to increase unless prevented by some remedy or constraint; ... it designates in labour, and in the very hardship of that labour, the only means of overcoming the fundamental insufficiency of nature and of triumphing over death .... *Homo œconomicus* is not the human being who represents his own needs to himself, and the objects capable of satisfying them; he is the human being who spends, wears out, and wastes his life in the imminence of death. (1970: 256–7)

In other words, the *homo œconomicus* of classical political economy is not the *homo œconomicus* as subject of interest so central to Foucault's narrative of the emergent liberal art of government (and the monotonous liberal and neoliberal paeans to Adam Smith). The felicitous coincidence of the representation of interests in market exchange predates both economics as a science and the liberal art of government which, instead, presuppose production, the Sisyphean toil and trouble which spends limited human life on increasingly infertile lands in confined space.

So a second feature of the Malthusian effect will indicate the relationship between the biopolitics of the population and what might be called a bio-economics of scarce resources and production. A third feature, as Alison Bashford has recently brought to our attention, is that this struggle to produce or secure the resources, concerns land and space and, we might add, territory (2012: 102). As she puts it, for Malthus 'population determinants were in the end about land and space ... There was a permanent struggle for room and food, and he might well have called the struggle for living space *Lebensraum*'. Rather than the emergence of population replacing territory, the very notion of population, as enunciated by its most famous progenitor, was inextricably linked to the appropriation of land and the establishment of territory. For example, while Malthus wrote against 'the right of exterminating, or driving into a corner where they must starve' of Indigenous populations, he advised that if the United States continued its increase in population, 'the Indians will be driven further and further back into the country, till the whole race is ultimately exterminated, and the territory is incapable of further extension' (1804: 5). Rather than a movement from territory to population in the art of government, we have the interconnection between human fertility, scarce resources and confined space. So not only does Malthus indicate a biopolitics of the population and a bio-economics of scarcity but a bio-spatiality of territory.

Moving from economics as a science to the art of government, Malthus's view of population also provides a programmatic ideal for the reform of those practices that encourage the population to increase without regard to its means of subsistence, namely poor relief, in both England and in France. There is a significant literature on this Malthusian ideal and the campaign against non-institutional forms of relief in the first third of the nineteenth century, starting with J.R. Poynter's *Society and Pauperism* (1969). In this respect, the Malthusian event is central to the definition of the proper and gendered 'form of life' of the property-less poor. This is incarnated in the 'independent labourer' who is governable to the extent that he is made to take responsibility for himself, his wife or the mother of his children, and his children, and who cannot expect public charity or what was called 'outdoor relief' to do so.

Malthus's role in liberal-colonial art of government is also noteworthy (Bashford, 2012: 99–102; Flew, 1982: 14). There are Malthus's extensive references to the lives of the savages found in the accounts of their voyages by James Cook, Vancouver and Lapérouse and the reports of magistrates and colonists. But the circle between theory and practice is completed with his appointment to the first British chair in political economy at Haileybury College (actually, Professor of General History, Politics, Commerce and Finance), established by the East India Company for the purpose of two years' general training for colonial administrators.

The degrees to which Malthus and his principle reshaped the notion of population, entered into the epistemological conditions for the emergence of classical political economy, and thus the earliest economic science, set certain key parameters for the transformation of poor relief and philanthropy, or affected the training of colonial administrators, are all, of course, open, revisable matters for historical investigation and debate. However, it indicates a liberal art of government in a *tête à tête*, as Foucault puts it, with political economy that is very different from the one proposed by Foucault in his lectures on governmentality. Alongside, or even instead of, an art of government that sought to govern through the subject of interest, or free subject, there was an art of governing (particularly applied to the poor, the indigent, the pauper, the native, the savage) that sought to govern through a civilized subject of prudence, or a responsible subject, and that brought that subject's procreative and labouring body, its concupiscence and restraint, fertility and infertility, lassitude or industry, and capacity for or lack of reason, into play. Instead of, or adjacent to, a free subject hoping to better its own condition, is one, confined in space, limited in resources and burdened by fertility, spurred by the idea of avoiding a slip into misery. And, alongside or even replacing a form of knowledge of the natural and necessary regularities of the market, of fluctuations of prices and wages, that presented a limitation on government and worked through the pursuit of self-interest, could be found a form of knowledge of the economy in which a fundamental scarcity would be manifest in recurrent and catastrophic events, such as war, epidemic and famine. Indeed, this catastrophe is manifested in the very life of the savage, and would be the lot of the domestic poor, that is, the great mass of the population, were they not led to a form of life of procreative prudence, morality and civility, personal and familial responsibility and foresight, and unremitting industry. As such it is the duty of the civilized to prevent the further deterioration of the condition and character of the indigent and to bring, however difficult, improvement to those of the savage.

In Malthus, there is a biopolitics of the population; but there is also a bio-economics of scarcity and a bio-spatiality of territory. The Malthusian effect is found at the intersection of fertility and subsistence, soil and land, appropriation and territory. It is thus a crucial one for the gendered, proletarian and colonial genealogies of the liberal art of government. And the event as bio-catastrophe is its enduring legacy.

4.6 A final aspect of *The Essay* by Malthus is its theodicy, that is, its squaring of the principle of population with divine sovereignty. In its first edition, Malthus spelt out a teleology that went somewhat deeper than the principle itself, postulating a movement from 'inert, chaotic matter' to an awakened mind, from which he infers the 'animating touches of the Divinity' (1982: 202). While the 'original sin of man is the torpor and corruption of the chaotic matter in which he may be said to be born', Malthus concludes that it 'seems, however, every way probable that even the acknowledged difficulties of the law of population tend rather to promote than impede the general purpose of Providence' (pp. 202, 206). They do this because they 'excite universal exertion and contribute to the infinite variety of situations, and consequently of impressions, which seems upon the whole favourable to the growth of mind' (p. 206). More specifically, the principle of population, and the vice and misery it produces, is conducive to the development of an industrious conduct of life and the faculty of reason. God's providential government of the mundane world takes such a form that humans have unrelenting material wants to lead them to develop order out of disorder, to undertake a life of constant industry and moral virtue, and so be led to rational conduct and the telos of 'mind'. Malthus's narrative thus conciliates between God's heavenly sovereignty – manifest especially in the principle of population – and a world of catastrophic events, in the form of the wars, famines and diseases that keep the population down to the means available for its subsistence.

Foucault is correct, then, to view the naturalness of population as presenting limits to what we can expect of sovereign or governmental decision and action, in which there is a kind of everyday *tête à tête* between the state and the laws and the regularities found within the population. But if he had examined Malthus in detail (or recalled his own earlier conclusions), and the notion of the event Malthus initiated, which had consequences for the constitution of economics, the government of poverty, and the knowledge and government of the savage life of colonial subjects, he would have discovered the fundamental and divinely inspired dilemma in which humans are irrevocably placed and which law, sovereign power and constitutional government can do nothing to change, but which should form their very basis.

There is, then, a liberal government of the event, such as a food scarcity, which would not simply be a technical element in the *dispositif* of security (Foucault, 2007: 33), and in which security of the population would cease to be opposed to 'the safety of the sovereign'. The event would be the means by which liberal governing through the economy becomes operable. Liberal forms of political power are exercised not only with security as their highest end, as Bentham noted (1950: 96), but in a permanent condition, not so much of exception but of necessity, which is, with Malthus, bio-economic insecurity. For classical political economy, the ultimate source of this insecurity is not war, social and political discontent, or occasional famines and natural disasters, but the notion of the economy itself, constituted by humans' relations to nature as one of a fundamental scarcity.

In Malthus we find a perfect illustration of the bipolar character of power. On the one hand, a providential order manifested by the principle of population, which dictates the different rates of growth of population and subsistence. On the other, a worldly government, such as that applied to the indigent life and its amelioration, or the savage life and its improvement. And it is the event, in the form of bio-catastrophe, which is the manifestation of that providential order that requires and dictates the parameters that the worldly government would take. Malthus, not Smith or Abeille, is our great teacher in the role of the event in liberal arts of government. And at the heart of that government is not so much freedom as a technical artefact but individual responsibility and moral conduct in the face of a divine plan.

4.7 The Malthusian effect in the fields of knowledge and governmental management leads us to qualify Foucault's characterization of a liberal art of government as one that solely or principally concerns the security of the population, and that governs through the natural processes of the economy, and its subject of interest, or free subject, *homo œconomicus*. It will lead us to question two other propositions advanced in his lectures: that economics is an 'atheistic discipline … without God … without totality', and that 'it begins to demonstrate not only the pointlessness, but also the impossibility of a sovereign point of view of the totality of the state that he has to govern' (Foucault, 2008: 282).

Foucault arrives at these conclusions after a discussion of Adam Smith. His claims here concern the phrase 'the invisible hand'. If we focus on the hand, in this metaphor, he argues that Smith's view is something like that of 'a providential god who would occupy the economic process a bit like Malebranche's God occupies the entire world' (2008: 278). However, by stressing the invisibility, he suggests, we arrive at the idea that knowledge of economic totality is denied both to any of the economic agents participating within it, or, importantly to any political agent. But given that Smith himself views 'political œconomy' as 'a branch of the science of a statesman or legislator' (1976, vol. 2: 428), it would be a mistake to make him, and particularly this metaphor (or at least its anachronistic interpretation), the exemplar of a new form of governing. Indeed, if we place the emergence of economic science not with Smith and the Physiocrats, but with Ricardo, deploying Malthus's principle of population in his differential theory of rent, then Malthus's providential event as catastrophe would be a better example of the cosmological premises of economic science than Smith's invisible hand guided by individual self-interest. In this framework the sovereign (or statesman or legislator, to use Smith's personae) might not be able to know the totality of interactions in the market, but he or she can know the cost of transgressing divinely given laws of population and the benefits of following them. Moreover, with Ricardo, while economics might not be able to know in detail every economic transaction, it can make a theoretical demonstration of the distribution of income in the form of profits on capital, the rents on land, and the wages of labour.

Even if we stay with the invisible hand metaphor, moreover, Foucault's position is untenable. There are in fact three references to the 'invisible hand' in Smith. The first is the famous passage in the *Wealth of Nations* in which every individual is 'led by an invisible hand to promote an end which was no part of his intention' (Smith, 1976, vol. 2: 456). The second is the less noted passage from *Theory of Moral Sentiments* of 1759, which clearly links the economic and ethical to the theological aspects of Smith's thought, as Alec Macfie noted (1971: 596). Here the 'invisible hand' ensures that in respect to the 'necessaries of life' that 'when Providence divided the earth among a few lordly masters, it neither forgot nor abandoned those who seemed to have been left out in the partition' (Smith, 2002: 215–16). The third and little-known instance was in a probably earlier essay on the 'History of Astronomy', which refers to the 'invisible hand of Jupiter' discerned by polytheistic religions, heathens, and savages not in the natural order but in 'irregular events' that 'were ascribed to his favour, or his anger' (Macfie, 1971: 595). While this use departs from the later versions in that it views a divine presence in occasional events and not in the natural order of market and society, it retains the theological element.

Foucault's genealogy of liberalism marks a closure in his discussion of political symbolism, as we have noted. By contrast, Giorgio Agamben, whose work in this area we shall examine in later chapters, offers a succinct summary of the examples of the hand metaphor in his research into 'economic theology'. These include St Augustine's occult hand sign by which God governs, Salvian's divine government like a hand and a rudder, Aquinas's hand of the Governor; and Luther's creature as the hand of the hidden God (Agamben, 2011: 284). Finally, he cites Bossuet, who we might translate thus: 'God takes into the highest heaven the reins of all minor kingdoms. He has all hearts in his hand.' Agamben notes, moreover, that Smith makes clear the source of the invisible hand in those he calls the 'ancient Stoics'. Indeed, from them Smith learns that 'as the world was governed by the all-ruling providence of a wise, powerful and good God, every single event ought to be regarded as making a necessary part of the plan of the universe ... that the vices and follies of mankind, therefore, made as necessary a part of this plan as their wisdom or their virtue and by the eternal art which educes good from ill, were made to tend equally to the prosperity and perfection of the great system of nature' (2002: 44).

It has been established since Tribe that Adam Smith's 'invisible hand' is read anachronistically and superficially as prefiguring later economic science and notions of the beneficial pursuit of self-interest at the expense of the role of the state (Tribe, 1978: 101–4). Smith's approach should be regarded, as we have noted, as a branch of the science of a statesman or legislator' (1976, vol. 2: 428). Moreover, it could be argued that his political economy is but a part of his moral philosophy concerned precisely with the 'sympathy' that unites humans in fulfilling their natural needs including those of self-preservation. Given this, it would be a mistake to continue to view the invisible hand as simply the benign opacity of self-interested action, without either God or sovereign (as Foucault does). Rather the invisible hand is that of Divine Providence working through the 'sympathy' between individuals, and with which the actions of the statesman or legislator must be aligned. Again, in a manner not that different from Malthus, we find a figure in which divine government and mundane government, sovereignty and economy, universal plan and event, interact in the operation of power.

'The King reigns, but he does not govern'

4.8 We have seen that Foucault wished to cut off the king's head in political theory. His excursus on population allows him to put forward an alternative maxim.

> The more I spoke about population, the more I stopped saying 'sovereignty'. I was led to designate or aim at something that again I think is relatively new, not in the word, and not a certain level of reality, but as a new technique. Or rather, the modern

political problem, the privilege that government begins to exercise in relation to rules, to the extent that, to limit the king's power, it will be possible one day to say, 'the King reigns, but he does not govern,' this inversion of government and the reign or rule and the fact that government is much more than reigning or ruling, much more that the *imperium* is, I think, absolutely linked to the population. (2007: 76)

We are not yet in a position to fully understand this phrase, 'the King reigns, but he does not govern' but it is clear it must be understood in a way that is completely different from Foucault's. However we can note a couple of points here. Just as we saw earlier the substitution of the word population for territory, we witness here the substitution of the word government for sovereign. In other words, Foucault's account itself remains trapped within a bipolar narrative that is concerned to disconnect the analysis of what is novel or new in modern forms of power from territorial sovereignty. He reads this maxim as indicating a bipolar and epochal transition in forms of power in which reigning becomes something much less, and much less important, than government. However, as we shall see, there are other ways of reading this maxim that do not erase the question of reigning and the question of sovereignty, whether earthly or divine, in liberal arts of government, and that are exemplary of a very different, if complementary understanding of power.

Population does not replace sovereignty, human or divine, and lead one to privilege government. In fact, Malthus's population principle presupposes a set of linkages between sovereignty and government. It presupposes a divine sovereignty that makes the world according to providential laws, such as those of population, which lead humans to reason and to virtue, and which thereby necessitate the parameters of the activities of mundane government. Conversely, in its worldly form, the exercise of sovereign power must not interfere with the laws by which God governs the world. It is not a question of the discovery of population allowing us to displace sovereignty by government but the way the principle of population captures the multiple inter-relations, connections and oppositions in a field of power defined by both (divine and worldly) sovereignty and governmentality (the government of self and others). That, together with the crucial role of the event in the stitching together of these poles of power, it must be said, *contra* Foucault, are Malthus's principal lessons.

In other words, 'the King reigns but he does not govern' indicates the sovereign reign of the Divinity who establishes the laws of the world that require humans to constitute their worldly government in a specific way, and, conversely, the withdrawal of worldly sovereign power in the face of divine government of the world.

Foucault's legacy

4.9 Both sides of the initial contrast offered by Foucault between the Prince and his territory and the security of the population, must be rejected. This is not to say that the local insights offered by Foucault (in his lectures on governmentality) in his readings of Adam Ferguson, reason of state theorists, the Ordoliberals, and others, are without value. Nor is it to say that the production of various concepts – of liberalism, pastoral power, biopower, governmentality, etc. – do not make a significant contribution to the contemporary discussion of power. Quite the contrary, they frame it and provide its starting point and have done so, not least for the present author. We should moreover allow that Foucault was trying out and testing concepts, propositions, and hypotheses in the lectures we have been examining, and which he never would have expected to publish.

However, it remains incumbent upon us to attempt, if not to complete, then to modify and extend his genealogies of power, even to correct them, and to indicate the necessary changes and new pathways of investigation. It is clear that both sides of the proposition of a movement from 'the safety of the Prince' to 'the security of the population', and thus from sovereignty to government, cannot be sustained in view of contemporary scholarship. This small example, which nonetheless has a key role in Foucault's genealogy of the art of government, indicates the recurrence in his work, including in lectures in which he actively seeks to combat its presence by introducing the notion of the *dispositif*, of a bipolar and epochal account of power, which must now be definitively rejected. Only when we have done that does the possibility emerge of an analytics of power that can understand the mutual inter-relationships between legal-sovereign and economic-governmental axes of relations of power and the terms that allow and shape their interaction. In developing this kind of analytics, we need to be alert to the continued presence of theological motifs in secular government and to be able to make intelligible the relation between providential governing and mundane governing.

Foucault attempted, but failed, to escape the signature that marks the concept of power by searching for a new, immanent, power that would allow humans to govern and act upon themselves with the maximum autonomy, and which would dispel the hold of sovereignty on political analysis and minimize the actuality of domination. This approach led him to look beyond the juridical-institutional structure of sovereignty and its commands to those relations of power that sought the production of identity and subjectivity through forms of true knowledge and techniques of government. This in turn would lead from 'soul'-producing corporeal forms of domination to government as the indirect shaping of conduct. While Foucault illuminated the detailed features of the landscape of the transformation of power, this movement beyond the vocabulary of sovereignty to that of government found its correlate in a vulgate language that marks the contemporary condition of the social and political sciences: that in which power has given way to mere 'governance'.

4.10 Foucault's legacy concerning power is a difficult one to explain and to assess. It is almost impossible to doubt his brilliance today. His texts proliferate as his lecture series are published and can be added not only to his major works but also to his prolix 'sayings and writings', his interviews and seminars. All of this adds up to something less than a well-circumscribed *oeuvre* with definite conclusions, findings and propositions. Rather, it is an enormous parchment on which is inscribed what he called 'experiences', which have to some extent become or continue to be our own. This work is a palimpsest, scribbled on, crossed out, modified, erased and overwritten, with conclusions forever provisional. We have examined some of his major sayings and writings on power, and even in this corner of his work there is the question of his continuity and discontinuity – of his changing mind and direction – so that there seems no limit to what we can derive from his thought, no objection that cannot be answered on the basis of an obscure fragment of it, no criticism that cannot be answered by charges that its maker is reading Foucault the wrong way or has neglected a crucial passage. Against his own will, Foucault has become a canonical thinker. His work can truly be all things to all people. He can be *the* theorist of power *and* the very thinker who definitely rejected the concept of power and the idea of theory. He can be implacably opposed to an analysis in terms of the state and someone who offered a new analysis of the state. He has been read as an anti-institutional radical and as offering an endorsement of neoliberalism.

There is, nevertheless, an overall physiognomy that emerges from his thought on power in the last decade of his life. There is a broad shift away from the notion of power towards one of government. This is supported by Pasquale Pasquino's testimony and in the fragments that constitute 'The Subject and Power'. There is an apparent rehabilitation, to a certain extent, of the analysis of the state, although he seeks to do this on the basis of techniques of governmentality. There is some care to avoid the political, if not analytical effects of state-phobia and theoretical anti-statism, and their potential for an anti-governmental eschatology. There is a sympathy for and learning from aspects of liberalism and neoliberalism but a rejection of their state-phobia and failure to grasp the specificity of the welfare state. There are even indications that he could draw upon the sovereigntist traditions of the 'state of exception', both in his methodologies and in his analysis of liberalism, yet there is a major continuity in his reluctance to let go of the juxtaposition of his own analysis of the new to the now revealed to be archaic notions of sovereignty and the juridical analysis based on it. While the '*dispositif*' seeks to introduce contingency, multiplicity and heterogeneity into his analytics of power, the general 'economies of power' of law, discipline and security he identifies already imply a rejection of a sovereigntist model of power as unified and homogenous. As Foucault distinguishes one new power from another, conceptualizes them and re-inscribes them within one another, or even as he tries to advance an immanent and 'economic' analysis of power, he does so with the ghost of the sovereign haunting him.

This ghost itself takes many forms and no doubt changes. It is a conception, reality and image. As a conception, Foucault called it the 'juridico-discursive conception of power' (1979: 82), the 'juridical-political theory of sovereignty' (2003: 34), and the 'theory of the state' (2008: 76). As reality it is the feudal state of justice, the Absolutist Monarchy, the stake of struggles. As an image it is that of the symbolics of blood, Machiavelli's 'Prince and his territory', the King's head, the cold monster. No doubt one could derive, very meticulously, a complete account of the sovereignty–state–law–right theme in Foucault's work.

Foucault ceaselessly tries to escape from the very set of binaries which continue to constitute his thought on power, between old and new, transcendent and immanent, juridical and economic, negative and positive, repressive and productive, domination and power, and so on. It is the transcendent sphere of sovereignty, with the law as its command, and the state at its mundane centre, that paradoxically constitutes, by its opposition, the central persona of Foucault's thought. The very terms he uses, such as *dispositif* or 'economy' of power (the second etymologically related to the first through the Latin *dispositio*), suggest the privilege of immanence in an economic-governmental framework of power.

In any historical account of the formation of modernity or its part, it is necessary to address the theme of secularization. In broad outline, Foucault presents a dual model of secularization of the exercise of political power. The first is of the progressive replacement of the medieval 'theological-cosmological continuum' by atheistic rationalities of rule such as reason of state and, later, Physiocratic political economy. The second proposes the persistence of pastoral power within modern states, and indicates the shift of the pastoral from a religious to a secular context. As a consequence, while Foucault links the 'shepherd-flock' game of the pastorate to the modern welfare state, he neglects the continued theological suppositions underlying classical political economy, such as those associated with Malthus. This confusion, as we shall see, is tied to the ways his genealogy of power marks the new as a domain of governing through self-government, but to understand that we shall have to address the debate on secularization itself.

4.11 As this physiognomy takes shape, we begin to see a picture of ourselves or at least of the direction of the social and political sciences since Foucault's time. It is a time of the recession of critical and radical thought and analysis where the softer and more acceptable vocabulary of 'governance' displaces the analysis of domination, power and the state. It is a time where theory and critique are rejected and abjected, where empirical analysis is increasingly narrowed and elicited, and where liberalism, especially economic liberalism, despite or perhaps because of all kinds of crisis, has become more confident in its invincibility.

However, we can discern a number of exemplary moves. Most of these are based on ones already played by Foucault himself. The first might be called the 'reinscription thesis', in which the positing of the new form of power, by simple virtue of its supposed current pre-eminence, reinscribes earlier forms within it and thus, to some extent, and with qualifications, saves the analysis of power from its association with its diabolical forms, particularly sovereignty, but also the old, state-driven biopolitics with its racism and eugenic ordering of populations (cf. Dean, 2007: 87–8). Essentially, this is no different from the claim that the liberal arts of government, through their critique of sovereignty and hierarchical forms of power, have made power safe or safer when compared to the 'pathological forms' Foucault diagnosed – National Socialism and state socialism. This leads to a straightforward reproduction of liberal self-understanding that liberal values and limited government prevent the possibility that 'the despotism of the state that is always an immanent presence in all governmentalities is manifest in all its bloody rationalities' (Rose, 1999: 23). At this point the allegedly non-normative diagnostic of technologies of government merges with the normative rationality of liberalism itself.

A second move is similar to the way in which Foucault would produce a new, 'new power' concept that stands in contrast to earlier new power concepts and fulfils a desire to ensure the archaism of sovereignty. This new power might be manifest as the actuarial calculation of risk displacing the legal assignation of responsibility as in Ewald's (1991) account of the welfare state. From a sociological viewpoint, it might be grounded in the individual and processes of individualization that give the individual the capacities to critically reflect upon and transform him- or herself and to thus become a life-planner or a cosmopolitan (as in Ulrich Beck), or a subject who makes and remakes one's life, as in what Anthony Giddens called a 'life politics'. The latter has become, with due consideration given to developments in biomedicine, a new vital politics, or an 'ethopolitics' (Rose, 2001). It is unsurprising that, following the structure of Foucault's thought, those who assert a new, downscaled biopolitics, life politics or 'ethopolitics' would consider that the old 'statist' biopolitics has now become outmoded – thus giving the bipolarity of power a further twist but retaining its fundamental architecture. In Max Weber's language, the governmentality paradigm that set out to investigate the conditions of the conduct of life has found itself rationalizing the politics of the style of life; the *Lebensführung* (life-conduct) has become the *Lebensstil* (lifestyle) (cf. Hennis, 1983).

The notion of ethopolitics indeed subordinates biopolitics to a liberal governmental rationality that seeks to work through the choices of individuals and groups. It gives new centrality to the self-management by newly responsibilized individuals and small groups, thus reducing the scale of biopolitical programs and undermining or negotiating the authority of state and of experts over them. Such a concept would seek to discount, according to Bruce Braun, 'whether the conditions of ethopolitics – for secure bodies that are open to "improvement" – include the extension of sovereign power elsewhere in the name of security' (2007: 25). Focusing on limited practices within certain spaces in liberal-democratic societies ignores the dependence of such practices and spaces on gendered and racialized appropriations of reproductive and 'clinical labour' outside and within such spaces, as Catherine Waldby and Melinda Cooper have demonstrated (2008). According to Matthew Hannah, this 'ethopolitics' then is a kind of lifestyle politics for privileged insiders, 'showing that the luxury of individual life-engineering is premised on sovereign interventions in poorer parts of the world aimed at prophylactically altering futures' and the 'commodification of the biological future inherent in women's bodies' (2011: 15). As in Foucault, the 'discovery' of a new form of power accompanies a downgrading of the significance of an older, once new, form of power, and a denial of the continued salience of sovereignty. In all such accounts, what is new or contemporary about our present is no longer the hierarchical, statist forms of power, expertise and authority, but the minor politics and practices of vital movements of self-government and self-ascription. The self-abnegation of power is coming closer.

A third move is to dissolve the explanatory capacity altogether of the concept of power itself and to replace it with others. One can do this with 'government' in Foucault's more embracing sense, but more broadly with its unsubtle cousin 'governance'. One can also do this with a range of concepts that follow Foucault's stress on immanence, manifest in his notion of the *dispositif*, such as those of 'actor-network', 'assemblage' (Latour, 2005), and, more recently, 'performativity' (Callon, 2006), which investigates the constitutive role economics has as a theoretical-practical ensemble in relation to its own objects. Bruno Latour, as we have seen in our introduction, denies the explanatory force of the concept of power with a kind of smug irony. Such attempts to deny the signatory character of the concept veer towards technicism, economism, and a largely uncritical understanding of the present.

That Foucault sought to conceptualize power in relation to a host of problems is not merely the delusion of his 'transatlantic destiny'

(Latour, 2005: 86, n. 106), a charge which amounts to blaming the Americans. In fact, the problems pertaining to power raised and unresolved by Foucault have been productive ones not only for those who stand in lineage to this thinker, which now has become a veritable academic aristocracy with major and minor principalities and fiefdoms, all more or less governed with 'good police' as the cameralists would have said, but also for the vast empire of the social and political sciences. It appears that it is only by standing at the end of this trajectory initiated by Foucault that it is possible for some to realize that all those statements about power and its forms were nothing but a slip of the tongue – indeed, we might say, one extended Foucauldian slip.

4.12 Perhaps we can say that Foucault was caught in the dilemma we have identified which is presented by the signature of power. Recall that the signature of the concept of power is for it to split into antinomies and then to return these to a unity in opposition to another term. No doubt, dialectical thought is one way of dealing with this: antithesis, synthesis and overcoming, its key terms. Initially at least, Foucault's approach is rather to establish the central antinomy by which sovereignty and law stand on one side and the new power and new conceptualization of power stand on the other. The latter is productive of a further antinomy, such as discipline and biopower, or even biopower and governmentality, which then can be subsumed under the larger term, renewed and strengthened, in their fight against the main enemy. The cost of this is that of excluding, rejecting or abjecting that which is taken to be old, archaic and outmoded, and essentializing the new. The core of the new is the ethical and political self-creation of the subject.

It is unsurprising that so great a thinker as Foucault recognized this trap and sought to escape it in two ways. First, he replaced an axial model of new and old power with a transformation intrinsic to the reasoning implicated in the exercise of power itself, particularly the major form of governmentality he discusses, liberalism. Now it is not a meta-historical transformation that leads away from the theory and practice of sovereignty but the logic of liberal governing itself through its critique of sovereignty, police and reason of state. The problem here, as Ian Hunter suggested (1998: 246), is that it accepts liberalism's self-description as a critique of state reason. It can tell us very little about the conditions that make this liberal critique of the state possible, including the state and the international system of sovereign states that create the spaces for the imagination of a national economy, population and society, as domains through which to govern.

Foucault's other move is to 'de-transcendentalize' sovereignty, law and the state so that they can be understood as merely composed of practices of governmentality or become elements, techniques or technologies of government, or form a local *dispositif* as one among several. Here he traces the figure of a whole constructivist version of politics and political formations, which imagines that everything can be explained on this flattened plane of immanence. But this move still begs the question of the *claims* of the state to be the unitary and supreme authority within a given domain, that is, to sovereignty, and for that authority to rest upon a lawful constitution. By arguing that the state can only be understood in terms of its composite governmental elements, Foucault is precluded from an analysis of an institution whose claim to unity, autonomy and supremacy is central to its definition, and which is already limited by the existence of other such entities in the international system and the possibility of other sources of power within its own domain, including capitalism (Du Gay and Scott, 2010: 12–13). Paul du Gay and Alan Scott have argued that to take an academic observation as a description of the operation of the state would not only be extremely disabling from the viewpoint of the state, but a recipe for chaos and re-theologization (p. 13). While, as we have seen, Foucault discerned precisely these possibilities in national, democratic-republican and revolutionary eschatology, which were made possible by the 'discovery' of civil society, he does not translate that political observation into an analytical one.

Hunter argued that Foucault's work on governmentality appears to fall precisely within those paradigms that have sought a restriction of the state by civil society, rather than those who recognize the juridical-political improvisation that allowed the establishment of a civil society (1998: 260–1). The relative absence of reflection, in Foucault's account of liberalism, on the neutralization of confessional conflict and the development of religious toleration within the domestic domain, or the de-moralization of war between states, might well indicate this. In any case we can conclude that in his efforts to escape the claims of the state to a 'transcendent' sovereignty, Foucault was led to elaborate a whole series of concepts adequate to an analysis of different 'economies of power'. While this was quite productive in the analysis of certain local practices and rationalities, it would prove unable to respond to or analyse certain fundamental problems of public security that would again come to trouble the great occidental powers in the early twenty-first century.

Foucault's third move, to return the analysis of power to ethics by way of a free self and its techniques of self-governing, reinstates, at the very end of this arc of his thinking about power, the basic dichotomy of conceptions of power as power to and power over, as capacity and as domination. An ethical approach to power relations, as he said in 1984, tries to minimize the states of domination in the exercise of the power as a game between liberties, that is, between loci of capacities. In any case, while he recognized the presence of this signature in his analytics of power, Foucault was not able to escape it. The route he followed in trying to do so was, however, not without real value.

Foucault was caught in an actual problem of this signature that marks the concept of power. His thought on power was the ongoing attempt to find a way out of it. In locating and recognizing it, and in his struggles with it, he has not only provided us with significant empirical analyses but also key concepts of thinking about power in our present-day societies, some of which we have précised in these three chapters. But due to his dogmatic antipathy to what he viewed as the juridical-political theory of sovereignty, he was not able to resolve that problem, thus lending his work to a reductive interpretation and use that subtracts its radical intent and makes it all too digestible. In certain disciplines, and under the force of extraordinary events, the limitations of this use and interpretation of his conceptualizations of power became all too clear.

Problem points

4.13 Foucault remains the essential horizon for our thought on power in so far as he articulated a language through which we continue to make substantive domains of power relations thinkable today: discipline, biopower, pastoral power, and, yes, sovereignty. However, our investigations reveal a number of 'problem points' that force us to take our investigations here to another stage.

1 The first and chief among these, and to which all the others are related, concerns the key terms of the triad sovereignty–state–law once we have rejected the bipolar and epochal understanding of power. As we concluded in the previous chapter, certain questions

must be posed again: Why state? Why law? We can also add old questions in relation to threats to security and public order and the undertaking of necessary action: Who decides? Who judges? Foucault offers us little by way of answers to these questions.

2   This is closely related to the lack of concentrated focus on the categories of politics and the political, and the dual tendencies to reduce the political to an ethical demand to practise games of power with minimum of domination and to gradually discard the vocabulary of power in favour of government. Even if we were to retain Foucault's mature view of power as a game between liberties or a structure of action upon the action of others, we must investigate its links with political power.

3   While it is easy to grasp and criticize his bipolar and epochal narrative, Foucault's tendency to reduce territorial sovereignty and the conception of the state to different forms of immanence – a *dispositif*, a set of techniques of governmentality, different economies of power – must also be rejected. This immanence is a false one in that it is only available in relation to a rejected plane of transcendence. We need a version of immanence-transcendence that is both able to account for government and its economies *and* the claims of sovereignty. This means that the claims of the state to supremacy and autonomy within a particular domain need to be understood, both in the constitution of the conditions of domestic government within the territorial state, and in relation to the system of states within the international order. Given the generally acknowledged crisis of those claims today, we need to be especially attentive to the transformations in the plane of transcendence of power.

4   Foucault's work raises the centrality of liberal arts of government and neoliberalism to our political present, but exists in an indeterminate relationship with them, neither quite critique nor rationalization. We need an understanding of liberalism that departs from its self-understanding as a critique of state power and state reason or risks becoming at best an analytical transposition of forms of liberal normativity.

5   It is a mistake to oppose biopolitics to sovereignty as does Foucault. As we have demonstrated with Malthus, the biopolitics of the population links divine sovereignty (the providential

plan for eternal life) to the mundane government of the forms of life (savage life, indigent life, civilized life) arranged in a temporal continuum and territorially confined. Conversely, the divine or natural government of the world demands a worldly sovereignty in response to the event as biopolitical catastrophe, that can align human conduct with the providential order. The catastrophe is not the exception to liberal government but its *raison d'être*.

6   Similarly, we should not oppose biopolitics to a liberal economic government. With Malthus and classical political economy, *homo œconomicus* is engaged in a bio-economics of survival and subsistence under the imminence of death. In that respect, the notion of the economy does not so much represent a limit to the biopolitical imperative to optimize life but becomes its main vehicle. For liberal domestic and colonial government, for the government of the indigent life and the savage life, a biopolitics of the population is founded on a bio-economics of scarcity and a bio-spatiality of the territory.

7   There are secularizing (classical political economy, reason of state) and counter-secularizing elements (medieval scholasticism, pastoral power, eschatology) in Foucault's genealogy of the art of government. This indicates a site for interrogation rather than a coherent thesis in relation to the problem of secularization.

8   Finally, Foucault has confirmed our starting hypothesis that the concept of power is caught in a signature that keeps referring it to antinomies, which themselves form unities in relationship to yet another term. In fact, he has given us a further and useful elaboration of this signature but has tried to limit it to the problem of the displacement of sovereign power. We need to be attentive to other ways of addressing this feature of our concepts of power.

In the next two chapters, we draw on Carl Schmitt's work, not to grasp the totality of his *oeuvre* in itself, but as a mode of address on these problem points found in Foucault's work: sovereignty in particular, but also the political, law, liberalism and secularization. We shall not lose sight of Foucault and, at times, the exposition will take the form of comparison. Schmitt is a man of ghosts and spectres, including his anti-Semitism and relationship with Nazism, with sharp, jagged formulations grounded in what has recently been called 'ongoing founding events' (Bussolini, 2011). But in a period of the assertion of an international unipolar political order, the conduct of a war on terror, the new status of the enemy combatant, the legitimacy of extra-juridical killing, and the exceptional spaces and populations within and at the fringes of the liberal world, his work has been called upon to contribute to a critical ontology of ourselves or a critical history of the present. Moreover, Schmitt would recurrently return to the very maxim that Foucault used to sum up the displacement of sovereignty: 'the King reigns, but he does not govern'. That fact alone should make the price of admission to his work worth it. Schmitt lived a long life in the very shadows from which Foucault failed to escape – those of sovereignty.

5

ENEMY SECRETS

5.1 If Michel Foucault attempted to neutralize the *montre froid* of the state, Carl Schmitt spent not only his intellectual career, but his very existence, engaged with it in one form or regime or another. He sought to save it from collapse during the Weimer Republic in books on jurisprudence (2004a) and constitutional doctrine (2008a). He compromised himself in relation to the National Socialist party and regime and had reason to fear for his life from both that regime and the American occupying forces. He was arrested and interned by both the Russian and American post-war occupations, twice by the latter, and interrogated, as we now know, four times at Nuremberg, but released without charge (Bendersky, 2007). Schmitt responded to the question by his interrogator of whether he was ashamed of certain of his writings during the Nazi period: '[w]ithout question, it was unspeakable. There are no words to describe it' (Kempner and Schmitt, 1987: 107).

In a poem on his sixteenth birthday in 1948, Schmitt wrote (1987: 130):

Thrice I sat in the belly of the whale

I confronted suicide at the hand of the executioner

In his book on Hobbes, Schmitt traced the mythology of the Leviathan to the biblical story in which the term for the state was a sea-beast, a great fish or a whale (2008b). Tracy Strong identifies the three occasions referred to in the poem (2005: xxxi, n. 59). The first was 1934 during the purge of the SA, which led to Schmitt's defence of Hitler's action in a newspaper article. The second was in 1936 during the attacks on him by the organ of the SS, *Das Schwarze Korps*, and the third was during his post-war interrogation, in which he believed he would be hung.

So we turn from someone who believed there had been an over-valuation of state, sovereignty and law, to a legal and political thinker who had not only asserted the specificity of sovereignty but also believed he had been inside the belly of the Leviathan three times. Foucault's failure to outrun the shadow of the sovereign obliges us to discover an old enemy who sought to understand sovereignty, state and law, and whose experiences would give him nightmares into his old age.

Politics and police

5.2 The evidence of Michel Foucault's engagement with Carl Schmitt is very slim. It consists of a single reference on a handwritten manuscript inserted between two of the lectures of 1979, and even here the initial of his forename is mistakenly written as 'K' (Sennelart, 2007: 400, n. 140).

The note identifies two definitions of politics, which give meaning to the phrase 'everything is political' (Sennelart, 2007: 390). The first supposes 'the state is everywhere'; the second, the 'omnipresence of a struggle between two adversaries', which Foucault attributes to Schmitt. Finally, asserting the perspective of resistance, he argues that 'everything can be politicized' and that politics is 'born with resistance to governmentality'. If governmentality concerns the technologies through which conduct is acted upon, then as resistance to governmentality, politics will take the form of 'counter-conducts', of ways of acting upon and governing oneself, elaborated in the 'struggle against the processes of conducting others' (Foucault, 2007: 201). Consistent with his enduring concerns for anti-institutional struggles, for minor and minority politics, and for the rights of the governed, Foucault's concept of politics concerns modes of 'subjectification' and 'de-subjectification'.

These notes indicate that Foucault was acquainted with Schmitt's *The Concept of the Political* (1996a) and its maxim. 'The specific political distinction to which political actions and motives can be reduced is that between friend and enemy' (Schmitt, 1996a: 26). As may be observed, however, this is not quite a definition of politics but a statement of what is essential about the political. Schmitt maintained that the political can be approached through the antithesis, friend/enemy, just as other activities, moral, aesthetic or economic can be approached through antitheses such as good and evil, beautiful and ugly, profitable or unprofitable. However, as Leo Strauss was the first to note, the political is not simply a sphere – that of politics – among others in the liberal totality of human culture (1996: 86). 'The political is the most intense and extreme antagonism, and every concrete antagonism becomes that much more political the closer it approaches the most extreme point, that of the friend-enemy grouping' (Schmitt, 1996a: 29). Like Foucault, Schmitt argues that all human spheres and actions have the possibility of being politicized. 'Every religious, moral, economic, ethical or other antithesis transforms into a political one if it is sufficiently strong to group human beings effectively according to friend and enemy' (p. 37).

On this basis, Foucault's conceptualization of power as a game between liberties and Schmitt's view of the political are not as different as they might first seem. Foucault coins the neologism, 'agonism', from the Greek, *agonisma*, meaning combat, to approach the fundamental nature of relations of power (2001: 342). Schmitt traces the arc by which these tensions, parries, thrusts and reversals enter into a fundamental antagonism in which what is at stake is of the utmost seriousness. 'The friend, the enemy and combat concepts received their real meaning precisely because they refer to the real possibility of physical killing' (Schmitt, 1996a: 33). The political is not merely a game; its manoeuvres are not merely the taunting, reactions and holds of the wrestler. It would seem the political is deadly serious, the point at which the game's stakes are raised to the highest order.

Foucault, it is true, said very little about the political per se and did not very clearly distinguish the political and the governmental (Hindess, 1997). If the 'politics of identity' discovers the political in everyday life – so that, 'the personal becomes political' as feminism would say – Schmitt by contrast places the political in the realm of 'high politics' and existential drama: firstly in the relationships between two 'organized peoples' or, in modern times, states, and only secondly, in the most extreme forms of conflict within states, that is open civil war. Schmitt's conception of the political as 'high politics' equates with what we might call foreign affairs, if we suppose the domestic front to be one of peace, harmony and order,

It is clear that Schmitt elaborated the enemy side of the distinction more than that of the friend. In the late Weimar period, he distinguishes between the enemy as *hostis* (the public enemy) and the enemy as *inimicus* (the private enemy) and reads Jesus Christ's injunction to 'love thy enemies' as addressing private quarrels rather than public or political enmity (1996a: 29). In a sentence that chillingly reads from the playbook of the contemporary anti-Islamic right: 'Never in the thousand-year struggle between Christians and Moslems did it occur to a Christian to surrender rather than defend Europe out of love toward the Saracens or Turks.'

In *The* Nomos *of the Earth*, published in 1950, Schmitt discusses the concept of *justis hostis* in the development of a non-discriminatory concept of inter-state war under European public law, the *jus publicum Europæum* (2003: 153 ff.). This was in effect a limitation of war in inter-state law, and thus a renunciation of the criminalization of the opponent. By the 1960s, and the age of anti-colonial wars of independence, Schmitt distinguished between the conventional enemy, the *justis hostis* of inter-state warfare, the real, often imperial or invading, enemy of the partisan, and the absolute enemy, an enemy who is the enemy of humanity and therefore must be destroyed at all costs. With the collapse of European international public law in the early twentieth century, and the proscription of war for national purposes, Schmitt contends, the enemy takes this general and abstract form. In this case, the political is directed not against another political entity, or state, but against those outside of humanity and its values, who thus appear as the last enemy. 'Enmity becomes so frightful that perhaps one no longer should speak of the enemy or enmity, and both should be outlawed and damned before the work of destruction can begin', Schmitt writes at the end of *Theory of the Partisan* (2007: 94).

Using these vocabularies in a complementary way, one could say that the arts of government of the state, according to Foucault are, at least in part, a practice of power relations that seeks to manage, prevent, limit or control the possibility of the political (in Schmitt's sense) emerging and threatening the state internally, and about reflecting upon and strategizing within the external political game. From Schmitt's viewpoint, resistance to governmentality would only become truly political when the resistance or counter-conducts that contest the art of government challenge the existence of the political unity, the state, itself. Certainly 'insurrections of conduct' are found in all types of revolutionary situations, from the Reformation to the French and Russian Revolutions, as Foucault himself notes (2007: 228).

There are many alternative definitions of the political and politics that stress how political activity is often about binding people together rather than the antagonisms that place them in situations of existential hostility. The role of the politician for Plato in *The Statesman* is described as an art of weaving together the different characters of humans by common beliefs, honours, interchanges and pledges, and thus to draw them together 'by friendship and community of sentiment into a common life ... omitting nothing which ought to belong to a happy state' (Plato, 1952: 195). But this aim, which we could liken to the notion of establishing 'good police', that is the good order within a community, which obtained in medieval and early modern Europe, is the 'friend' component of the other feature that makes things political. 'That feature', wrote Paul Hirst, 'is struggle, and struggle means the reciprocal action of parties opposed to one another' (1988: 274).

Foucault thought and wrote explicitly about power and power relations in a relatively brief time period, which we might delineate by the decline of theoretical Marxism and the ossification of political conflict during the entrenched stage of the Cold War. It was also a time when economic crises would disturb the unprecedented affluence of the 'West' at the end of the post-World War II 'Long Boom'. He wrote to support, rather than represent, local, identity and anti-institutional politics, and was not particularly concerned with fundamental antagonisms over inequality or class conflict. In this sense, it is perhaps unfair to contrast him to Schmitt who lived through four different political regimes in Germany, failed Marxist revolution, Nazi dictatorship, defeat in two world wars, and the division of Germany into two ideologically opposed and armed camps. He imagined himself to be, as he told his interrogator at Nuremberg, an 'intellectual adventurer' (Kempner and Schmitt, 1987: 103). However, in the early twenty-first century intensification of the political, specifically during the United States-led 'war on terror', which justified the administrative detention without trial of 'enemy combatants' and sanctioned the use of torture and the expansion of extra-juridical killing of those considered a threat to humanity, Schmitt seemed to have put his finger on aspects of power relations that were either simply missing, or not placed in the foreground, not only in Foucault but also in most of the contemporary human sciences. As a *Chronicle of Higher Education* headline put it without too much delicacy, 'A fascist philosopher helps us understand contemporary politics' (Wolfe, 2004).

There is a certain continuity between Foucault's power relations as agonistic games between liberties and Schmitt's political relations as antagonistic enmity between parties. It would be possible to link the two and examine the thresholds at which the former turns into the latter and the way the political and its management form a part of relations of power and techniques of governmentality more broadly.

However, Foucault's conception of the political as a resistance to governmentality, and the formation of counter-conducts and different ways of acting on oneself, forms a local politics of struggle and resistance, which is appropriate to the anti-institutional and identity movements to which he attached his work. But Schmitt's definition indicates a political beyond local power and self-formation contests, an eventuality which can be managed, deferred, and even prevented, by forms of governmentality, but which cannot be abolished by them, that of the relationship between sovereign states.

5.3 It might be thought that Schmitt's restriction of the political to the high politics of foreign affairs presents an essential limitation in his work. However, he introduces a second term to describe the production of unity within the state, that of 'police'. Within the classical model of the European state 'there was indeed only police and no more politics, unless one were to designate as politics such things as court intrigues, rivalries, frondes and attempts at rebellion on the part of malcontents, in short, "disturbances"' (Schmitt, in Deuber-Mankowsky, 2008: 149–50). Police and politics are both, he contends, derived from the Greek word, *polis*.

In this identification of internal or domestic politics as 'police', Schmitt would seem to anticipate Foucault's own understanding of the objectives of *raison d'État* (reason of state) in the seventeenth and eighteenth centuries. On the one hand, reason of state is practised as a limited art in the domain of international politics and the relations between competing states. Where Schmitt would find states facing each other as equal sovereigns in European public law, Foucault discovers the development of new military and diplomatic techniques such as permanent armies and diplomacy. In this sense, reason of state was a reflected practice of the political, of friend–enemy relations. On the one hand, like Schmitt, Foucault designates the internal aspect of reason of state by the term police. Externally, reason of state accepts a set of limited objectives of ensuring the state's independence within the complex of a balance of forces of states of different size; internally, however, 'there is no limit to the objectives of government when it is a question of managing a public power that has to regulate the behavior of subjects' (Foucault, 2008: 6–7). Police will fulfil a set of functions that Schmitt will designate by a phrase from Thomas Carlyle: 'The absolutism of the state is, accordingly, the oppressor of the irrepressible chaos inherent in man, or as Carlyle said in his drastic manner, anarchy plus police' (Schmitt, 2008b: 21–2).

Both sides of the police/political distinction that Schmitt makes might be said to have a biopolitical function. In a twist on identity politics, Schmitt views the enemy as existentially defining one's own identity and requiring individuals to be willing to sacrifice their lives. The political relation of friend and enemy is thus a biopolitical one. Yet this is neither a case of 'to foster life and let die' or 'to take life and let live' (as it is in Foucault's language) but to 'give one's life and kill'. It is this existential, biopolitical sense that made the conduct of war totally abhorrent for Schmitt:

> There exists no rational purpose, no norm no matter how true, no program no matter how exemplary, no social idea no matter how beautiful, no legitimacy or legality which could justify men in killing each other for this reason. If such physical destruction of human life is not motivated by an existential threat to one's own way of life, then it can not be justified. (Schmitt, 1996a: 49)

For Foucault, the history of police and the cameralist *Polizeiwissenschaft* also belongs to the history of biopolitics in a number of ways. Police will be one of the first formations of domestic governmental rationality to take population and the numbers of the inhabitants within the state as its object (2007: 323–4). It addresses all the different aspects of life: its necessities, the health of the population, professions and work, and the circulation of goods. It is thus concerned with 'an immense domain that goes from living to more than just living' (p. 326), which includes humans' 'convenience, amenity, felicity' (p. 327) or finally, 'well-being' (p. 328). Biopolitics is thus not only the existential threat to a way of life by external enemies, which demands a willingness to sacrifice one's life, but the optimization of life within the state.

For Schmitt, many of his references to police after World War II were predominantly negative ones. For example, he described the allied bombings of German cities as indicating 'the fact that war had been transformed into a police action against troublemakers, criminals, and pests' and the re-emergence of the medieval doctrine of just war (2003: 321). In a language that will ramify through the critiques of the global order by the radical Left in our century, Schmitt lamented the collapse of the state system in the twentieth century, with its non-discriminatory concept of war, and the appearance of a 'global civil war' in which war will be replaced by such police actions (2007: 93, 95).

Foucault, however, alerts us to a further feature of the early modern conception of police that is far from these negative connotations. He observes that police 'must ensure the state's splendor', which is 'the visible beauty of the order and the beautiful radiating manifestation of a force' (2007: 313, 314). But why should this be the case? If police is simply about the effective internal ordering of the state and the well-being of the population, then why should it seek to give the state such light, radiance, and brilliance? This is something which neither Foucault nor Schmitt will ever ask. If the inter-state domain of the political would appear to form a transcendent plane in relation to the immanence of domestic police, why would the latter also seek its own kind of transcendence?

Secrets and power

5.4 Schmitt says surprisingly little about the concept of power per se, although it could be argued that the nature of power, particularly political power, is manifest throughout his writings on sovereignty, constitutional and international law and the political.

The view of power he enunciates is certainly difficult to digest because it presents what could be described as the antithesis of contemporary views of power, many of which owe their derivation to Foucault, and broader views of power as systems of governance or complex networks, or as assemblages, and as the more or less gentle, non-consensual but also non-violent, shaping of conduct. His characterization of the political in terms of the friend–enemy relationship, with the possibility of 'real killing', as he puts it, is an affront to our view of politics in liberal-democracy as a process or procedure of election, representation, deliberation, and policy-making. In one brief, explicit discussion in 1957, commenting on a chapter on power by the theologian Erich Przywara, Schmitt draws us to a characterization of power that is the antithesis of the liberal governmental imperative to make power open, public, accountable and transparent. In so doing he makes us aware of another duality found within the signature of the concept of power: power as open, visible and manifest as opposed to power as secret, hidden and latent.

Schmitt asserts that 'power is the "secret sinister end"' (2003: 336). 'The impulse to secrecy and to learn the secret is the first tendency of any power, whatever form of government or method of administration it services. No ruler can escape this impulse, which becomes greater and more intense the stronger and more effective power becomes.' Schmitt's sources for this view are Carl Friedrich; Hannah Arendt, who comments that 'real power begins where secrecy begins' (1951: 386); and Max Weber with his analysis of the will to domination found in the Puritans' worldly asceticism. Secondly, Schmitt argues, power seeks an 'implicit centrality' which is not an academic or theoretical assumption, such as the one Foucault contested, but a kind of tentative and fragile project of construction undertaken by rulers themselves.

> From its compulsion to self-affirmation, daily and hourly power seeks to secure, to justify and to consolidate its position anew. This creates a dialectic, whereby the ruler, in order to maintain this position, is compelled to organize new security systems around himself and to create new anterooms, corridors, and accesses to power. (2003: 357)

These passages present an immediate counterpoint to the tendency to wish to view power in terms of visibility and publicity and to make power visible and public by our theorization. They call into question the attempt to make power visible as an epistemological object through clear definition and proper empirical study, as they do the liberal governmental project of placing power in the light of publicity, and using technologies of government and mechanisms of accountability to render it transparent and visible. In contrast to the liberal imagery and will to control power, we have the kind of power found in spy novels, in Franz Kafka, in surveillance instruments such as the now ubiquitous closed-circuit television camera which, in rendering certain activities and potential threats visible, protects an area in which access is not public but restricted, and the activities within which are not visible but hidden from the public. This notion of power belongs to the secret police and security services, both in authoritarian regimes and their liberal-democratic equivalents. It is also the power of the 'court society' of the absolutist monarchy in the France of Louis XIV with its intrigues, status hierarchies, rooms and antechambers, sequestrations and rituals described by Norbert Elias (1983). One could think that Schmitt had all this in mind when he continued:

> The inescapable dialectic consists in the fact that, through such security measures, he [the ruler] distances and isolates himself from the world he rules. His surroundings thrust him into a

stratosphere, wherein only he has access to those over whom he rules indirectly, while he no longer has access to all the others over whom he exercises power, and they no longer have access to him. (2003: 337)

Schmitt comes close to grasping the signature of the concept when he immediately suggests a third proposition. 'The tendency of power to secrecy corresponds to a counter-tendency, which is to visibility and publicity.' This is not only the assumption of liberal normative approaches to power but also the task of political thought since Plato. The two suffixes, -*archy* and -*cracy*, try to make clear, respectively, the source of power and the power holder. Thus the study of power seeks to identify its source, which for Schmitt has a 'theological foundation', in words such as monarchy or oligarchy, and the 'anthropological power' of those who hold it in words such as democracy and aristocracy. This reflection on power stops short with Schmitt's assertion that neither -*archy* nor -*cracy* can exist without *nomos*, which in his view, penetrates and in some sense subjugates them (2003: 358; on *nomos*, see §6.1).

Schmitt here challenges us to recognize the tendency to secrecy and invisibility, the locked doors, the restricted areas, the darkened passageways, antechambers and mazes where power is manifest as much as in the kinds of visibility and publicity of liberal normativity. There is continuity with Foucault, who already began to write the history of this relationship of visibility and power when he proposed an inversion of visibility in the functioning of the disciplines. Against the excessive, spectacular, exaggerated expression of potency and might, often related to triumph, found in the solemn appearance of the sovereign and the hidden shadows of his subjects, Foucault proposed the invisibility of a disciplinary power that exposed its subjects to a compulsory visibility and inspection (1977: 187–9). Bentham's well-known diagram of the Panopticon was emblematic for Foucault of this form of power in that it rendered its inmates or other subjects in a field of perfect transparency while keeping the presence of their guard or supervisor hidden. Schmitt would emphasize the paranoid hiding of power and Foucault its fields of visibility and its controlling scopophilia.

This problem was resolved for Foucault when he turned to the liberal problematic of security, which, according to him, no longer expressed a detailed concern with the individual but focused rather on 'the population and its specific phenomena and processes' (2007: 66).

Rather than the emblem of the modern form of non-juridical power, the Panopticon had retreated, like, as we have seen, so many other figures before it, to the world of sovereignty and its archaisms.

> The idea of the panopticon is a modern idea in one sense, but we can also say that it is completely archaic, since … [it] basically involves putting someone in the centre … who will be able to make its sovereignty function over all the individuals … the panopticon is the oldest dream of the oldest sovereign … The central point of the panopticon still functions, as it were, as a perfect sovereign … The government of populations is … completely different from the exercise of sovereignty over the fine grain of individual behaviours. It seems to me that we have two completely different systems of power. (Foucault, 2007: 66)

The hidden/visible binary of forms of power is thus again collapsed into a unity by Foucault in his search for the new, non-sovereign, sense of power – this time it is collapsed into the side of sovereignty itself. Schmitt's couple of pages, by contrast, allow the binary of these 'tendencies' to remain a feature of all kinds of exercise of power, albeit taking different forms, thus affirming the necessity of attempting to read the *arcana* of power.

5.5 The discussion of the secret and power has important resonances in both Foucault's extended discussion of reason of state and in Schmitt's *The Crisis of Parliamentary Democracy* (1985). In a discussion of the sovereign's knowledge of the elements that constitute the state, Foucault notes that often this knowledge was considered effective if it was not divulged and that the new science or knowledge of the state, which could be called 'statistics', was often included in the *arcana* of power (2007: 273–5).

When Foucault takes up the liberal critique of state reason, it is a critique in part of its omniscience, not its *arcana*. Schmitt by contrast argues that one of the fundamental principles of liberalism, openness, is elaborated precisely in respect to the doctrine of state secrets, *arcana rei publicae*, elaborated in the literature on *Staatraison*. 'The postulate of openness finds its specific opponent in the idea that *Arcana* belong to every kind of politics, political-technical secrets which are in fact just as necessary for absolutism as business and economic secrets are for an economic life that depends on private property' (1985: 37–8).

From this point of view, liberalism is a critique of the tendency to secrecy of power, based on the principle of openness. In this sense, freedom of the press is of equal if not greater import than other political techniques that promote freedom and openness of opinion in liberalism: freedom of speech, freedom of assembly, and parliamentary immunity. Paradoxically, 'the contradictory demand for a secret ballot appears. Freedom of opinion is a freedom of private people; it is necessary for that competition of opinions in which the best opinion wins' (Schmitt, 1985: 39). Yet it is not only that paradox which can be cited, but also precisely the spatial figure of access to power that Schmitt would approach in his papers on the *nomos* in the 1950s (see §5.4). In *The Crisis of Parliamentary Democracy*, he cites the assertion of a nineteenth-century French politician, Comte de Cavour, that 'the worst chamber is still preferable to the best antechamber' as a feature of constitutional regimes, and then makes the observation: 'Today parliament itself appears a gigantic antechamber in front of the bureaus or committees of invisible rulers' (1985: 7). Whatever the empirical validity of such a proposition concerning particular parliaments, it is enough to remind us that among the first attempts to empirically investigate and critically theorize the exercise of power in post-World War II America was the discovery of non-decision-making and latent conflicts. Peter Bachrach and Morton S. Baratz would ask: 'Can the researcher overlook the chance that some person or association could limit decision-making to relatively non-controversial matters, by influencing community values and political procedures and rituals, notwithstanding that there are in the community serious but latent power conflicts?' (1962: 949). While these authors would view non-decision-making as a possible feature of the procedures and rituals of liberal democracy, Schmitt of course would view it as a persistent, if not necessary, one.

For Schmitt, the question of openness and secrecy is one of the tools by which he shows some of the aporias of liberalism and its claims and hence forces apart the terms liberalism and democracy. Democracy, in his view, depends on some kind of identity between the governed and those governing, or 'the assertion of an identity between law and the people's will' (Schmitt, 1985: 26). Liberalism on the other hand is a set of political techniques such as open public discussion, a division of powers, and the theory of the *Rechstaat*, and a 'consistent, comprehensive metaphysical system' based on individualism, rationalism and universalism (p. 34). The problems he diagnosed for his own time and place, writing in 1923 and 1926, before, during and after major crises of the Weimar Republic, can be presented in terms of this antithesis of democracy and liberalism.

The first problem is the conflict between liberal universalism's belief in the equality of humanity and the democratic identity of ruler and ruled, which implies 'only the equality of equals, and the will of those who belong to the equals' (Schmitt, 1985: 16). Democracy thus rests on a necessary exclusion of those considered 'unequals': in the past, slaves, women, propertyless men, and Indigenous populations; today, refugees, illegal immigrants, certain prisoners, children, the mentally ill. A second is between the idea of representation inherited from the Catholic Church by way of monarchy and that of the identity or democratic homogeneity of rulers and ruled, as Chantal Mouffe has definitively shown (1993: 106–7). 'If democratic identity is taken seriously', Schmitt states, 'then in an emergency, no other constitutional institution can withstand the sole criterion of the people's will, however expressed. Against the will of the people especially an institution based on discussion by independent representatives has no autonomous justification for its existence, even less so because the belief in discussion is not democratic but originally liberal' (Schmitt, 1985: 15).

The belief in discussion and openness, for Schmitt, arises from liberalism's metaphysical system (1985: 34). In the sphere of economics, it posits that economic competition and free trade leads to social harmony and the maximum of wealth. In politics, the application of this same 'game of freedom' takes the form that 'the truth can be found through an unrestrained clash of opinions and that competition will produce harmony'.

As we have seen (§2.7), Foucault suggests parliamentary democracy is a part of a set of technologies appropriate to the participation of the governed in a liberal governmental economy. Like Schmitt he indicates a kind of necessary non-correspondence between liberalism and democracy. Where Foucault however remains uninterested in the theory of democracy per se, perhaps because it is simply a 'democratization of sovereignty' as he calls it, and thus associated with the rejected juridical-political theory, Schmitt still wishes to chart the democratic imperative in contemporary societies and its associated concepts of the will of the people, popular opinion, legitimation, and so on. Democracy as concept appears to have little salience in Foucault's analysis while Schmitt keeps the term in play, and he gives positive value to direct democracy by acclamation. Both, however, view liberalism as a critique of sorts – in Foucault's case, a critique of too much government, of sovereignty, of the imperatives of the police state, and of biopolitics. In Schmitt's case, it is the critique of politics and the political itself. In *The Concept of the Political*, he notes 'there exists a liberal policy of trade, church, and education, but absolutely no liberal politics, only a liberal critique of politics. The systematic theory of liberalism concerns almost solely the internal struggle against the power of the state' (1996a: 70).

Liberalism thus portends a kind of anti-state or anti-governmental 'eschatology' rooted in its notion of civil society, as Foucault puts it (2007: 356). Both Foucault (2008: 310) and Schmitt (1996a: 61) cite Thomas Paine's 1776 pamphlet, *Common Sense,* and its formulation that links society with human goodness and government as a necessary evil to restrain human wickedness. Both note that liberalism directs its critique to specific states and forms of political power. For Foucault, however, liberalism develops an art of government, rooted in an immanent knowledge of society, population and economy, which might provide us with a way beyond the hierarchies and dominations of sovereignty and discipline. For Schmitt, it does nothing but negate the state and the political, for it is 'neither a political theory nor a political idea ... but has attempted only to tie the political to the ethical and to subjugate it to economics' (1996a: 61).

Schmitt thus indicates an almost identical fate of the political to that of Foucault in the twentieth century. Where the latter notes the centrality of economics to the art of governing, and comes to look for political struggles in the ethical action of self on self and the formation of 'counter-conducts', the former indicates a kind of false displacement of the political which will manage to rear its head in ever new, and sometimes frightening, ways. Citing Walter Rathenau's claims that 'destiny today is not politics but economics', Schmitt responds that 'it would be more exact to say that politics continues to remain the destiny, but what has occurred is that economics has become political and thereby the destiny' (1996a: 78). Moreover, the polarity of economics and ethics 'serves newly emerging friend-enemy relations and cannot escape the political' (p. 79). These relations will designate the enemy as an 'outlaw of humanity' in a war that will 'turn into a crusade and into the last war of humanity'.

The signature of the concept of power keeps referring us to a field of irreducible antinomies. Now we can add latent and manifest, visible and hidden, open and secret, to that field. Moreover, Schmitt uses them to intensify the opposition between fundamental political concepts of liberalism and democracy in order to make them appear antithetical. No doubt there is something crude about the way he does this but it is still a way of addressing this signature that marks our concepts of power. If Foucault seeks a displacement of the pre-eminence of sovereignty by a liberal-economic art of government founded on an ethical subject, Schmitt discovers the locus of the decision, and the presence of the political, in precisely this same sovereign power.

Legitimacy and sovereignty

5.6 The problem of legitimation is fundamental to the juridical-political theory of democratic sovereignty. For Foucault, however, it appears that questions of legitimacy and legitimation are barking up the wrong tree. They are a part of the vocabulary of sovereignty and, in democratic theories of sovereignty, they rest on the notion of the consent of the governed or will of the people in the exercise of properly acquired and executed power of the state. For the idea of legitimation, Foucault substitutes the idea of the technologies of power, the effective means by which spaces and objects of government are constituted and acted upon, and through which conduct is directed and shaped. This general picture of Foucault's thought is complicated a little by the recognition that certain technologies, such as those necessary for the implementation of a market society in post-war West Germany, could themselves provide the basis of legitimation. Like democracy, however, legitimacy and legitimation are largely ruled out of the central frame of Foucault's power analytics, and identified with the problematic of sovereignty.

Schmitt however has a very specific view of legitimacy and frames it in a new antithesis between legality and legitimacy. In doing so, he appears to follow Max Weber's distinction between legitimate and illegitimate domination. While domination for Weber is 'the probability that certain specific commands (or all commands) will be obeyed by a given group of persons' (1968: 212), every system of domination 'attempts to establish and cultivate the belief in its legitimacy', which is to say that it seeks to provide a basis for the exercise of authority (p. 213). Weber distinguishes ideal types of legitimate domination or authority. Traditional authority thus rests on 'an established belief in the sanctity of immemorial traditions' and charismatic authority on the 'devotion' to the exceptional character of the individual person

(p. 215). In the case of rational authority, legitimation 'rests on a belief in the legality of enacted rules and the right of those elevated to authority under such rules to issue commands' (p. 215).

In *Legality and Legitimacy* (2004a) Schmitt uses Weber's account to drive a wedge between the two concepts. He reads Weber as identifying legality as a valid form of legitimacy and cites him as saying that 'the most widely prominent form of legitimacy today is the belief in legality' (Schmitt, 2004a: 9). Against this, he understands legality as a system of justification closely associated with the liberal parliamentary system, which, by itself, contains no reason for a belief in it. Legality then would need to be supported by concrete forms of legitimation such as the traditional authority of the monarch or the charismatic authority of the 'people's plebiscitarian will'. As John P. McCormick remarks, Schmitt can see nothing intrinsic in legality that could secure its legitimacy: '...legality possesses neither procedurally formal nor moral-practical rationality' (2004: xxv). For Schmitt, the aporias of legality – which mean a *coup d'État* might be deemed legal, and a parliamentary dissolution illegal – 'document the breakdown of a system of legality which ends in a formalism or functionalism, without substance or reference points' (2004a: 10).

Schmitt maintains the antithesis of legality and legitimacy beyond the immediate crisis of the calamitous endgame of the Weimar Republic until, as we shall note, his very last works (see § 6.8). His search for securing the basis of legitimacy of an existing legal order will take many forms: from political theology, to the sovereign, the Reich president, and the *Führer*; and from the concrete order to the *nomos* and the Earth as mother. What is characteristic however is the way Schmitt approaches the signature of the concept of power: to locate the distinction and to drive it into open antithesis and conflict. It is a rough enough method but it yields, at least in impression, powerful insights.

5.7 Foucault focuses our attention on the liminal or 'in-between' space, a space between limits: governmentality exists *between* power as a game of liberties and states of domination. Sovereignty too forms a limit in the narrative of the genealogy of government. Schmitt also seeks limit concepts and defines sovereignty as a 'borderline concept' but his intention is anything but the sidelining of it (2005: 5). 'Sovereign is he who decides the state of exception', as George Schwab's elegant translation puts it (p. 5). Sovereignty, as borderline concept, pertains to the 'outermost sphere'; it 'must be associated with a borderline case and not with routine'. There is nothing vague about this. Sovereignty concerns the making of a decision when, and under what circumstances, 'a case of extreme peril', or 'a danger to the existence of the state', obtains (p. 6). But it also means that the sovereign is the one who decides on the resolution to that situation. 'He decides whether there is an extreme emergency as well as what must be done to eliminate it' (p. 7). For Schmitt, moreover, not every police measure or emergency measure amounts to a state of exception. In order to cross that threshold, such a measure would need to suspend the entirety of the existing order and call for absolute authority (p. 12).

Schmitt presents an important clarification of Foucault's diachronic contrast between the safety of the Prince and the security of population. The latter is certainly correct when he places rationalities of security at the centre of modern arts of government of the state, but his formulations tend to sever security from sovereignty by virtue of their juxtaposition. Schmitt, however, reminds us that such observations cannot make sovereignty completely disappear from the picture. For him, the sovereign decides, under the pressure of the exceptional case, that is, not in relation to an academic observation or scientific form of knowledge, the practical meaning and content of terms such as security and public order and when and how they should be applied to life. In face of discussions of what constitutes the common good, 'sovereignty (and thus the state itself) resides in deciding this controversy, that is, in determining definitely what constitutes public order and security, in determining when they are disturbed, and so on' (p. 9). While it is appropriate to establish the empirical existence and transformation of different rationalities of government, as Foucault does, this move cannot avoid sovereignty as the structure of decisions that define the thresholds at which public order and security obtain, what their content is, and how, in any given situation, they might be achieved.

For Schmitt, in deciding the exception, the sovereign also defines the norm, or what is normal, and the 'normal everyday frame of life' to which it is applied (2005: 13): 'For a legal order to make sense, a normal situation must exist, and sovereign is he who definitely decides whether this normal situation actually exists.' The sovereign decides not only the exception but also the norm. This is an important point but it does not mean that the sovereign somehow determines in detail the normal frame of life. There is no analytical equivalence here between exception and norm. 'The rule proves nothing: the exception proves everything. It confirms not only the rule but also its existence, which derives only from the exception. In the exception, the power of real life breaks through the crust of a mechanism that has become torpid by repetition' (Schmitt, 2005: 15). It is only in the exception that the law and its norms are brought into contact with life, that the rule and the general can be understood, and the 'essence of the state's authority' can be revealed (p. 13).

Both Schmitt and Foucault regard sovereignty as a limit concept. For Foucault, it is a kind of limit against which the conceptualization of what is new or contemporary about power relations in our present can be specified and analysed. For Schmitt, it defines a limit between the law and what is outside the law. It first looks outside the law and the legal order, to what is beyond and not contained by them, and to a situation of such emergency and necessity that the entire edifice needs to be made inoperable, that is, to be suspended. But it also looks toward the founding of the legal order, and the definition of a normal situation and a normal frame of life. In this sense, although the sovereign 'stands outside the normally valid system, he nevertheless belongs to it' (Schmitt, 2005: 7). It is only in this second and partial sense, that we could define law as the expression of the will of the sovereign.

The defining feature of sovereignty for Schmitt, then, is not its reliance on law or even a right of life and death, a *jus vitae ac necis*. This again serves as a point of distinction from Foucault's view that seeks to define sovereignty according to 'the right to decide life and death', which was ultimately 'derived from the *patria potestas*', the right of the father of the Roman family 'to "dispose" of the life of his children and his slaves' (1979: 135). Schmitt considers this option but drops it precisely because the right of life and death can belong to other 'non-political' units such as the household:

> The authority to decide, in the form of the verdict on life and death, the *jus vitae ac necis*, can also belong to another nonpolitical order within the political entity, for instance, to the family or the head of the household, but not the right of a *hostis* declaration as long as the political entity is an actuality and possesses the *jus belli*. (Schmitt, 1996a: 47)

The defining feature of a political entity, such as the state, is its right to decide the enemy and to make war; its right of war. The *jus belli* implies the possibility of 'the right to demand from its own members the readiness to die and unhesitatingly to kill enemies' (Schmitt, 1996a: 46).

Schmitt thus departs not only from Foucault's view of sovereignty but also Max Weber's famous definition of the state as the claim to the monopoly of legitimate force or violence. The sovereign, rather, has the 'monopoly over this last decision' (Schmitt, 2005: 13). Internally, this means to decide when conflict is so extreme as to be a threat to the public interest, public security and safety, and to act to secure and restore a normal condition. In its relations with external entities, it means to decide to declare war and mobilize its members in the defeat of the enemy.

For Schmitt then, the unpredictability and unknowability of the exceptional case makes sovereignty relevant and important. As long as the normal situation obtains, sovereignty can be forgotten about and fade into the background. Liberal constitutionalism attempts 'to repress the question of sovereignty by a division and mutual control of competences' (2005: 11). Rationalism will say that only the rule is of scientific interest and the exception is of none (p. 14). If Schmitt is correct about this, we can predict that in times of relative peace and security within the secure borders of liberal democracies, and a perceived pacification of those outside these borders, not only lay people but political and social scientists will start to imagine, theorize, analyse and diagnose the displacement of sovereignty by softer, flatter, less unitary, more subtle, and more acceptable kinds of human organization and power. In the absence of the exception, it is harder to make the case for attentiveness to sovereignty. However, Schmitt would argue, it 'is precisely the exception that makes relevant the subject of sovereignty, that is, the whole question of sovereignty' (p. 6).

In many governmentality studies claiming allegiance to Foucault, liberalism, understood as an art of government, provides limits to the omniscience and omnicompetence of state sovereignty or, its surrogates, police and reason of state. This is because sovereignty is understood simply as the locus of generating commands as laws or regulations. Schmitt provides us with an alternative way of approaching the limits to a power that would claim supremacy within a domain: that of the exception. But the exception does not undermine the relevance of sovereignty or present limits to it; it underlines it, and is the event or occasion that most emphasizes the intense relevance of sovereignty. And, unlike and in stark contrast to the study of governmentality, sovereignty does not claim to be all-knowing of everything occurring within its purview, but only competent to decide and act upon what cannot be predicted or fully known. Sovereignty implies only a limited competence or capacity, to make a decision, in unknowable and unpredictable circumstances, on the exception, not unlimited competence and infinite knowledge.

Alongside and underlying a right of death, and a monopoly of force, we have then the monopoly of the final decision. Against a view of sovereign power that expresses its command in law and regulations, we have a sovereign that both belongs to and stands outside the law and the legal order. For Foucault, the liberal critique of sovereignty and the state makes possible the flourishing of the arts of government. For Schmitt the liberal critique of sovereignty risks neutralizing its unique political function and capacity thereby opening the path to civil lawlessness and anomie.

Government, the pastorate and the King's reign

5.8 Carl Schmitt clearly has a forceful concept of sovereignty, but does he have one of governing or government in any sense recognizable to those who have followed the genealogy of the arts of government of the state? What does he add, if anything, to the discussion of the 'government of men' or the 'government of the living'?

When Schmitt does turn to the notion of government in his *Constitutional Theory* (2008a), first published in 1928, it is, as might be expected, what we would call executive government, or *the* government. Schmitt addresses the relationship between an elected representative assembly and government in this sense and finds a number of options under democracy. These include the possibility of the subordination of the government to the parliament. Under parliamentary democracy, the 'popular assembly (the parliament) is a committee of the people (enfranchised voters), while the parliamentary government is a committee of the popular assembly (of the parliament). State organization appears as a committee system with three levels: people, popular assembly and government' (2008a: 292).

Schmitt then proceeds to discuss two alternative relations between parliament and government: one, the Westminster system of cabinet government in which the majority party forms government which leads the parliament; and the second, the idea of a *counterpoise* between government and parliament, such as imagined by the Weimar Constitution, in which the people decide between the two and act as a 'higher third' (2008a: 293–4). Hence, Schmitt uses the term 'government' in the sense of one component of the division of powers and an attempt to specify who constitutionally can act as sovereign in any given situation. This is a fairly standard use of the term although Schmitt draws attention to the possibility of an antagonism emerging here between parliament and government.

However, on other occasions, Schmitt's discussion of government and its genealogy took special notice of the Hebraic and Christian pastorate and the figure of the shepherd and the flock. Schmitt addresses precisely this figure as a symbol of rule on more than one occasion. In a 1957 essay, he notes that Plato, in *The Statesman*, distinguishes between the shepherd and the statesman. The shepherd nourishes the flock and is a kind of god to the animals he herds, while 'the statesman does not stand as far above the people he governs as does the shepherd above his flock' (Schmitt, 2003: 340). That the statesman does not nourish the people indicates the separation, for Schmitt, of politics from economics. In respect of the god-like character of shepherds, Schmitt concurs with Foucault's reading of Plato, that statesmen 'are themselves a part of humanity and therefore cannot be seen as shepherds' (Foucault, 2007: 145).

Schmitt however goes somewhat further by suggesting that the identification of the rule of the shepherd was linked to the 'nomadic age'. Thus he claims that *nomos* is etymologically linked to *nomeus* (the shepherd). He can only conceive nomadism as a search for pasture and land to settle on, not as a permanent movement on the face of the Earth. However, with settled communities, this earlier identity with the shepherd is overcome by the linking of house (*oikos*) with *nomos* in *oikonomia*. 'The rule of the patriarchal father over the house and family was a totality in that it united religious and moral authority, juridical *potestas* and dispositional economic rights' (2003: 340). Schmitt employs a language that would have been worthy of much later feminist critiques of the patriarchal welfare state. 'The transformation of the community into an administrative state responsible for total social welfare leads to a paternal totality without a house-father when it fails to find any *archy* or *cracy* that is more than the mere *nomos* of distribution and production.'

In focusing on the relationship of the citizen to the city and not the Judaeo-Christian shepherd-flock, Schmitt seems to depart from Foucault's view that the trajectory of pastoral power is relevant to our present and the forms of government that characterize it. His main adversary here is that which breaks with the pastorate, that is, economic and technical forms rule, which seems to him to be summed up in Friedrich Engels's claim that the 'government of men' would be replaced under socialism by the 'administration of things' (Schmitt, 2003: 341).

Yet this was not the first time Schmitt had recourse to the problematic of the pastorate. In the 1933 pamphlet, *State, Movement, People* (2001), he turns to the question of leadership, or *Führung*. To lead, he states there, 'is not to command, to dictate, to govern bureaucratically from the centre, or any other kind of rule' (p. 46). Again he rejects what he here calls the 'Roman Catholic' image of a shepherd and his flock in which 'the shepherd remains absolutely *transcendent* to the flock' (p. 47, original emphasis). Instead he picks from Plato the image of the pilot of a ship, the 'helmsman' or '*gubernator*', which in all Latin-influenced languages 'has become the word for "government", such as *gouvernement, governo, government*'. But again, the image is rejected, as too is that of the horse and horseman. In contrast the German and the National-Socialist concept of leadership comes from 'absolute ethnic identity between leader and following' (p. 48). The *Führer* is thus not a transcendental god over the impolitical and passive *Volk* but linked to them by 'an absolute equality of species' (*Artgleichheit*).

There is much that could be said about these passages from what is a slim volume concerned to give a popular account of the then-new National Socialist legal and constitutional order. It certainly ranks amongst the least edifying of Schmitt's writings. But what it does indicate is the way in which the rejection of the pastoral lineage, and the idea of government derived from it, leads Schmitt to seek to specify the bonds of the new order in this racial identity of leader and led which, while the basis of mutual loyalty, would at every turn need to define its enemies in similarly racial terms. In Schmitt's view then, Nazi biopolitics is not the result of the over-extension of state sovereignty and its cold bureaucratic rationality nor the 'demonic' combination of sovereignty and biopower, as in Foucault (2001: 311). Rather, it arises from the collapse of an effective constitutional sovereignty – and all its attendant transcendent, traditional and symbolic mechanisms of authority and legitimacy – at the end of the Weimar period, and the need for a direct identification and equality of leader and led capable of deciding internal and external enemies. The explanation of why the latter took the form of 'race' is not offered by Schmitt and awaits the project started by Foucault in *Society Must Be Defended* (2003).

In his concern for sovereignty, for the concrete basis of legitimacy, and the political as a distinction between friend and enemy, Schmitt not only instates force, antagonism and decision at the heart of his characterization of political power but leaves little room for a discussion of 'government' in the broader, sociological sense raised by Foucault's lectures. When following the genealogy of pastoral power, however, Schmitt indicates the elements of pastoral government through its rejection by Greek thought, its presence in the form of the Roman Catholic Church, its overcoming by the National Socialist concept of leadership, and its manifestation in the administrative-welfare state. Only the third of these four is absent from Foucault's account.

5.9 We have noted Foucault's interpretation of the maxim 'the King reigns, but does not govern' as stressing the movement he traces from sovereignty, prince and territory to the liberal economic government of populations. The same phrase is found at least three times in the writings of Schmitt, separated by over 40 years.

The first time it appears is precisely in the discussions of constitutional theory and with reference to the Belgian constitutional monarchy (Schmitt, 2008a: 315). This is a situation in which the monarch loses all effective power (*potestas*), which is now in the hands of the prime minister and other ministers. The monarch 'continues to exist as authority and, therefore, also to exercise the distinctive functions of a "neutral power" especially well' (p. 315). The maxim thus concerns not the transition from one side to another (that is, from sovereignty to government, as in Foucault), but the affirmation of the two sides of political power. Schmitt thus cites Max von Seydel's question concerning the maxim 'what then remains of the "*régner*" if one removes "*gouverner*"?', which he argues is answerable if one makes the distinction between *potestas* and *auctoritas*, and accepts a distinctive meaning of authority in respect to political power.

From the perspectives we have been following, this is a new distinction, which again activates the signature of the concept of power. This authority is not on the side of sovereignty for Schmitt for 'sovereignty and majesty by necessity always correspond to effective power' (2008a: 458). Authority 'denotes a profile that rests essentially on an element of *continuity* and refers to tradition and duration' (p. 459, original emphasis). For all the arguments we have considered regarding the displacement, pre-eminence or inscription-in-dominance of sovereignty, discipline, biopower and government, they are all forms of effective power, which now can be contrasted with this new opposite, authority. Classical versions of this binary are found in the contrast between the *auctoritas* of the Senate in the Roman republic and the *potestas* and *imperium* of the people, and the claim, later, by the Roman Pope of *auctoritas* for himself while leaving *potestas* to the Emperor. For Schmitt then, if one removes the governing, what remains of reign is this element of authority.

Seven years later, Schmitt again cites the expression as one of the instances of the applicability of political theology in the preface to the second edition of *Political Theology* (2005: 1–2). It refers to the idea of a 'neutral power' in the nineteenth century, much like the role of the monarch in constitutional monarchy, which he contrasts with contemporary liberalism that 'administers but does not rule'. The neutral power is thus a component of the processes of secularization of the position of the god-sovereign that has nothing to do with quotidian administrative tasks.

Thirty-five years after that, he is prompted to return to the phrase in his belated response to the claim by the theologian, Erik Peterson, of the closure of political theology. Like Foucault (2007: 85, n. 36) and Peterson, Schmitt traces its appearance first to Adolphe Thiers in 1829, the 'typical representative of the bourgeois monarchy'. He also finds it as a Latin phrase, *rex regnat sed non gubernat*, used against the Polish King Sigismund in 1600 (2008c: 67–8).

We shall return to the political-theological debate. However, what is clear throughout is that Schmitt's understanding of the *arcanum* of this phrase is not that it downplays the 'reign' aspect of political power but that it preserves, in however attenuated a fashion, a place for a sovereign and, by analogy, divine element in political power even in liberal, economic and technocratic rule. While it is 'grotesque', he argues, to compare the bourgeois monarch, Louis Philippe, with 'Hellenistic emperors, Roman Caesars or Persian caliphs' (as did Peterson), the parallel between a constitutional monarch of a parliamentary regime and 'the idea of a passive being from a higher sphere is striking' (Schmitt, 2008c: 68).

While Foucault seeks a transition from the dominance of one form of power to another in this maxim, and makes it emblematic of the pre-eminence of the government of populations over territorial sovereignty, Schmitt comes back to it to assert precisely the opposite: the continuing eminence of the sovereign and, behind that, of the divine being, as the source of authority in the most secular forms of rule, even where that sovereign exercises no effective power.

In the moment of extreme crisis, with the collapse of the sovereign state of the Weimar Republic, Schmitt discovers that governing will now be based not on a Christian-like pastoral relationship of ruler and ruled, but on the non-pastoral racial identity of the leader and his followers, the absolute equality of species. For Schmitt, the state racism of National Socialism is not a result of the delirium of the combination of sovereignty and biopower, as Foucault advanced in *Society Must Be Defended* and the first volume of *History of Sexuality*, but the collapse of sovereignty and a new biopolitical relation of *Führer* and *Volk*. Nazi biopolitics compensates for sovereignty by racializing the enemy as a threat to the way of life of a racialized people and leader.

This is perhaps as close as Schmitt will come to a concept of post-sovereign biopolitics – a politics based on the equality of equals defined by their common racial character and the inequality of those unequals who do not share it. In one sense, sovereignty is already a biopolitics, for in deciding the exception, the sovereign decides on the 'normal frame of life', and on the enemy, which is a threat to that way of life and to life itself. When the constitutional sovereign is replaced by a leadership based on the racial identity of leader and follower, then the enemy will be constituted as a racialized enemy, no longer a just enemy but a biopolitical enemy.

(Dis)agreements

5.10 If the signature of our reflection and analysis of power is the production of binaries, distinctions, and antinomies, then Schmitt's work positively celebrates and revels in them, and forces them to antithetical and antagonistic extremes. We have found that:

1   Schmitt uncovers distinctions, binaries, and oppositions: friend and enemy, politics and police, open and secret power, liberalism and

democracy, legality and legitimacy, exception and norm, authority and effective power, and reign and government.

2 Many of these antitheses are intensified, with one side positively marked as the political and the other the neutralizing or depoliticizing one. Thus democracy is the identification of rulers and ruled, while liberalism is an ethical or economic denial of political antagonisms. The enemy is definitive of political identity, whereas a cosmopolitan world of universal friendship denies the very absolute enmity it requires. The exception is the defining feature of sovereignty, whereas the norm is thought 'without passion' and made rigid through repetition. The legitimation of the concrete system of authority is opposed to its 'mere legality'. The political as 'high politics' is opposed to lowly police matters.

3 Schmitt's work provides us with a strong sense of the way relations of power are already marked by events that have continuing hold or purchase on them. In that sense there is a 'transcendental' side of power relations: of authority, of the position of sovereign, the state, the monarch, the president, of the constitutive act of establishing a concrete social order. Against these, he will downplay or be actively hostile to the immanent side of power relations: governing that becomes administration, legitimacy reduced to mere legality, liberal neutralizations of the political by means of economics and ethics, war redacted to become police action.

4 The structure of Schmitt's thought is found then in the intensification of oppositions and the privilege given to reign, sovereignty, legitimacy and democracy over governing, economy, legality and liberalism. His inability to resolve the riddle of the maxim, 'the King reigns, but he does not govern', comes from his inability to give positive value to the immanent, governmental-economic side of political power, the precise opposite of Foucault, except, on the collapse of all other authority, to diagnose National Socialism as making leadership immanent to racial identity.

5 The crisis of this transcendental axis of constitutional sovereignty, however, reveals the inner weakness of Schmitt's political thought, where the immanent, governmental axis is re-imagined either as a biopolitical racial identification of leader and impolitical people or the administrative state colonized by welfare-state demands, or, as he put it in 1932, the qualitative total state or quantitative total state (1998). There is little or no place for the analysis of civil prudence and wisdom, and the arts of governing.

If there is a massive weakness in Schmitt's failure to understand the more immanent aspects of relations of power, there are a number of other ways in which he presents an addition, a counterpoint, or even a corrective, to Foucault.

1 Schmitt offers a non-patriarchalist conception of sovereignty. Where Foucault founded sovereignty on a right of life and death, *jus vitae ac necis*, inherited from the Roman father, Schmitt insists on the *hostis* declaration, the *jus belli*; the right to declare war.

2 Schmitt views sovereignty as a limited and singular competence not a general claim to omniscience and omnipotence that will be checked by the liberal arts of government. The unknowability and unpredictability of the exception lies at the heart of the exercise of sovereign power.

3 Sovereignty is no longer opposed to security in Schmitt, as it is in Foucault's juxtaposition of the territorial sovereignty of the Prince and the governmental security of populations. The sovereign's competence consists of knowing the thresholds at which public order and security obtain or do not obtain, irrespective of the academic or epistemological content of notions of security, and the ability to act to restore them.

4 While both view liberalism as critique, they have very different ideas of the target of critique. For Foucault, it is a critique of sovereign claims to omniscience and omnicompetence; for Schmitt, it is critique of the political and of the state. For Foucault, this critique makes possible the inventiveness of a liberal art of government based on an immanent form of knowledge, political economy; for Schmitt, it leads to ever-new neutralizations and de-politicizations that threaten to dissolve sovereign authority itself.

5 This view of sovereignty provides different views of National Socialism. For Foucault it arose from the deadly articulation of sovereignty and biopolitics, a demonic combination of sovereign and pastoral power. For Schmitt, it resulted from the radical undermining of the competency of sovereignty, which then prepared the way for the racial identity of leader and people and decisions based on biopolitical enmity.

It is quite extraordinary how many overlaps, interconnections, points of agreements and disagreements there are between Schmitt and Foucault. What is more extraordinary, however, is that both are forced to address the signature of power. This means that they reproduce and multiply the tendency of the concept of power to beget ever-new antinomies without quite being able to grasp or accept the bipolar character of the concept of power with which they are forced to work. The contrast between Schmitt's *nomos* and governmentality, his paradigm of political theology and the heated debate over secularization, and in that regard the legacy of Max Weber, will bring us closer to understanding the contemporary shape of this concept of power.

6

SECULAR ORDERS

6.1 There are times when Foucault's characterization of the juridical-political theory of sovereignty reads as if he is actually citing Schmitt, but with a minus sign attached. To take an example: 'The theory of sovereignty is bound with a form of power that is exercised over the land and the produce of the land ... [it] concerns power's displacement and appropriation not of time and labour, but of goods and wealth' (2003: 36). Elsewhere, he argues sovereign power was 'a right to appropriate ... a right of seizure: of things, time, bodies and ultimately life itself; it culminated in the privilege to seize hold of life in order to suppress it' (1979: 136). This conception of power is under the shadow of the sovereign, which Foucault flees from, but which continues to be cast across his thought. In these statements, Foucault could have been alluding, almost word for word, to one of Schmitt's key essays of the 1950s, in which he uses the Greek word, *nomos*, to investigate the preconditions of every social order, which he etymologically breaks down into three parts.

> Each of these three processes – appropriation, distribution and production – is part and parcel of the history of legal and social orders. In every state of social life, in every economic order, in every period of legal history until now, things have been appropriated, distributed and produced. Prior to every legal, economic, and social order, prior to every legal, economic, or social theory are these elementary questions: *Where and how was it appropriated? Where and how was it divided? Where and how was it produced?* (Schmitt, 2003: 327–8, original emphasis)

If appropriation or seizure is a feature of the 'deductive power' of sovereignty, as it is according to Foucault, and sovereignty has either been displaced by or put under the dominance of more modern kinds of power, then it cannot be a feature salient to contemporary analysis and the present. With Schmitt, however, acts of land-appropriation (*Landnahme*) literally provide an ongoing foundation of power and domestic and international law. Hence the question of colonization, conquest, military victory and other means of the direct taking of land remain the basis for all aspects of contemporary social and economic organization, and must be taken into account in order to understand ongoing power formations.

> The history of peoples, with their migrations, colonizations, and conquests is the history of land-appropriation. Either this is the appropriation of free land, with no claim to ownership, or it is the conquest of alien land, which has been appropriated under legal titles of foreign-political warfare or by domestic-political means, such as the proscription, deprivation, and forfeiture of newly divided territory. Land-appropriation ... is what John Locke called *radical title*. As a 17th century Englishman, Locke had in mind the land-appropriation of England by William the Conqueror (1066). (Schmitt, 2003: 328)

Schmitt's reference to John Locke is significant given he is generally understood to be a thinker who is associated with the concern for the legitimacy of civil government, and its distinction from tyranny. Thus Barry Hindess has argued that 'a broadly Lockean view of political power and a corresponding style of political critique have played, and continue to play, a major role in Western political thought' (1996: 48). In his discussion of radical title, however, it is probable that Locke also had in mind the contemporary land-appropriations in colonial America which he would justify, as Richard Tuck has shown (1999: 176), on the grounds that 'a commonwealth could only claim jurisdiction over the territory under its control if that territory under it had been at some point brought into private ownership through cultivation'. On these terms, Locke would establish a right to settle and a means to void many of the claims that might be made by or on behalf of the American Indians. Schmitt cites Locke's proposition that 'Government has a direct jurisdiction only over the land' which he takes to be in support of his own claim: 'According to Locke, the essence of political power, first and foremost is jurisdiction over the land' (Schmitt, 2003: 47, n. 5).

Indeed, if we examine Locke's chapter on 'Property' in the second of *The Two Treatises of Government*, we find discussions of the necessity of a 'means *to appropriate*' the Fruits, Beasts, and Water given by God to the 'World of Men in common' in 'their natural state' (1960: 304, section 26, original emphasis). We also find the term used to described the '*chief matter of Property*' in 'this *appropriation* of any parcel of land' (p. 308, s. 31, original emphasis). In this sense, the original and divinely given law enables these acts of appropriation:

> The Law man was under, was rather for *appropriating*. God commanded, and his wants forced him to *labour*. That was his *Property* which could not be taken from him where-ever he had fixed it. And hence subduing or cultivating the Earth, and having Dominion, we see are joined together. The one gave Title to the other. So that God, by commanding to subdue, gave authority so far to *appropriate*. And the Condition of Humane life, which requires Labour and Materials to work on, necessarily introduces *private possessions*. (Locke, 1960: 310, s. 35)

In these and the following sections, Locke bases government on property, property on labour and land-appropriation, and appropriation on natural law and divine command. In this respect, the ongoing grounded-ness of human community and law in a concrete spatial order made possible by land-appropriation radically advanced by Schmitt is hardly novel. Nevertheless it can be distinguished from every immanent conception of power as an assemblage of heterogeneous elements, and is the latter's precondition.

In different times and places, for Schmitt, the 'sequence and evaluation' of the three questions – of appropriation, distribution and production – changes. At certain times distribution and consumption are emphasized; at other times, production. While classical economic liberals and socialists focused on production, contemporary liberalism, and the imaginary of an age of consumption, seeks to employ the vocabulary of consumer choice. However, Schmitt's key point is that an ongoing necessary condition for any social, legal or political order is an appropriation of part of the Earth, on which a community can be located, from which it can be sustained, and upon which a legal title can be established. Hindess (1996) has argued forcefully that power as capacity and power as right (or legitimate power) are the two principal conceptions of power in 'Western political thought'. Schmitt and Tuck's reading of Locke captures a third: power as appropriation. One could find this conception elaborated in Marx's writing on the expropriation of the peasantry, and his phrase the 'expropriation of the expropriators', and, for Schmitt, from different perspectives, Joseph Chamberlain and Lenin's writings on imperialism (2003: 330–1).

This elementary observation allows us to make several points regarding Foucault. First, that he seeks to deny the continuing significance or reality of appropriation, and land-appropriation, to contemporary power relations by making the deductive, seizing, appropriating, or taking-away elements of power relations a feature of a now archaic sovereignty which, even as it survives, is subjugated to the field of government. Second, we could note that his genealogy of economic government traces the displacement of the government of and through the family or household (derived from *oikos*) in early modern thought – mercantilism, cameralism, tracts of advice to and on the education of princes – by the economic government of populations in classical political economy. Governmentality arises first within a problematic of distribution to, or circulation between, households and moves towards the nineteenth-century concern for production, labour and the source of value, and finally, with neoliberalism to one of consumption, based on the idea of individual choice. For Foucault, no form of governmentality is elaborated in relation to processes of appropriation.

The clearest way of putting this to help with our understanding of different approaches to power would be to say that Foucault wishes to know *what happens* in relations of power and thus asked the question of the *how* of power. By contrast, Schmitt wants to know the spatial orders and orientations entailed in power and thus asked the question of the *where* of power. The notion of order becomes not only a key to Schmitt's thought but to the way in which the sovereign and governmental dimensions of power have been stitched together in the twentieth century (see §6.13, §7.8–§7.11).

To express things in this way, however is simply to demonstrate a fundamental difference between two thinkers: one insists that the exercise of power is marked by an ongoing founding event of appropriation, no matter how distant in time; the other proposes that the most significant and relevant ways of exercising power in the present are completely absolved of this original element. A first step is a comparison of the histories of which *nomos* and governmentality are a part.

Nomos and governmentality

6.2 *Nomos* and governmentality could be regarded as the respective master-concepts of both Schmitt's and Foucault's later work on power. If Foucault's lectures on governmentality are the initial exemplar of the 'immanentism' of post-structural approaches to power and state power, Schmitt's 1950 book, *The Nomos of the Earth* (2003), is a history of and a lament for the juridical organization of power and sovereignty in European international public law, that is, for a legal order of global proportions. While Foucault views the emergent liberal arts of government as a possible escape from the older transcendent powers of sovereignty and law, and early modern forms of domination such as discipline and biopower, Schmitt views the end of this European public law, the *jus publicum Europæum*, as an unprecedented crisis leading to a re-moralization and re-theologization of war and the possibility of transformation of traditional war into what he would call 'global civil war' both in this book (2003: 296) and in the *Theory of the Partisan* (2007: 94–5).

The Nomos of the Earth is in many ways Schmitt's magnum opus. While it rests on 'essentially jurisprudential foundations', it is 'indebted to geographers', he writes in the foreword (2003: 37). 'The ties to mythological sources of jurisprudential thinking', he nonetheless continues, 'are much greater than those to geography' (p. 38). The concept of *nomos* thus continues a trajectory in Schmitt's work that ties his reflection on concepts of power to symbols and mythology. Thus Schmitt used the biblical, Jewish and cabbalistic, mythology of the Leviathan to investigate the limitations of Hobbes's state theory and writes of 'political myths of the most astonishing kind often fraught with downright magical intensity' at the very time he was being denounced by the SS (Schmitt, 2008b: 8). In 1942, he takes up the mythology of land and sea in a book intended as a children's fable for his young daughter, Anna, in which the elemental character of human existence is imagined in relation to each of the four classical elements of earth, water, fire and air (1997). The post-war book on *Nomos* begins precisely with the idea that in 'mythical language, the *earth* became known as the mother of law' and explores the way in which international law comes to rest on the antithesis of firm land and free sea, *terra firma* and *mare liberum*. For Schmitt the appropriation of land, and the establishment of law, state, and the international system of states, are all accompanied by spatial imaginings and mythologies, what Christopher Connery has called 'geo-mythography' (2001). For Schmitt, not only does power seek mythological representation but mythology makes possible forms of spatial order and intensifies and extends power relations across the characterless sea and the deeply inscribed earth. In order to restore the 'energy and majesty' of *nomos*, Schmitt crosses jurisprudence, legal history, geopolitics, philology and mythology (2003: 67).

In contrast, the Foucauldian concept of governmentality emphasizes governmental reason or rationality, even if it uses the term in a non-normative sense. It emerges from the relatively restricted fields of secular discourses of rule but retains elements of the Judeo-Christian pastorate. However, despite this 'rationalist' understanding, if we can call it that, of the genealogy of the art of government, Foucault resorts to both philology and mythology. Thus, in order to displace the *monstre froid* of the state, Foucault returns to the political etymology of the word 'government'. For Schmitt, Nietzsche's image lifts the problem of the state only into an irrational domain of the 'impressionistic-suggestive style of the nineteenth century' (2008b: 5). Perhaps we can say that this also characterizes Foucault's interest in the analysis of political mythology: it is necessary to forsake the irrational images of the state and sovereignty in order to understand the critical rationalities of government.

6.3 There are fundamental differences between Foucault and Schmitt, commencing with the scale and nature of their political concerns. Foucault, starting from the local, anti-institutional struggles and the politics of identity, hoped later to use this approach as a way of analysing the state, which would eventually even consider the relations between states and the government of the international sphere; Schmitt, starting with the definition of sovereignty, moved to understanding the place of equal sovereigns in an inter-state, global legal order. In one, we find the conservative ethos of lament at the collapse of this organized system of power relations between sovereigns; in the other, the hope, against the odds, of a non-normalizing and de-subjectifying form of power and resistance beyond sovereignty, discipline and domination. There is most of all a difference of genre: the tentative hypothesis of the lecture hall and the realized grand thesis of the opus. Yet, beyond this, and in the most unlikely ways, there are elements of a common history here.

Schmitt and Foucault both present alternatives to the Kantian or normative view of the history of international law as the progressive limitation of the sovereignty of territorial states by liberal values and human rights, which would restrict war, enable global commerce and bring about a pacific and cosmopolitan world order. While Foucault regards law as a part of the technology of governing the international order, Schmitt views law as linked to, and marked by, acts of appropriation that constitute the *nomos*. Thus both view the emergence of the international system in the seventeenth and eighteenth centuries as replacing a medieval view of the cosmos grounded in what Schmitt calls the *respublica Christiana*; for Foucault, this view, following St Thomas Aquinas, is of the great 'theological-cosmological continuum' between God, the sovereign, the pastor and the father (2007: 234). This makes way for the modern inter-state system of law, which Schmitt calls the *jus publicum Europæum*, and which entails a view of sovereigns as legal persons, and 'brackets' the moral evaluation of war (that is, the 'just war') for a non-discriminatory conception of the enemy as the *justus hostis* or just enemy (e.g. 2003: 142–3). Similarly Foucault regards early modern international government, as a component of doctrines such as *raison d'État*, as breaking with notions of just war and the idea of a universal Christian Empire, as forming a Eurocentric global perspective, and as concerning the relations and 'balance' between European sovereign states (2007: 291, 297). Instead of the system of law itself, he focuses on the technology of governmental regulation, which includes the technique of 'balance' between states of different size and 'force', and new diplomatic and military means, including permanent diplomatic staff and standing armies, as well as what he calls the law of nations, the *jus gentium* (2007: 298–9). In both cases this transition has its historical conditions in what Schmitt called the 'land appropriation of the New World' and Foucault 'the discovery of America' and 'the constitution of colonial empires' (2007: 295).

Schmitt was immensely influential on Hans Morgenthau and the formation of the post-World War II discipline of international relations, as Martti Koskenniemi has shown at length (2002, 2004). Schmitt, along with conventional international relations wisdom, views state sovereignty as the great achievement of the classical age and of Western rationalism, whereas Foucault sees a displacement in forms of thinking about rule based around the sovereign by a new 'reflexive prism' provided by the internal and external aspects of reason of state

(2007: 276–7). For Schmitt, the catastrophes of the twentieth century were the bitter fruit of the disarray of Eurocentric international law, the triumph of a space-less universalism, a re-moralization of war in new forms of the just war, and the collapse of the distinction between inter-state war and civil war. For Foucault, too, the liberal art of government would make competition and trade the principle of a global order, replace the Europe of balance with the notion of progress and give rise to the Kantian hope of securing perpetual peace by a commercial globalization. Well before the current discourse on globalization, Foucault concluded with respect to Kant that '*La garantie de la paix perpetuelle, c'est donc en effect la planétarisation commerciale*' [The guarantee of perpetual peace is therefore in effect commercial globalization] (Foucault, 2004a: 60).

The structure and conclusions of the international genealogies of governmentality and the *nomos* of the Earth thus offer us ample room for comparison. Both have to deal with the place of Christian theology in the formation of Western political thought and practice, and its continuing significance. For Foucault, there is the transformation of the Christian pastorate, the secularization undertaken by political thought, and the continued presence of anti-state eschatology in the liberal order grounded on the notion of civil society. For Schmitt, there is the figure of the *katechon*, which holds back or restrains the Apocalypse, and the course of the de-theologization, and likely re-theologization, of the political.

The antithetical formulations of power lead us to consider their respective genealogies: of governmentality and liberal arts of government; and of *nomos* and international law. These genealogies force us to look more closely at the various ways in which we can approach the transformation of power through the viewpoint of secularization. Both posit the continued eminence of theological elements in contemporary forms of power and rule, but to very different effect.

Political theology

6.4 Carl Schmitt published two books with the term 'political theology' in the title. The first was published in 1922 and the second in 1970, that is, toward the beginning and at the very end of his book-publishing career. There are several other occasions on which he refers to the term but these remain his most important statements. Of particular importance is a work published at around the same time as the first of these books, *Roman Catholicism and Political Form* (1996b).

For our purposes, the discussion of political theology really begins with the third chapter of *Political Theology*:

> All significant concepts of the modern theory of the state are secularized theological concepts not only because of their historical development – in which they were transferred from theology to the theory of the state, whereby, for example, the omnipotent God became the omnipotent lawgiver – but also because of their systematic structure, the recognition of which is necessary for the sociological consideration of these concepts. The exception in jurisprudence is analogous to the miracle in theology. Only by becoming aware of this analogy can we appreciate the manner in which the philosophical ideas of the state developed in the last centuries. (Schmitt, 2005: 36)

Schmitt's initial position posits a relationship between the concepts of the modern state and theological concepts, which is one of analogy rather than causality. He speaks, for instance, not only of the analogy of the miracle and the exception, but of 'a conceptually clear and systematic analogy' between the personal sovereignty of the monarchy and 'theistic theology' when he cites the Catholic counter-revolutionary philosophers of the nineteenth century (2005: 37). More broadly, he speaks of a sociology of legal concepts as positing a 'systematic analogy between theological and juristic concepts' (p. 42).

Schmitt uses the term 'analogy' several times in these passages and explicitly rejects any notion of causality moving in either direction between theological and political concepts. 'Both the spiritualist explanation of material processes and the material explanation of spiritual phenomena ... must necessarily culminate in a caricature' (2005: 43). The sociology of juristic concepts, by contrast, 'aims to discover the basic, radically systematic structure and to compare this conceptual structure with the conceptually represented social structure of a certain epoch' (p. 45). Schmitt along the way rejects psychological reductionism and theories of reflex or mirroring. The key presupposition of this kind of sociology is instead expressed in the following manner. 'The metaphysical image that a definite epoch forges of the world has the same structure as what the world immediately understands to be appropriate as a form of its political organization' (p. 46). Given his later discussion of pagan political mythology, we can observe here that political theology, in its initial formulation, makes little or no distinction between theology and metaphysics.

At the same time, however, Schmitt advanced a thesis in *Roman Catholicism and Political Form* (1996b) that would act as a complement and a corrective to that of Max Weber's *The Protestant Ethic and Spirit of Capitalism* (1985). If *Political Theology* dealt with a sociology of juristic concepts, *Roman Catholicism* would address a kind of genealogy of political form. In place of Weber's 'elective affinity' between the individualist, Protestant ethic and an inner ascetic spirit consistent with economic acquisition, Schmitt would advance a fundamental relation between the juridical rationalism embodied in the Roman Catholic Church as a public institution and the form of the modern state (Ulmen, 1985: 27–9).

In this book, Schmitt discusses the Church as a kind of 'economy of forces' (to borrow, as we have seen, from Foucault) given material and institutional form. The term he uses, however, is *complexio oppositorum*, a complex of opposites, a structure which is capable of positioning and encompassing apparent antinomies (1996b: 7). Thus the political form of Church is both autocratic and democratic, its history is both of accommodation and intransigence, and its staunch adherents range from the supporters of authoritarian dictatorship (such as Donoso Cortés) to the theologists of the poor from Ireland to Latin America. It is theologically complex as well: the Old and New Testaments. 'The Marcionite either-or is answered with an as-well-as' (p. 7). Even 'the antithesis of man "by nature evil" and "by nature good" – this decisive question for political theory – is in no sense answered by a simple yes or no in the Tridentine creed' (p. 8). Schmitt's characterization of the Roman Catholic Church would satisfy the test of the most stringent postmodern theorist: it proposes no essentialism of the human subject, and its logic has a 'rhizomatic' character even as its form is 'aborescent', as Gilles Deleuze and Felix Guattari might have put it (1981).

For Schmitt, the Church is the exemplar of key political notions of form, of representation and of office. It evinces 'a specific formal superiority over the matter of human life such as no other imperium has ever known' (1996b: 8). Further, it demonstrates 'a capacity to embody the great trinity of form: the aesthetic form of art; the juridical form of the law; finally the glorious achievement of a world-historical form of power' (p. 21). The concept of representation – which is taken up again in the electoral systems of liberal democracy – is crucial to this.

The pope is not the Prophet but the Vicar of Christ. Such a ceremonial function precludes all the fanatical excesses of an unbridled prophetism. The fact that the office is made independent of charisma signifies that the priest upholds a position that appears to be completely apart from his concrete personality. (Schmitt, 1996b: 14)

In this sense the Church upholds a kind of rational-legal form of authority around the office of the priest and the 'vicarious' position (hence 'vicar') of the hierarchy of the Church's office to Christ. However, as Schmitt points out, the idea of representation is governed by conceptions of personal authority and the personal dignity of both the representative as well as the person represented (1996b: 21). Thus Schmitt continues with reference to the office of the pope:

Nevertheless, he is not the functionary and commissar of republican thinking. In contradistinction to the modern official, his position is not impersonal, because the office is part of an unbroken chain linked with the personal mandate and concrete person of Christ. This is truly the most astounding *complexio oppositorum*. (1996b: 21)

In this respect, the Roman Catholic Church manages to combine the charismatic authority of Christ with the rational-legal authority of canon law, the Church and its offices.

There are thus two dimensions to the political theology Schmitt enunciated in the early 1920s. A synchronic sociology of juristic concepts which seeks the clear and systematic structural analogy between theological-metaphysical and political concepts; and a diachronic genealogy of political form which follows the secular mutations and adaptations of concepts of canon law, vicarious representation and priestly office.

6.5 We know that Carl Schmitt attended Max Weber's lectures in Munich, including 'Politics as a Vocation' and 'Science as a Vocation'; participated in his *Dozentenseminar*; and held private conversations with him on politics and the state (Ulmen, 1985: 5). Jürgen Habermas would cause something of a scandal by calling Schmitt the 'legitimate pupil' of Weber in the 1960s (1971: 66; see §6.14). It should come as no surprise that Schmitt would remain close to Weber's ideas and draw out his propositions in relation them, including Weber's view on secularization. The first key element of this view is the limited historical thesis of the elective affinity between the Puritan ethical life-style and life-conduct and capitalist economic activity. The second is the broader characterization of the direction of modernity in terms of rationalization and disenchantment, in which the latter means the 'de-magicalization' of the world and the disappearance of absolute or transcendent values. In contrast, Schmitt finds that the theological remains operative both in the way the secular state acts as inheritor of the canon law and the political form of the medieval Roman Catholic Church, and in the inherited structure of our political concepts. The eminence of the latter arises from Schmitt's thesis of neutralization: the striving for a 'central sphere' that will be one of neutrality, on which all sides can agree, and which will neutralize a previous 'central sphere' that has become riven by irreconcilable antagonism (2010). Thus the secular state in the seventeenth century – the great product of Western rationalism – emerged from the apparently hopeless theological disputations and confessional civil wars of the Reformation and counter-Reformation.

Schmitt hence poses two secularizations: the first a rationalization and the second a neutralization. The rationalization of Protestant asceticism neutralizes the rationalization of the Catholic Church. In a juxtaposition, G.L. Ulmen interprets Schmitt's relation to Weber in the following manner: 'the *economic ethos* promoted by Protestant asceticism was fundamentally antagonistic to the *political ethos* of Catholic decisionism, even as the liberal concept of culture was fundamentally antagonistic to the concept of culture that arose with the modern state' (1985: 28, original emphasis). For Schmitt, neutralization continues confessional civil war by other means while, for Weber, rationalization means that culture loses its spiritual bearings. Weber criticizes the irrationalities that accompany the rationalizations of modern capitalism, whereas Schmitt criticizes the depoliticizations that are associated with liberal neutralization. For the former, the world becomes a soulless mechanism, without transcendence; for the latter, secularization means the continued salience of confessional conflict.

For Schmitt, the state and state system in European law are the great achievements of the neutralization of theological dispute. What were once assiduously built conceptual edifices for the ages became merely private matters of belief in the 'heroic age of occidental rationalism' of the seventeenth century (2010: 83). Liberalism conducts a further neutralization, that of the political itself. Thus the 'negation of the political, which is inherent in every consistent individualism, leads necessarily to a political practice of distrust toward all conceivable political forces and forms of state and government, but never produces on its own a positive theory of state, government, and politics' (Schmitt, 1996a: 70). The theory of the state is replaced, according to Schmitt, with the political romanticism of the state as a 'work of art' (1986: 113). In Weber, secularization is borne by the persona of the Puritan individual. While this 'tormented liberal' laments that 'the light cloak' of the Puritan calling 'should become an iron cage', he is careful not to replace a one-sided materialism with a romantic critique of rationalization and technology (1985: 181). While secularization leads Schmitt to a critique of political romanticism, it leads Weber to a critique of economic romanticism (Ulmen, 1985: 22). He will look to St Paul's idea of charisma as way of counteracting the movement of rationalization.

In *Political Theology II*, Schmitt will characterize Weber's writings on charismatic legitimation as entirely derived from Paul as their 'theological source' and 'the most striking example of a new political theology' (2008c: 74). This may be so. However, the historical analysis of the notion of 'the calling' in *The Protestant Ethic* would seem to initiate another project: that which might be called 'economic theology' (Ulmen, 1985: 44) again, Weber's source will be Paul.

Secularization

6.6 In 1949 Karl Löwith initiated the post-war discussion of secularization in Germany by offering a resounding endorsement of the theological and eschatological sources of the philosophy of progress. He sought 'to show that philosophy of history originates with the Hebrew and Christian faith in a fulfilment and that it ends with the secularization of its eschatological pattern' (Löwith, 1949: 2). In a famous epilogue to his *Meaning in History* it turns out that modernity can be neither consistently Christian nor consistently pagan. It eliminates from Christianity 'creation and consummation' while it assimilates endless and continuous movement but not the circularity of the ancients. 'The modern mind has not made up its mind whether it should be Christian or pagan. It sees with one eye of faith and one of reason. Hence its vision is necessarily dim in comparison with either Greek or biblical thinking' (Löwith, 1949: 207).

In what amounted to a very positive review of Löwith's thesis in the following year, Schmitt states:

> Following Karl Löwith, we are convinced that paganism is not at all capable of any form of historical thought because it is cyclical. The historical loses its specific meaning within the cycles of eternal recurrence. We know that the Enlightenment and the positivist belief in progress was only secularized Judaism and Christianity, and it obtained its '*eschata*' from these sources... This is how we interpret the infinitely meaningful proposition by Löwith: the further we go back from today into the history of human historical thinking, the more the conception of an act of planning ceases to exist. Divine providence, which the human being can recalculate or even predict, is after all also just a human act of planning. (Schmitt, 2009: 168)

Löwith indeed gives an excellent brief understanding of the idea of the *eschaton*. It combines both senses of the word end, as the finishing of a process and as the completion of a goal, as *finis* and as *telos*. 'Not only does the *eschaton* delimit the process of history by an end, it articulates and fulfils it by a definite goal'. It is thus like the compass that gives orientation in space: 'the eschatological compass gives orientation in time by pointing to the Kingdom of God as the ultimate end and purpose' (1949: 18).

Against the figure of the *eschaton*, Schmitt places the *katechon*, derived from Paul's second letter to the Thessalonians (2009: 169). The *katechon* is both restrainer and deferrer in historical understanding. In *The* Nomos *of the Earth*, Schmitt notes that the medieval Christian Empire understood itself as 'the historical power to restrain the appearance of the Antichrist and the end of the present eon' (2003: 60) and the office of the emperor for the German and Christian Kings 'was inseparable' from the *katechon*. In broader terms, the figure of the *katechon* appears alongside all eschatological thinking: in the Cold War, the United States might be viewed to have acted as a *katechon* on the international communist revolution; alternatively, the Cold War might be the *katechon* that restrained further catastrophe after the collapse of the *jus publicum Europæum* and the ensuing World Wars. More recently, the United States can be presented as restraining the 'anti-humanity' forces of terror or checking the rise of China during the hastening of liberal globalization. According to Schmitt, however, we must 'be careful not to transform this term into a general designation of simply conservative or reactionary tendencies' (2009: 169). In other words, it is not merely a technical concept of history or political science. 'The original historical force of the figure of a *kat-echon*, however, remains and is capable of overcoming the otherwise occurring eschatological paralysis.'

6.7 According to Hans Blumenberg, Löwith's thesis 'has had a protracted dogmatizing effect in Germany since its first appearance' (1985: 22). Thus, in *The Legitimacy of the Modern Age*, first published in 1966, he set out to prove the independent legitimacy of modernity and to put paid to this secularization thesis in a significant contribution to the philosophy of history in its own right. For Blumenberg, the future hoped for in the modern idea of progress arises from an immanent set of developments rather than the transcendent and awe-provoking intervention of the Second Coming and Apocalypse. Moreover, he contends that this notion of progress first arises in two spheres of human practice: in cooperative long-term scientific inquiry guided by method, as is the case of the observations of Copernicus; and the arts as embodying the creative spirit of their particular age, as in the eighteenth-century *querelle des anciens et des modernes* about whether modern poetry was superior or inferior to that of the classical world. From these points, a generalization of the notion of a 'possible progress' radiates to different domains of society and technology. The legitimacy of modernity rests on human 'self-assertion', a term which 'means an existential program, according to which man posits his existence in a historical situation and indicates to himself how he is going to deal with the reality surrounding him and what he will make of the possibilities that are open to him' (Blumenberg, 1985: 138).

Blumenberg does not deny that there are theological and eschatological elements in many of the particular ideas that express this self-assertion, including the idea of an inevitable progress that is universal and necessary. Indeed he shows links between the teleology of human self-preservation and that of divine providence, and the mechanistic idea of the world and that of absolute divine will, and notes the messianic character of Marxism and its promise of a secular and worldly paradise (Wallace, 1985: xx–xxv). However, these are not to be interpreted as necessary features of modern rationality animated by self-assertion and the possibility of progress, but rather a 'reoccupation' of the positions within the medieval Christian schema. This is to say that the idea of progress is distorted by a compulsion to take a stance that reproduces the absolutist quality of theological positions. 'The idea of "reoccupation" says nothing about the derivation of the newly installed element, only about the dedication it receives at its installation' (Blumenberg, 1985: 49).

6.8 Löwith is not, however, Blumenberg's only opponent. In the course of the presentation of this book, Blumenberg had occasion to return to Schmitt's 1922 thesis as 'the strongest version of the secularization theorem' (1985: 92). He immediately locates a weakness in and exploits as a loophole Schmitt's conception of the relation between theological and political concepts by way of analogy. In Blumenberg's view, the analogy does not imply a transformation of the theological into the political but rather a response to the problem at hand. For him, 'the choice of linguistic means is not determined by the system of what is available for borrowing but rather by the requirements of the situation in which the choice is being made' (p. 93). This would seem an entirely well-founded observation. We would need only to consider the case of secular, Enlightenment political absolutism, which rather than a simple analogical transference of theological into political absolutism could be viewed as a response to the concrete problem of the conflict between competing theological absolutisms – that is, of religious civil war. According to Blumenberg, 'the phenomena of linguistic secularization cannot be an extensively demonstrable recourse to theology as such; rather it is a choice of elements from the selective point of view of the immediate need in each case, for background and pathos' (pp. 93–4). This would thus explain the case of the French Revolutionaries who 'needed not only a reservoir of political expressions but a pagan one' and hence used Roman costume and Roman phrases (which Schmitt had noted). Moreover, the counter-revolutionary tradition of the Restoration imagined the sovereign decision as a *creatio ex nihilo*, not as a secularization of divine creation (after William of Ockham) but as 'metaphorical interpretation of the situation after the revolutionary zero point' (p. 93).

Schmitt's analogical reasoning is not enough to carry the weight of the transformation of the theological to the political, and can thus be defeated by the practical, problem-solving logic Blumenberg invokes. The problem for Blumenberg, as Löwith and Schmitt would no doubt point out, is that pagan traditions know no notion of linear progress. Why, then, does modern 'self-assertion' express itself in these terms if not in some continuity with Christian eschatology? Can it be simply a reoccupation of the same positions, or is there a deeper logic at work?

Perhaps sensing his own weakness, Schmitt felt compelled to devote a postscript to Blumenberg in his last book, *Political Theology II* (2008c). There he confirms the relationship between his sociology of juristic concepts and his genealogy of political form. His elaborations of political theology:

> bring to light the classical case of a transposition of distinct concepts which has occurred with the systematic thought of the two – historically and discursively – most developed constellations of 'western rationalism': the Catholic *church* with its entire juridical rationality and the *state of the jus publicum Europaeum*, which was supposed to be Christian in even Thomas Hobbes' system. (Schmitt, 2008c: 117, original emphasis)

Blumenberg, Schmitt concludes, has not posed the question of the legitimacy of the modern age, but 'rather its legality – because of its explicit link to the exception and interruption of the unquestionable nature of "law"' (2008c: 118). Further, for Schmitt, there is an 'autism' in Blumenberg's argument. 'Its immanence, directed polemically again a theological transcendence, is nothing but self-empowerment' (p. 120). Schmitt's tactic of driving distinctions into antitheses again operates so that immanence is not only opposed to transcendence but is a source of aggression towards it: 'the inner aporiae of the contradictions in planning and novelty are indeed great and must radicalize and inaugurate the immanent aggression of the unfettered new' (p. 121). Self-empowerment is here equivalent to the 'Greek word *tolma* ... an expression that implies audacity and joy in the danger of having no need for justification'. The legitimacy of the modern is the need to have no other justification other than its radical newness. But this newness could only be defined according to the old and thus modernity would not be able to absolve the world of enmity.

In regard to the first criticism that he is concerned only with the legality not legitimacy of modernity, Blumenberg responds that this is a criticism that puts into question the status of the book's problematic and its historical claims, and thus 'could hardly be stronger' (1985: 96). Blumenberg agrees that the legality–legitimacy distinction is fundamental to their disagreement because it means, for Schmitt, that legitimacy is diachronic, a 'relation of foundation producing the inviolability of systems of order out the depths of time', while legality is the synchronic hierarchy of norms. Under such a distinction, the only possible legitimation of modernity would be the Middle Ages by other means. This makes germane Blumenberg's response to the second criticism of self-assertion as self-empowerment against theology. He tones down his initial arguments (Müller, 2003: 163) and claims his notion of 'self-assertion' is not 'self-empowerment', that is, a kind of *coup d'État* or seizure of power against established forms of legitimately conferred authority. It is rather the idea of a self-founding epoch in discontinuity with what it regards as its own prehistory (Blumenberg, 1985: 97). For Blumenberg, modernity can legitimate itself by its own means, in discontinuity with what went before it, and without regard to what Schmitt sums up as the 'traditions, customs, fatherhood and necromancy of the old' (2008c: 119).

We have thus aggression against aggression. For Schmitt, Blumenberg proposes an aggressively immanent legitimation of modernity; Blumenberg responds that his project is a defensive one against the thesis of secularization, 'the syndrome of the assertions that this epochal conformity to reason is nothing but an aggression (which fails to understand itself as such) against theology, from which in fact it has in a hidden manner derived everything that belongs to it' (1985: 97). Schmitt, for his part, uses this as an occasion for an all-out attack on the immanence of this idea of modernity:

> The process-progress does not only produce itself and the new human being, but also the conditions for the possibility of its own novelty-renewal. This it is the opposite of creation *out* of nothing, because it is the creation *of* nothingness as the condition for the possibility of the self-creation of an ever-new worldliness. (2008c: 129)

The project of modernity as an immanent self-assertion, according to Schmitt, rests upon a nihilism, in the words of Jan Werner Müller 'in which function had been completely substituted for substance, a world that permanently deconstructed itself' (2003: 162). It would be a world of 'utmost aggressiveness'.

Blumenberg argues that what really separated them was that, for Schmitt, 'secularization is a category of legitimacy. It gives access to a depth dimension of history for the benefit of present moments endangered by their contingency' (1985: 97). For him, political theology is a 'metaphorical theology'; the political theologian is in the 'enviable position' of finding a ready-to-use stock of concepts he would otherwise have had to invent. The legitimacy of the 'quasi-divine person of the sovereign' is 'no longer legality, or not yet, since he has first to constitute or to reconstitute it' (p. 101). Political theology is then really only a theology. If Schmitt accuses Blumenberg of positing the modern age as an act of aggression towards theology and transcendence, Blumenberg charges Schmitt with justifying the often unjustifiable acts of the sovereign decision by an implicit appeal to a higher promise of legitimacy of politics as theology.

6.9 This debate was joined by Odo Marquard's playful call for 'an enlightened political polytheism', a kind of liberal and pluralist political theology in which religious choices amount to what sociologists would characterize as a kind of late-modern or postmodern lifestyle politics (Müller, 2003: 166–8). Ernst-Wolfgang Böckenförde distinguished between a juridical political theology like Schmitt's sociology of juristic concepts; an institutional political theology similar to Schmitt's analysis of political form; and finally an ethically motivated political theology, which could account for the Christian preconditions of liberalism and mixed values and orientations of human beings.

This labyrinth might seem some way from our understanding of the concept of power. What is at stake, however, is absolutely crucial to our investigation. In a very broad sense, the legitimacy of modernity rests on the immanent human capacity to address an existing situation to change it in the future. In other words it rests fundamentally on a notion of power as a capacity to achieve certain ends. This is not so far from Hobbes's notion: 'The Power of a Man … is his present means to obtain some future apparent Good' (1996: 62). While Blumenberg would deny it (1985: 99), for Schmitt this amounts to the claim that it is neither reason nor freedom, the new rationality nor the new individualism, which founds modernity and its powers, but the new and innovative, that is, novelty itself. Thus the last line of the postscript of this, his final book, reads: *stat pro ratione Libertas, et Novitas pro Libertate*

[Freedom stands for Reason, and Novelty stands for Freedom]
(2008c: 130).

In this argument, then, we have the conflicting schemas of historical
time in which the audacity of modern power as human capacity
to construct a new solution contests and undoes the archaism of
a divine-sovereign power linked to a legitimacy and an authority founded on the continuity of tradition. However, neither
Blumenberg nor Schmitt is entirely fair to his opponent and in their
unfairness they miss what is common ground. Blumenberg accuses
Schmitt of effectively dressing up the unjustifiable political decision
in theological garb in order to secure obedience. In doing so, he
under-estimates the degree to which the final decision is a problem for constitutional law and the practical conduct of politics in
unforeseen and unpredictable circumstances – circumstances, we
might note, that are often used to characterize contemporary life.
Schmitt indicates a continuing problem for the actual exercise of
political power in a world where unexpected and unprecedented
events can occur and where there can be no clear and direct communication from a univocal God. Thus sovereignty is defined as
a singular competence, the capacity for decision, rather than as
omnipotent.

On the other side, Blumenberg has done more than reduce legitimacy to legality, as Schmitt contended. Rather he indicates a new
source of legitimacy in the creation of new solutions to humans'
existential situation. Indeed, this is the point of agreement between
Blumenberg and Schmitt and at which their respective problemat-
ics of modernity and political theology become radically indistinct.
The legitimacy of modernity for the former is the potential for radical novelty and innovation with no longer any need for reference to
the inheritance of tradition and law. The legitimacy of the decision
for the latter is also one ultimately grounded in a kind of radical
novelty: that of the exception to the law and its generality. In this
respect, Schmitt is right to pose the problem of a legitimacy more
fundamental than legality and Blumenberg is correct to claim that the
legitimacy of the modern age is not mere legality. In their debate they
both propose and produce a concept of legitimacy which is no longer
founded in tradition, theology, charisma or even law and reason, but
one founded on the capacity to address new, unanticipated, problems
and respond with new solutions. Where Blumenberg posits this as the
legitimacy of modernity, Schmitt views it as a fundamental feature of
political authority.

Yet, it is perhaps possible to accept both Schmitt's and Blumenberg's theses here of 'analogy' or 'reoccupation' of the theological in the political, if we allow that political concepts are produced in relation to an immediate need and a concrete situation and still manage to carry the mark of their sources which, depending on the case, might be shown to be theological. Thus it is necessary to attend to the signature of the concept as well as its meaning, purpose and use. While recent history, with its re-theologization of conflict in the war on terror, would no doubt appear to validate Schmitt over Blumenberg, the latter's critique indicates that what Schmitt is lacking is an understanding of the signature that marks political and juridical concepts – such as the one we have proposed for power – which means that the practical use of a concept and its transference to another domain may carry a determinate conceptual structure within it. Secularization can indeed be a 'reoccupation' of theological positions rather than simply a transfer from theology to politics, while still leaving open the possibility that empirical investigation of the history of concepts and their contexts can resolve whether particular secular or profane concepts carry within them their theological sources.

The power of the new

6.10 The debate over modernity and secularization summarized in the preceding sections turned on the question of the independent legitimacy of modern societies and hence of the relations of power that characterize them. To raise the question of legitimacy is thus to raise the question of the legitimacy of forms of power, such as those of sovereignty or the governmental-economic powers of liberal governing. With Blumenberg and Schmitt, these problems also concern whether novelty itself constitutes its own legitimation, and thus whether the search for a new kind of power needs no other justification than its very newness.

The substantive forms of power seek, as Max Weber said of what he called 'domination' or authority, to secure the compliance of those over whom they are exercised. They might do this by appealing to 'material or affectual or ideal motives', but, as Weber argues (1968: 213), no system of domination would limit itself to these. 'In addition every such system attempts to establish and to cultivate the belief in its legitimacy.' Moreover, to ask questions of legitimacy is to ask questions of 'the kind of legitimacy which is claimed, the type of obedience, the kind of administrative staff developed to guarantee it, and the mode of exercising authority'. For Weber, as for Schmitt and Blumenberg, legitimacy does not refer us to legality and the juridical-political theory of sovereignty. They do not look to the idea of power as right such as that found in Locke, but to the concrete organization of substantive forms of power, of which law may play a part. In this respect, they all stand in contrast to Foucault, for whom legitimacy is only a category of juridical-political theory and not an element in the organization of power relations. In fact, he argues, from 'the Middle Ages onwards, the essential role for the theory of right has been to establish the legitimacy of power' (2003: 26).

The debate on secularization thus provides us with a very different perspective on Foucault's genealogy of power relations. We were astonished to find the intransigence of his flight from sovereignty. We were equally astonished at the speed with which he would discover *new* and different conceptions and forms of power relations from those of discipline to the forms of regulation envisaged by the American neoliberals. In contrast to the three German thinkers, Foucault rejects problems of the legitimacy of power because in his view these questions are intimately tied up with the juridical discourse of state-right-sovereignty. However, if legitimacy is a historical-sociological and not a legal category, law (or 'legal-rational authority') being only one of its forms, then, even on his own terms, Foucault should not have been so concerned. But rather than pose to him the question of what is the legitimacy claimed by the forms of power he discovers, such as discipline, biopolitics and governmentality, which will only yield a reformulation of his own work, we can ask him, what kind of legitimacy does he hope to discover every time he finds and marks a new, post-sovereign power?

This question makes Foucault's project, which stands at the commencement of our contemporary projects in the analysis of power, very clear. Discipline, biopower and governmentality are all elaborated in a journey towards the specification of a new kind of exercise of power that will allow for difference, minority and multiplicity, and maximize the capacity for the self-making of identities. This new power will no longer subjugate through the command of the law, 'subjectify' through the capture of the body, or normalize through a knowledge of the regularities of populations, but allow the maximum autonomy in self-creation, and indeed, to use Blumenberg's term, 'self-assertion', in ever new ways. This is the sense in which Foucault's project is a 'critical ontology' of our selves and of our present (2010: 21).

The charismatic authority of Foucault and his work should not be under-estimated. But its continuing claim on the present rests on precisely the same motivation that drove him to move so quickly from one characterization of relations of power to another. This is the search for a new power, beyond the forms of domination inherent first in sovereignty and later in discipline and biopolitics. It is the move to a form of new power that will afford us the greatest possible opportunities to create ourselves as different kinds of subjects. The drive toward the present in Foucault's genealogy of power is not a concern to identify the modern or the postmodern but to grasp the possibilities of the new, of undertaking an 'experimental attitude', as he calls it, of going beyond the limits of identity we have been bequeathed (1997: 316). This going beyond limits needs no other justification than the audacity of newness itself – one which of course rejects the now old socialist 'programs for the new man'. Foucault concludes: 'I shall thus characterize the philosophical ethos appropriate to the critical ontology of ourselves as a historico-practical test of the limits we may go beyond, and thus as work carried out by ourselves upon ourselves as free beings'. In place of Blumenberg's 'self-assertion' of modern humans, we have the 'self-empowerment' of free beings.

In this move, Foucault captures precisely our present predicament with regard to the analysis of power. Many contemporary conceptions of power, from myriad claims of a 'governance without government', to actor-network, complexity and systems theory, gain legitimacy because they rest on little more than the pure creative possibilities of novelty; of a new which intellectually and politically does away with the old, which is coded in terms of sovereignty, hierarchy and transcendence. This metaphysics of the new that absolves all our struggles with old power takes theoretical, ethical, economic and technical forms. In this respect, we have become heirs to Blumenberg but without his subtlety and qualification, and without the context of one of the most intense intellectual-historical debates of the twentieth century.

6.11 There are difficulties in placing Foucault's genealogy of the arts of government in relation to the historical schemas of secularization that can now be cleared up. The first, and most obvious of these, is his relation to the discipline of history and the philosophy of history. In his various expositions of archaeology and genealogy, he rejects a totalizing and teleological history on the one hand and the search for origins on the other (1972; 1984: 76–100). From this point of view secularization would seem to constitute precisely that totalizing 'meta-narrative' that Foucault would reject and it would thus be illegitimate to apply such a framework to his work.

There are also elements that suggest an equivocation. On the one hand, Foucault is tempted by a version of secularization in which modern forms of government and power, or at least aspects of them associated with certain kinds of professional expertise, are an extension of a pastoral power that has been freed from what Schmitt would call the political form of the Church. In 'The Subject and Power', Foucault explains this very clearly when he responds to the claim that 'the pastorate has, if not disappeared, at least lost the main point of its efficacy':

> This is true, but I think we should distinguish between two aspects of pastoral power – between the ecclesiastical institutionalization that has ceased or lost its vitality since the eighteenth century, and its function, which has spread and multiplied outside the ecclesiastical institution. (2001: 333)

The notion of salvation is hence reborn as 'health, well-being (that is, sufficient wealth, standard of living), security, protection against accidents' (Foucault, 2001: 334). Pastors are found in the state, in private philanthropic organizations, and in 'complex structures such as medicine', both selling private services and in public institutions. Professional expertise, forms of knowledge, and social and political institutions are thus historically linked to the transformation of a religious form seeking a theological end. In this respect, Foucault would seem to advance a strong version of secularization, what Böckenförde called an institutional political theology and Schmitt a sociology of political form. Thus he advances the proposition that the loss of the institutional form of the Church released the contents of the pastorate onto the welfare, health and caring professionals and markets in expertise and services. What he had initially called biopolitics is an outcome of this secularization process.

It is when he comes to identify what is new in the new power of government that Foucault shifts to an anti-secularization thesis. Governmentality is born from the critique of sovereignty first by early modern thought and practice and later by liberalism. Reason of state, characterized as 'the devil's reason' by Pope Pius V, (*ratio status* as *ratio diaboli*) asserts the immanent rationality of governing the state in Foucault's account (2007: 242). Liberalism, moreover, continues the attack on the transcendent dimension of sovereignty by mobilizing a form of knowledge, political economy, which he characterizes (mistakenly) as an 'atheistic discipline'.

But even in this part of the narrative there is some ambivalence. Reason of state is a form of secular reason that allows the art of government to break open the great 'theological-cosmological continuum' and to place history and politics in multiple spatialities and open time (Foucault, 2008: 290). But in its critique of the 'statism' of reason of state, liberalism not only further breaks with the rigidities of sovereignty to found an art of government but also, by grounding government in a natural-historical domain of civil society, makes possible a new range of anti-state eschatologies, including those taking democratic, nationalist and revolutionary forms.

The impression, however, is that Foucault upholds the secularization thesis by asserting the Christian-religious taint on those powers he once called discipline and biopower – a taint transmitted through the release of the pastorate from the political and institutional form of the Church. But he also holds the possibility of the contestation of those powers, of their critique and the emergence of a form of resistance and struggle, and even perhaps a form of power (such as that envisaged by American neoliberalism) that is no longer mortgaged against secularization. Like Blumenberg, this could be described as one of self-assertion but with the slightly different meaning in which our identity or, as Foucault said so often, our soul, is no longer an outcome of corporeal disciplines or practices of confession, but to the maximum extent possible a product of our own ethical self-practice.

Foucault's thesis on the emergence of the art of government thus amounts to a dialectic between the secularization of pastoral power and forms of power that will allow the flourishing of self-created identity in the present. In this respect his secularization thesis confirms only the liberal rationalization of the state of the nineteenth and twentieth centuries at the expense of the statist neutralization of confessional conflict that was its condition and preceded it by two centuries in European history. From the point of view of the former, the economy becomes central to governing and politics because it dissolves all theology within a purely atheistic rationality which, when applied, can continue the disenchantment of professional expertise and knowledge. Over the course of the nineteenth and twentieth centuries, the genealogy of the art of government can chart the rise of pastoral expertise and the enclosures or territories in professions and bureaucracies it creates in the welfare state, and their penetration by and subjection to a host of formal rationalities derived from economics and its associated techniques of auditing and accounting. Professional expertise and bureaucratic competencies are thus rendered calculable and comparable. In our discussion of Malthus, we have already found there are problems with this thesis. If Schmitt looked to the formation of the state as the fundamental political neutralization of confessional conflict, Foucault sees liberalism as an economic neutralization of expertise that completes the secularization of the Christian pastorate.

Schmitt and neoliberalism

6.12 The link between Carl Schmitt and neoliberalism, in its two main forms, is a matter of some discussion and investigation.

The relationship between the 'rule of law' and the exception in neoliberalism has been explored by those concerned to show the theoretical links between Schmitt's theory of law and his critique of liberal democracy and Hayek's notion of the rule of law (Cristi, 1984; Scheuerman, 1997). The principal point of connection is the distinction, found in both Schmitt and Hayek, between general legal norms and individual legal commands and measures and the diagnosis that the democratic-welfare state, first glimpsed by Schmitt in its nascent and precocious Weimar form, undermines the classical liberal rule of law (Scheuerman, 1997: 173). For both of them, social and economic policy is closer to particularistic measures than general law, and undermines both the political authority of the state and civil society as an autonomous sphere of freedom. While Schmitt would recommend the movement to an authoritarian solution, Hayek will argue paradoxically for a return to a classical rule-of-law ideal and, in his last work, a state-institutional framework using an authoritarian upper house, reminiscent of Schmitt's plebiscitary democracy, to maintain the rule of law and the distinction between legislation and administration (pp. 178–83). Considering neoliberalism as praxis rather than theory, Schmitt's conception of a 'commissarial dictatorship' as a temporary state of exception to preserve democracy would also find resonances in the practice and statements of members of the Chicago School (including Milton Friedman and Hayek) in their advice and participation in 'reform' under regimes such as that of General Pinochet's Chile in the early 1970s (Fischer, 2009).

Direct links have also been made between Schmitt and Ordoliberals such as Eucken, Müller-Armack and Rüstow (Ptak, 2009). Schmitt's critique of the Weimar democratic-welfare state as the 'quantitative total state' which was weak because parliamentary democracy had allowed it to be colonized by plural interest groups, was directly referenced and taken up by those thinkers in the early 1930s who would be become key members of the Ordoliberals. At the very least, as Ralf Ptak reminds us, the Ordoliberals did not repress the critique of the democratization of economy and society and shared precisely the same enemies as Schmitt (and later, the Chicago School): Marxism, Keynesian economic theory and the administrative or welfare state (2009: 111–12). If we have found Schmitt deficient in his relative neglect of the economic-governmental domain of power, it might be that his sovereign-tist view of power opens a space of complementarity with what became the neoliberal conception of the role of the state. The Ordoliberals, such as Wilhelm Röpke, were particularly fond of Benjamin Constant's saying: 'The government beyond its proper sphere ought not to have any power; within its sphere, it cannot have enough of it' (cited in French in Röpke, 1996: 32). To under-line the relationship between German neoliberalism and Schmitt's political theory, consider two speeches given in the fateful year of 1932. Alexander von Rüstow made what Carl Friedrich (1955: 512) would later call a 'programmatic declaration' under the title 'Free Economy – Strong State' (*Freie Wirtschaft – Starker Staat*). Schmitt delivered an address to an association of German business-men entitled 'Strong state and sound economy' (*Starker Staat und gesunde Wirtschaft*) (1998). The latter took the position that only a strong state can preserve and enhance a free-market economy (Cristi, 1998: 31). As he wrote at around the same time: 'Only a strong state can generate genuine decentralization, bring about free and autonomous domains, and guarantee the independence of the bodies of autonomous administration' (Schmitt in Cristi, 1998: 35n). Rüstow responded that unlike the old liberalism that had demanded a space for its own development *contra* 'the excep-tionally strong state [i.e., absolutism], the new liberalism that is justified today demands a strong state, a state that rises above the economy' (in Cristi, 1998: 194). Neoliberalism, in both its major branches, relies upon the fundamental antitheses between general law and particular measures, legislation and administration, and ultimately strong state and market economy. The key to thinking their linkage will be the notion of order (§7.10).

6.13 Many lines of these twentieth-century German discussions lead back to Max Weber. We have observed that one way of characterizing Carl Schmitt's political theology is to contrast it with Weber's economic theology. Foucault's discussion of the German Ordoliberals also traces the important influence of Weberian economic history and sociology in formulating problems of the 'economic-institutional ensemble in the history of capitalism' (2008: 166). Indeed Foucault contrasts Weber's problem of the 'irrational rationality of capitalist society' as it is inherited by Max Horkheimer and the Frankfurt School and by Walter Eucken and the Freiburg School, so that while the former searched for a 'social rationality' that will 'nullify economic irrationality', the latter seek to discover or recover the 'economic rationality' that will 'nullify the social irrationality of capitalism' (p. 106).

Perhaps the Ordoliberals trace the circle that links Schmitt and Foucault. After the publication of his lectures on neoliberalism, the Walter Eucken Institute in Freiburg issued a very favourable discussion paper on Foucault's treatment of Ordoliberalism. It concluded that 'all the Foucaultian suggestions should be acknowledged, that his genealogical endeavours represent a remarkable expansion of the economic issue of freedom – in the narrow sense of the word' (Goldschmidt and Rauchenschwandtner, 2007: 26). The outcomes of this genealogy, however, should not be limited to the 'aesthetics of the self', but should 'once again and with great effort strive towards an ethic of the polity'.

The Ordoliberals, in a manner not noted by Foucault, also became the bearers of Weber's economic theology. Rüstow finds a pagan and pantheistic economic theology in laissez-faire capitalism (1942: 269–70). In an extraordinary tour de force, he presents a genealogy of the idea of 'invisible harmony' from pre-Socratic philosophy, Heraclitus, the Pythagoreans, to Hellenistic Stoicism, early Christianity and to *l'ordre naturel* of the Physiocrats, in which he also detects a second 'theologico-metaphysical line' – that of Taoism. He cites Spinoza's formula, *Deus sive natura*, God as nature, and identifies it with Adam Smith's 'invisible hand' (p. 270). Rüstow's view of early liberalism's economic theology is

as an optimistic one, without original sin and standing on its head
the moral distinction between virtues and vices (Palaver, 2007: 218).
Envy becomes a virtue by leading to emulation, which promotes
competition and therefore prosperity.

Rüstow insists, however, first of all that this 'economic machinery',
including the beneficial principle of competition, must be made to
serve 'the "vital situation" of man', and second that a 'strong and prudent state policy of policing the market should be instituted' (1942:
279, 281). Every 'free economic system needs a market police' so that
'a true maximum of economic and social justice could be attained by
means of such a combination of just initial conditions and free efficiency competition' (pp. 281, 282).

In reviving the possibility of a pantheistic liberal economic theology, Rüstow indicates a historical alternative to Schmitt's monotheistic political theology and Foucault's atheistic governmental
reason. However, as we know, Ordoliberalism will insist, contrary
to classical or laissez-faire liberalism, on the enframing of the market within a legal and political order that will promote competition,
generalize the model of enterprise, and establish a decentralization
of economic activity. Rüstow presents this, using a term with more
recent connotations, as 'the Third Way', between 'broken down liberalism and collectivism' that leads 'towards a new life of human
dignity' (1942: 278). In seeking to overcome the 'mistaken sub-
theological pseudo-universalism of liberalism', he appears also to
suggest that this Third Way seeks a reconciliation of economic with
political theology. In this way, the program of Ordoliberalism looks
less like a third alternative to liberal governmental reason and political theology, pantheism (or even atheism) and monotheism, market
competition and state authority, than an attempt at an interlacing
of both sides of the formation of power, in the form of the politics of
life, a *Vitalpolitik*.

The power of, and over life, in this instance and others, is neither
Foucault's historically singular application of power to the life of
the population in opposition to a transcendent sovereign power,
nor a universal feature of Occidental politics (a view often identified with Agamben), but a kind of constant relay between a transcendent and universal order (examples of which we have found in
Locke, Smith and Malthus) and the government of singular forms
(e.g., savage life, indigent life) and orders of life (e.g., economic life,
molecular life).

A strange contemporaneity

6.14 There are stark divergences between Foucault and Schmitt on the question of appropriation, between their concepts of *nomos* and governmentality and on the respective focus on governmental rationality and the different forms of political mythology, metaphysics and theology. It is perhaps strange that a 'nominalist' historical approach in Foucault will yield a concern for forms of reason, while a political 'realist' approach, such as Schmitt's, gives centrality to myth and theology. There is also the consequential question of the relationship between Schmitt's political mythology and his political theology, which we have not tried to analyse.

Nonetheless, there are fundamental similarities we have noted in their genealogies of the international sphere, and of international law and government, and much that can be learnt about the conceptualization of power through German debates on modernity and secularization. Let us try to summarize some of the main points that we have found here.

1 There is a kind of complementarity between the diametrically opposed language of Foucault's analysis of power and Schmitt's specification of the conditions of every social and political order, with the vocabulary of 'appropriation' being the key zone of contention. However, if taken together, a challenge for the conceptualization of power relations is to understand power both in relation to the ongoing foundational character of the *nomos* and the fluidity and singularity of new ways of governing and being governed, of governmentality.

2 The genealogies of *nomos* and of governmentality each posit different kinds of secularization and neutralization: the former, a political neutralization of theological conflict that establishes a secular state and the just enemy; the latter, an economic neutralization of expertise that follows the release of the contents of the pastorate from within the political form of the Catholic Church. Despite the basic differences in analytical vocabulary and intent, both Schmitt and Foucault insist that we need to understand the continuing theological presence in the contemporary exercise of power.

3 However, Foucault's genealogy of the arts of government functions as a critique of political theology. It charts the emergence of an

atheistic governmental rationality always suspicious of the state and its theological-like claims to transcendent sovereignty. This first takes the form of reason of state and then of an early liberal economic rationality and critique. It finally proposes that, in its critique of the welfare state, neoliberalism initiates an economic rationalization of the theological remnants of pastoral expertise attendant upon the end of the monopoly of the Catholic Church.

4 The debate on secularization puts Foucault's genealogy in a different light. Despite its ambiguities, it is a historical philosophy of the emergence of the new through the progressive critique of the old, the theological, and the transcendent. Foucault posits in this history a dialectic between a transcendent power of sovereignty and state reason blocking the arts of government and the immanent forces of a liberal art of government with its techniques of self-government. This dialectic leads towards a potential overcoming in the form of the maximization of self-government and minimum of domination. While such a narrative might be appealing, it results in the considerable problems we have indicated for an analytics of power.

5 From Max Weber to Alexander von Rüstow and Walter Eucken, a third term in the debate emerges between political theology and governmental atheism – that of economic theology. While Rüstow posits a pantheistic early liberalism, and Weber the association of Protestantism and capitalism, Ordoliberalism traces a different figure. As a preliminary finding, Ordoliberalism seeks to weave together the anarchic and pantheistic economic-governmental domain it attributes to early liberalism with a monotheistic political theology. This framework is thus a key one for further attention.

6 Political theology is interwoven with economic theology as framework, concept and critique (as we found in our discussion of Schmitt's engagement with Weber). Thus they propose different secularizations in Europe: the first flowing from the economic ethic of Protestant asceticism and the second from the political ethos of Catholic decisionism; one leading to a diagnosis of spiritual loss, the other to civil war by other means. Economic theology is linked to the ongoing processes of rationalization and its attendant irrationalities, while political theology discovers the outcome of neutralization and criticizes its accompanying depoliticizations.

7   The 'analogy' between theological and political concepts, and the
    idea of the 'reoccupation' of the former by the latter, are not antin-
    omies. It is possible that political and practical solutions address
    concrete political problems and situations of modern societies
    and utilize concepts that are marked by their theological anteced-
    ents. This is a matter for historical and contextual investigation.
    Without this possibility, the debate on secularization, and indeed
    the genealogy of the arts of government, remains one of mutual
    antagonism between the aggressivity of the new and the dogma-
    tism of the old.

Strange as it may seem, Schmitt and Foucault could be said to be contemporaries. While there was a 38-year age difference, they would
die within a year of one another. But their contemporaneity lies in
the almost parallel reception and putting to work of these thinkers
over the last three decades on what, no doubt, are often very different
problems. Both of them have spoken to aspects of what still constitutes our present. We have noted Foucault's one comment on Schmitt.
We can only imagine what Schmitt would have thought of Foucault.
Perhaps he would have charged him with traces of political romanticism, economic and ethical liberalism, and the modernist belief in
the audacity (*tolma*) of the new. The evidence for the first would be
the attempt to analyse the deconstructed state as an 'art of government' with a telos of the self-creating, self-governing individual. The
evidence for the second would be the view of liberalism as a critique
of state, government and politics without being able, or willing, to
develop a new theory of the state. The support for the third would be
indicated by the suppression of the problem of legitimacy in Foucault
and the search for a novel form of power that is justified by nothing more than the possibility of self-creation or self-empowerment in
games of power.

   Schmitt teaches us to recognize and analyse those aspects of
power relations that cannot be reduced to the local, the contingent
and the new. These are the ongoing founding acts of appropriation,
of the constitution of law and legal order, of the decision on the
exception and the declaration of the enemy. He teaches us to examine relations of power in the rootedness of authority in tradition,
the continuity of the old at the advent of the new, and of the theologically eminent in that which is most secular. But to the extent
to which he cannot understand the twentieth-century expansion of

the economic-governmental axis as anything but a neutralization of the state and the political, Schmitt's conceptualization of power remains as rigid, dogmatic and authoritarian, as much as Foucault's was restless, elusive and anarchic.

In the early 1960s Jürgen Habermas offered the comment that Carl Schmitt was the 'legitimate pupil' of Max Weber (1971: 66). Later, on 'friendly advice', he was persuaded that he had really meant 'natural son' (p. 66, n. 4). Perhaps we could say that Schmitt in his political theology is more like the bastard son of Weber's political sociology, and Foucault is the heir to his postulate of the economic rationalization of government. But between them, and at the time of their deaths, the inheritance of economic theology remained unclaimed.

7

REIGN AND GOVERNMENT

7.1 The uproar which followed the translation of Giorgio Agamben's 'political writings' into English paradoxically indicates their anticipatory potential towards our present (Agamben, 2005b). It is understandable that his application of the state of exception to the contemporary United States would provoke 'predictably loud' responses (Raulff, 2005: 610). What was not so predictable was the response in certain quarters, particularly those claiming the heritage of Michel Foucault, to his engagement with the concept of biopolitics. Agamben was accused of illegitimately grounding biopolitics in the dark truth of thanatopolitics, a politics of death, and of being fixated on juridical questions under the spell of sovereign power (Rabinow and Rose, 2006: 201–2; Lemke, 2010: 59). Above all, his concept of biopolitics was regarded as totalizing, a concept without the necessary empirical support and historical nuance, basing itself on an essentialized conception of life and unable to grasp that today the main danger might come not from the state power's over life but from the withdrawal of the state in the face of the commercialization of biological existence and techno-scientific innovation.

Agamben himself answers these criticisms in three ways. He asserts that his focus on phenomena such as *homo sacer*, the camp, the state of exception and the Muselmann were not intended as exhaustive descriptions of contemporary power relations nor underlying principles but as paradigms in the sense of exemplars and emblems of aspects of our present and its potentials, their role being 'to constitute and make intelligible a broader historical-problematic context' (2009: 9). Secondly, he argues that while he practises the same methods as Foucault, it is natural to address law and theology as precisely the areas the latter did not address (Snoek, 2010: 46) While carefully listening to the call from Foucault to liberate analysis from the shadow of sovereignty, Agamben's response has been, on the contrary, to radically intensify the theorization of that very concept. Thirdly, in response to the claim of empirical insufficiency, Agamben affirms that his project is not an attempt to provide a concept of power adequate to a history of our present but a 'philosophical archaeology' which seeks a 'moment of arising' (*Entstehung* in Nietzsche, 'emergence' in Foucault) that will take the 'form of a past in the future, that of a *future anterior*' (2009: 83, 105–6). It is this methodological movement that gives his work a kind of hallucinatory predictive quality, which is not merely content to describe history for our present purposes of self-creation (after Blumenberg and Foucault) but to regress towards that *archē* that exists as an operative force in the present and the process of becoming. Agamben's main objective is not to offer an empirically adequate historical description of a phenomenon or concept, but to establish the conditions of possibility of it in a historical process or trajectory.

At least in the minds of certain followers of Foucault, there is indeed something like Mika Ojakangas's (2005) 'impossible dialogue' between Agamben and Foucault on biopower, when we consider the differences of timespan, the relationship to sovereignty and even the place of the 'camp' in contemporary relations of power in their respective discussions of biopolitics (Snoek, 2010: 47–8). While it has, nonetheless, become clear that there is a great deal more material to consider in assessing their relationship than the engagements found in *Homo Sacer I* (Bussolini, 2010a), even then a dialogue must start with an acceptance of different objectives and perspectives despite a sometimes common vocabulary. For Foucault, the genealogical 'emergence' of biopolitics in the eighteenth century is an index of a new form of power that escapes the shadow of the sovereign, and even the corporeal disciplines. In contrast, Agamben seeks not to offer an empirical description of a new form of power but to follow the intimate relation between such terms as power and life, sovereignty and biopolitics, as far back along a diachronic arc to the point of their indifference or 'indistinction' to better account for a 'moment of arising' that will continue to be eminent and active in the future.

In this respect, Agamben pinpoints early in his political writings Foucault's incapacity to articulate the two sides of power when the latter recurrently analyses whether they take the form of sovereignty and biopolitics, the 'city-citizen game' and the 'shepherd-flock game', 'totalization' and 'individualization', political technologies and techniques of the self (Agamben, 1998: 5–6). His problem is one that neither Foucault nor Schmitt can resolve, 'the hidden point of intersection between juridico-institutional and biopolitical models of power' (p. 6). Agamben cites Foucault's own term for this problem of articulation as a 'political double bind' and calls it his 'blind spot' or, more accurately, 'vanishing point'. Foucault's genealogy seeks the potential for an ethical and aesthetic self-creation in the emergence of the new – whether a form of power or of reasoning, a kind of counter-conduct or an ethical culture of the self. In this respect his explorations of power are driven by secularization in the broader sense of the word as self-assertion within the present and its radical novelty. Agamben, though dissatisfied with political theology, wishes to maintain the eminence of the theological in the present. He sets out on a quest for the *arcana imperii*, the continued presence and eminence of the distant moment of arising that regresses towards the future, the point where law and politics, on the one hand, and religion and theology, on the other, cannot yet be distinguished. Thomas Lemke is certainly correct to argue that the 'statist' orientation of *Homo Sacer I* is ultimately inadequate to grasp the conditions of contemporary biopower (2010: 59). The 'economic' orientation of *The Kingdom and the Glory: for a Theological Genealogy of Economy and Government*, which is the second part of *Homo Sacer II*, might compensate for the earlier absence of a consideration of how decisions on life are today handed over to 'the realm of science and commercial interests, as well as the deliberations of ethics committees, expert commissions, and citizen panels' (Lemke, 2010: 61).

It is Agamben's economic theology we intend to focus on here, given the conclusions we reached at the end of the previous chapter (§**6.14**).

Economic theology

7.2 The archaeology of twentieth-century political theology reveals that Schmitt engraved his 'lapidary sentences' on political theology, as Jacob Taubes put it (2004: 105), into the very stone of Max Weber's economic theology (see §**6.5**). The history of political theology is one of multiple contributions and denials, closures and openings. Marquard's liberal, polytheistic political theology responds to Schmitt's monotheistic one; Blumenberg's self-assertion of modernity opposes both Löwith and Schmitt's secularization theses. These debates have raised the necessity of resolving the problem of the status of modern political concepts, above all the concept of power, in relation to theological ones, and require us to grasp the historical-philosophical frameworks (of secularization, neutralization, analogy, reoccupation, etc.) within which that problem is posed. In the following section (§7.3), we turn to the biggest challenge posed to political theology, the claim of its closure that was made long before these debates by the theologian Erik Petersen.

The history of economic theology appears as somewhat more abbreviated. The term is used in the contemporary Anglo-American history of economic thought. On the one hand, it is used as a critique, in which the suppositions of famous economists, such as that of the beneficial outcomes of the pursuit of self-interest, are shown to be matters of faith rather than the result of forms of reasoning (Foley, 2006). On the other, there are those who draw the sociological and historical links between Christian, typically Protestant, religion and ministry and the economics profession, its mission and zeal (Nelson, 2004). For the latter one can speak, in purely analogical terms, of an 'economic priesthood', 'economic commandments' and so forth. Friedrich Hayek himself offered a version of a similar kind of economic theology when he dates the development of the market order from the recognition by 'the late sixteenth-century Spanish Jesuits' that the just price meant 'the prices determined by just conduct of the parties in the market, i.e. the competitive prices arrived at without fraud, monopoly and violence, was all that justice required' (1976: 73, 179, n. 15). As we have noted, it was the Ordoliberal, Alexander von Rüstow, who would take the concept beyond the analogical and merely historical to uncover the conceptual foundations of liberalism in a pantheistic and pagan economic theology (*Wirtschaftsheologie*) (§6.13).

It is in relation to this latter project that we can begin to place Agamben's scholarly interventions on economic theology. He argues that the eschatology of salvation, unearthed by Löwith, was 'nothing but an aspect of a vaster theological paradigm, which is precisely the divine *oikonomia*', or 'divine economy' (2011: 5). This paradigm was, he continues, known to Hegel who 'posited the equivalence of his thesis of the rational government of the world with the theological doctrine of the providential plan of God' and even more so, Schelling, who 'summarized his philosophy with the theological figure of *oikonomia*'.

Agamben's thesis is yet another (like Foucault and like Schmitt) to deal with the signature that marks our political conceptions and our concepts of power. Indeed, it is an explicit attempt to deal with the signature of power that produces an understanding of power as composed of either, or both, a 'transcendent' juridical-institutional pole of sovereignty and an 'immanent' economic-governmental pole of the power over mundane life. He wishes to demonstrate that Christian theology begets two functionally related antinomian paradigms: 'political theology, which founds the transcendence of sovereign power on the single God, and economic theology, which replaces this transcendence with the idea of an *oikonomia* conceived as an immanent ordering ... of both divine and human life' (Agamben, 2011: 1). For Agamben, political philosophy and the theory of sovereignty derive from political theology, and modern biopolitics and liberal economic government from economic theology.

Agamben thus opens a path not available to either Foucault or Schmitt: that, normatively, historically, and analytically, we do not have to choose between, or give pre-eminence to, either axis in the understanding of how power operates. As Thanos Zartaloudis has clearly spelt out, for Agamben it is only by an understanding of the centrality of economic theology that the Christian theological inheritance of philosophy and politics and law can be properly appreciated (Zartaloudis, 2010: 55–6). The difficulty we face of course is that in an intellectual culture of what we might call 'immanentism' – what Zartaloudis calls the denigration of 'the Kingdom of God' – the bipolar and antinomian inheritance remains unthought and unthinkable. However, it is not that this culture *under*-estimates the powers that are attributed to God and the sovereign. Rather the key problem of our modern conceptions of power is that they are drawn against a political and theological imaginary of a divine or worldly sovereignty as all-powerful.

To understand this, we must first approach economic theology from the question of the closure of political theology and the rejection of the possibility of an economic theology by both Erik Peterson and Carl Schmitt.

7.3 Well before the vigorous discussions after World War II on political theology, the inter-war German convert from Protestantism to Catholicism, the theologian Erik Peterson, sought to bring an end to political theology. He did this in a small volume, published in 1935, 'Monotheism as a Political Problem: A Contribution to the History of Political Theology in the Roman Empire' (2011: 68–105). While the title explains its subject matter, it was the final paragraph that announced its radical conclusion:

Only on the basis of Judaism and paganism can such a thing as 'political theology' exist. The Christian proclamation of the tri-une God stands beyond Judaism and paganism, even though the mystery of the Trinity exists only in the Godhead itself, and not in Creation. (Peterson, 2011: 105)

In a final footnote, Peterson will turn this conclusion against his friend:

To my knowledge, the concept of 'political theology' was intro-duced into the literature by Carl Schmitt, *Politische Theologie* (Munich 1922). His brief arguments at that time were not system-atic. Here we have tried to show by a concrete example the theo-logical impossibility of 'political theology'. (Peterson, 2011: 234)

Thirty-five years later, Schmitt offers, in his final book, a response to this conclusion and footnote, which will allow him to address what might be called a 'parting shot', or, as he puts it, 'to rip the Parthian arrow from his wound' (2008c: 32). In doing so, he clarifies the limits and limitations of political theology, and opens up a space for the consideration of the 'economic' legacy of Christian political theology.

Peterson's argument takes the form of an exegesis of texts of Aristotle, Philo of Alexandria, the early Church fathers, and finally of Bishop Eusebius from the time of the Emperor Constantine. The principle at stake is the 'divine monarchy'. Peterson argues that the divine monarchy 'had originated in the Hellenistic transformation of the Judaic faith in God' (2011: 104). We can see the immediate rele-vance to our concern for the concept of power when he finds the sub-stance of the divine monarchy in Aristotle: 'in the divine monarchy, the single rule (*mia archē*) of the ultimate single *principle* coincides with the actual hegemony of the single ultimate possessor of this rule (*archon*)' (p. 69, original emphasis).

Philo provided the most startling formulations of this idea by combining Judaic theology with pagan (or 'Peripatetic') material in order to make Judaism more comprehensible to the proselyte. 'The divine monarchy', states Peterson, 'stands in opposition to the assumption of a divine "polyarchy" (*polyarchia*), "oligarchy" (*oli-garchia*), or "ochlocracy" (*ochlokratia*) [mob rule]' (2011: 74). The metaphysical question of whether there are one or more principles of divinity is resolved; 'the decision even in the metaphysical world seems to have been arrived at from a political perspective', writes Petersen (ibid.).

After showing how early Church fathers failed in their attempts to join the traditional doctrine of divine monarchy with the dogma of the Trinity, Peterson turns to Origen and particularly his student, Eusebius, for the complete Christian elaboration of the doctrine of divine monarchy. These thinkers correlated the divine monarchy with the Roman Empire, firstly under Augustus. Christ's incarnation and becoming a Roman citizen by virtue of the first imperial census are linked to the end of multiple kings and kingdoms, including that of Israel, under the universalizing reign of the Pax Augusta. Polytheism belongs to the world of multiple sovereignties and multiple *poleis* [plural for *polis*]. For Eusebius, the cessation of national sovereignty and national gods under the reign of Augustus is thus providentially related to the appearance of Christ (Peterson, 2011: 93). Similarly, with Constantine, political monarchy is re-established and the divine monarchy secured. This is no longer a fulfilment of the eschatological prophecy, as it is for Origen, but a historical and political fact that unites 'empire, peace, monotheism and monarchy' (p. 96). With Constantine, Peterson concludes: 'To the *one* King on earth corresponds the *one* God, the *one* King in heaven and the *one* royal *Nomos* and *Logos*' (p. 94).

For Peterson, the later Greek fathers, such as Gregory of Nazianus, in defending the Trinity after the Arian controversy, developed the notion of a triune God and thus ensured that the link between the Christian proclamation and the Roman Empire was 'theologically dissolved' and a fundamental break with every political theology was made (2011: 103–4). Political theology appears as a kind of opportunistic legitimation of imperial and monarchical power indulged in by pagans and Jews, and the almost heretical early Christians.

However, Peterson remained aware of another possible relationship between theology and mundane existence; he discovered it in Paul's commandment to the Romans, 13:1: 'Be subject to the authorities'. He called this, without elaboration, the 'divine economy' (2011: 96).

7.4 In 1970, Carl Schmitt placed Peterson's book of 1935 in the context of the crisis of Protestantism that occurred after World War I. That crisis, expanded through the Weimar Republic, was the breakdown of the separation between religion and politics with the 'shattering of the two decisive domains, church and state' by the 'domain of *society* and *the social*' (Schmitt, 2008c: 139, original emphasis). This crisis would trigger various biographical pathways including Peterson's conversion to Roman Catholicism.

Schmitt compares Peterson's 1935 book, *Monotheism as a Political Problem*, with his 1931 essay on 'Divine Monarchy' and, in doing so, locates the former in relation to a new crisis occasioned by Hitler's coming to power and the totalitarian ambitions of National Socialism (Schmitt, 2008c: 43). For Schmitt, Peterson's later book, while not addressing this crisis explicitly, does so disguised in 'a very erudite theological focus'. What separates the 1935 book from the essay of 1931, however, is something quite extraordinary for the pathways we have been following on power. It is 'an interpolation in a politico-theological mode' (p. 62). What is this interpolation? It is precisely the maxim we have found in both Foucault and in Schmitt and which neither can properly resolve: 'the King reigns, but he does not govern'. For Peterson, argues Schmitt, the formula becomes the key to understanding monotheistic paganism, which, like Aristotelian metaphysics, is excluded from the impossibility of a political theology.

From the theological side, Schmitt accuses Peterson of ignoring Islam altogether and of refusing Judaism a proper theology (2008c: 76–7). While Bishop Eusebius is the main explicit enemy, Schmitt accuses Peterson of an unnamed, disguised enemy, behind the veil of his critique of Eusebius as a caesaro-papist, Byzantine and sycophant (p. 80). Indeed, Eusebius had been 'defamed' already by Franz Overbeck in an 'excoriation' of Adolf Harnack as theologian of the Prussian court (pp. 40–1). Schmitt twice cites Overbeck's portrayal of Eusebius as a 'hairdresser for the Emperor's theological periwig' (pp. 40, 81). According to Schmitt, Peterson regards Eusebius not as a theologian at all, but an ideologist, propagandist and orator (pp. 93–4). Peterson thus 'retreated from the crisis of Protestant theology into a rigorous negation of all that was non-theological' (p. 95). However, Schmitt argues in a long deconstruction of Peterson's final paragraph, this attempt at a theological closure of political theology places the latter in a performative contradiction because it is impossible to attempt theological closure without becoming political, that is, when deciding on the enemy, one is undoubtedly engaged in a kind of political theology.

What is interesting about Peterson and Schmitt is that they both ignore the content of the doctrine of the Trinity and its implications for the political. Peterson seeks closure on political theology at the very moment a kind of theological politics had thrown the Church into utter disarray, while Schmitt turns the problem into a jurisprudential one. In so doing, he claims inheritance of Max Weber's view of the relationship between canon law and secular law expressed as the 'relatively decisive factor' of 'the unique organization of the Catholic church as a rational institution' in the process of legal rationalization (cited in Schmitt, 2008c: 109). In the process, Schmitt turns a figure like Tertullian into a 'legalizing theologian' despite his interpretation of the Trinity (p. 111).

Schmitt thus saves political theology by a constant referral back to the juridical and institutional form of sovereignty. Indeed it is precisely that form that acts as the *katechon*, the restrainer of the coming of the Antichrist, particularly as international public law, the *jus publicum Europæum*. Peterson, by contrast, according to Schmitt, argues that it is the unbelief of the Jews that delays the Apocalypse and the Second Coming (Schmitt, 2008c: 92, 147, n. 9). Neither of these 'apocalyticians of counterrevolution', as Taubes called them (2004: 69), will be able to grasp the fundamental contribution of Christian theology to the operation of power because they stop short of the key secular inheritance of that theology: the notion of the *oikonomia* which the Church fathers used to explain the mystery of the Trinity. That, at least, is the fundamental argument advanced by Agamben.

7.5 In a memoir of his post-World War II relationship with Carl Schmitt, the Jewish philosopher of religion, Jacob Taubes, identified a commonality between Schmitt, Heidegger and Hitler. As Catholics, they were on the margins: 'German culture of the Weimar Republic and of the Wilhelmine period was of a Protestant and somewhat Jewish coloring' (Taubes, 2004: 103). They were all 'Catholics gone stale'. No doubt the two professional academics of this unholy trinity would find this analysis and comparison exceedingly odious. Taubes says of them that they 'were guided by a resentment, that's the first thing, but who with the genius of resentment also read the sources in a new way' (p. 104).

There is a macabre irony in Taubes's comment. He wrote an extraordinary letter to the aged Schmitt in 1979, who was living in Plettenberg in what he called San Casciano, naming the house after Machiavelli's place of exile where the latter wrote *The Prince*. This letter would lead very quickly to a meeting between the two at Schmitt's home in part, as Taubes put it, 'conducted under a priestly seal' (2004: 2). In his memoir, Taubes assesses the Peterson-Schmitt debate and reveals Peterson not as aiming at Schmitt as his disguised enemy but as a 'best friend' who issued him a 'coded warning' (p. 111). He had sent not a Parthian arrow but a Christian arrow. In the letter, Taubes called the Nazi 'race question' a political 'theo-zoology'. Even if his analysis of the three Catholics gone stale has the air of a sally or a *boutade* about it, this latter term should be taken seriously.

Taubes would come back to this term in his lectures on Paul delivered in 1987 under the imminence of his own death. There he tells of reading Paul's Letter to the Romans at Plettenberg with Schmitt and the latter's acknowledgement of his failure to appreciate Paul's words about the enemies of God: 'Enemies for your sake; but as regards election they are beloved, for the sake of their forefathers [II: 28]' (Taubes, 2004: 51). Schmitt had adopted not the text but the 'folk traditions of church anti-Semitism, onto which he, in 1933–36, went on to graft the racist theozoology'. This passage from Paul would seem to reverse the distinction between *hostis* and *inimicus*, public enemy and private foe. Taubes quotes the nearly 90-year-old Schmitt, whom he calls the 'most important state law theorist', as saying '[t]hat I did not know!'

We should be prepared to take seriously Taubes's inelegant compound, which indicates a form of reasoning in which a knowledge of the ordering of creaturely life ($z\bar{o}\bar{e}$) depends on, or presupposes, a providential order of eternal life, or simply a conception of life itself. As such a politics of life does not belong to either history (the biopolitics of the population – Foucault) or the transcendental order (the sovereign decision which, through the exception, constitutes the normal 'frame of life' – Schmitt) but to an interlacing and interweaving of the transcendent and the immanent, eternity and temporality, life as a universal and its singular forms.

Oikonomia

7.6 In what is an unlikely twist, both Erik Peterson and Michel Foucault reserve a privileged place for the eastern Church father, Gregory of Nazianus, in their respective historical investigations. In Foucault's case, he appears at the very beginnings of the genealogy of the arts of government in his account of the Christian pastorate (2007: 192–3). Foucault notes that Gregory speaks of an *oikonomia psychōn*, an 'economy of souls', which in Latin is *regimen animarum*. Foucault traces the derivation from the Greek *oikos* (household), and the managerial sense of the *oikonomia*. He soon, however, passes over the literal translation of the term and argues the best word is 'conduct' in its dual sense as an activity of conducting or leading and a form of conduct or behaviour. With this far from 'obvious' move, Foucault then puts to one side the notion of economy, which would not reappear for some fourteen centuries in the time of Quesnay and the Physiocrats.

Peterson places the same Gregory at the very climax of his story about pagan political theology. He cites Gregory's third *Oration* to argue that the triune God 'had no correspondence in the created order' and 'thus monotheism is laid to rest as a political problem' (2011: 103). As his English translator notes, it is doubtful that Foucault could have found the notion of an *oikonomia psychōn* in the *Orations* (2007: 217, n. 1). But what is truly extraordinary here is that the same text of the same Church father is being used to commence the genealogy of the arts of government and to bring a closure to political theology. The apocalyptic Catholic convert and theologian and the Nietzschean 'happy positivist' both act to deny the political and governmental implications of the theological conception of the economy.

Agamben commences his own genealogy precisely from these complementary removals or repressions. Foucault, he argues, misses an opportunity to 'complete' his genealogy by moving back in time to the Trinitarian paradigm to discover the 'origin of the notion of an economical government of men and the world' (2011: 110); this 'does not discredit his hypotheses, bur rather confirms their theoretical core to the very extent to which it details and corrects their historico-chronological exposition' (pp. 110–11). Peterson, Agamben suggests, stands at a threshold of the entwinement of the divine monarchy with the economy: 'the fact that it is absent in Petersen lets us infer something like a conscious repression' (Agamben, 2011: 114). In this sense, to use Peterson's own language we should look from the 'divine monarchy' to the 'divine economy'.

Oddly enough, it is Schmitt who discovers a political-theological element in the notion of the Trinity. 'At the heart of the doctrine of Trinity', he says (2008c: 123), 'we encounter a genuine politico-theological *stasiology*'. *Stasis*, Schmitt notes, has two meanings in

Greek, apparently diametrically opposed: 'quiescence, tranquillity, standpoint, status'; and *'unrest,* movement, uproar and civil war'. Peterson had cited Gregory's view of the three opinions about God: 'anarchy, polyarchy and monarchy'; the first two unleashed disorder and revolt, leading to dissolution, in God, and Christians confessed the Monarchy of God (2011: 103). Peterson represses the economic content of this divine monarchy; Schmitt finds in the character of the Trinity the possibility of civil war in God, a possibility, that is, of the political distinction between friend and enemy.

7.7 Agamben's exegesis of the theological *oikonomia* is long, detailed and rigorous. But it is intelligible as a genealogy of economic theology, which we will simply sketch here. He commences with the core meanings of the term *oikonomia* in classical Greek, Hellenistic and Roman texts, starting with the management of the household in Aristotle and Xenophon. Here he finds the semantic core that will determine any analogical extension (2011: 18–19). He then examines its first extension to the notion of arrangement in Hippocratic texts and among the Stoics, including Marcus Aurelius. The latter in part used it to mean the ordering or distribution of the matter of an argument in rhetoric. Cicero translates the term *oikonomia* with the Latin word, *dispositio,* from which, of course, the French word *dispositif* will be derived, used as we have seen by Foucault. Here it means 'more than a mere arrangement, since it implies, above and beyond the ordering of the themes (*taxis*), a choice (*diairesis*) and an analysis (*exergarsia*) of the topic' (p. 19). *Oikonomia* and *taxis,* economy and order, are thereby linked at a very early moment.

Agamben's extensive research into the translation of the term into the theological context starts with the contraction of a sentence by Paul into the syntagma *'oikonomia* of the mystery' (2011: 23) and then follows its gradual reversal into 'the mystery of the economy'. The first uses of the term to express the Trinity are recovered from a contemporary of Marcus Aurelius, the Christian philosopher, Athenagoras (p. 30), and from Ireneas, who seeks to remove the term from the Gnostics (pp. 31–3). However, it is with Hippolytus and particularly Tertullian that the 'technicization' of the term begins to take shape against the rigorous monotheism of the so-called Monarchians, Noetus and Praxeas (pp. 35–6). Hippolytus confers a new meaning on the term by the reversal of the Pauline syntagma, and Tertullian 'confers on economy all the semantic richness and ambiguity of a term that means, at the same time, oath, consecration, and mystery' (p. 40). Hence he uses the formula *oikonomia sacramentum*. The essential point here, for Agamben, is that the mystery of the Trinity is not resolved by ontological or metaphysical means, at least in these, the earliest stages of its formulation, but by economic-governmental ones, which emphasize not the divine being but its praxis. The mystery of the Trinity is the mystery of its economy.

With Origen, the essential nexus between *oikonomia* and history can be grasped so that when 'something like a notion of history – that is, a process endowed with a sense – appears for the first time, it is precisely in the guise of a "mysterious economy"' (Agamben, 2011: 44–5). *Oikonomia* is not just a synonym for a providential unfolding of history according to an eschatological design, but any historiographical sense of meaning and direction in history. It opposes Christian praxis to pagan fate, and posits a freedom that corresponds to and realizes a divine design. This mystery of freedom is nothing but the mystery of the economy. Clement of Alexandria extends this conception of providence, Agamben argues, and makes the most original contribution to the elaboration of the paradigm (p. 46). Clement seeks to save the 'economy of the saviour' from appearing as a myth or allegory and thus embeds 'the temporal economy of salvation in eternity' and, by so doing, 'initiates the process that will lead to the progressive constitution of the duality of theology and economy, the nature of God and his historical action' (p. 48).

Agamben's erudition here is impressive and his conclusions about the implications of these sometimes rough, strategic, and metaphoric formulations of the Trinity doctrine are fundamental and far-reaching. It is in the concept of *oikonomia* that a concept of the divine and its relation with all of creation emerges at the very end of the ancient world. But what is important is that this first articulation of the Trinity is achieved not in metaphysical terms, but as an economic apparatus and activity of government that is both mundane and divine. God is thought not through the being of the Trinity but through its praxis. Agamben concludes that the *oikonomia* conciliates between the 'unitarism of the Monarchians and Judaism' and the 'Gnostic proliferation of the divine hypostases', between the Gnostic and Epicurean non-involved god and the Stoic active god. The triune God thus can 'take charge of the world and found an immanent praxis of government

whose supermundane mystery coincides with the history of humanity'
(Agamben, 2011: 50–1).

The argument establishes that the early Christians were able to
propose a conception of divine power that articulated the monarchy
of God with his divine economy on earth, and in so doing required
both a divine sovereignty over the universe and an economic and
governmental management of the world. We could say, by analogy,
that in this sense Schmitt is basically a Monarchian in his political
theology and analysis of power in terms of a transcendent, juridical-
institutional form. But equally, Foucault, and much of our recent
thinking on power, is revealed as a kind of Gnostic, polytheistic,
proliferation of the sites (or 'hypostases') of power relations, which
tends to become, like Rüstow's analysis of early liberalism, a pantheism that makes power disappear into the nature of spontaneous
order or complex networks of government (or later, governance).
If we continue this analogy, then, what is needed is a conception of
power that can achieve the conciliations that were found by these
Christians. But we should note that this is more than an analogy for
Agamben and that these Christians are 'the first fully "economic"
men' (2011: 24).

In summary, for Agamben the *oikonomia* allowed the early
Christians to do three things. Firstly, it made possible a resolution to
the problem of the being and praxis of God that avoided either a strict
monotheism or a polytheism, a passive or hidden God, and an over-
interventionist one or an evil demiurge; secondly, it brought a sense
of direction and meaning to a historical process with the problem
of eschatological design; and thirdly, it allowed them to embed the
temporal process of human salvation within eternity. This articulation of the divine and the worldly, the heavenly God and God made
man, worldly salvation and eternal life, and above all God's being and
his actions, would only be resolvable from the viewpoint of *oikonomia* as praxis. These attempted resolutions, according to Agamben,
would also give rise to two other key related conceptual innovations
of 'order' and of 'providence'.

Order

7.8 One of the most difficult concepts to understand is 'order'
and yet it is central to the way we discuss and think

about politics and power. The word appears readily in our every-day lexicon: social order, political order, economic order, inter-national order, and world order. It sometimes seems to express a condition, which is ensured by a higher power, such as the state and its agencies, as in the phrase 'public order and security' and, at other times, it is an immanent domain with its own relations and sense, such as when we talk about an economic order or market order. It also expresses an action, such as the giving of orders, in the sense of commands, and of the activity of ordering, of arranging things.

Max Weber used the term as a central concept in a number of these senses. Firstly, he employs it to describe general social organi-zation, such as a legal, social or economic order. He also uses it in the compound *Lebensordnung* (life-order) to describe the different 'value-spheres' in the process of rationalization, such as the economic, political, aesthetic, erotic and intellectual spheres (1972: 323–59). Finally, it appears as legitimate order, which can be divided into laws and conventions, but which in itself implies an already meaningful and organized social relationship (1968: 31–3). His central concern in relation to the latter concept is how an actor might orient her relation-ship towards such an order, and an order's legitimacy depends on the probability that it will be followed.

Schmitt, too, used the word 'order' extensively in these senses. The definition of sovereignty, as we have seen, is concerned with a decision about public order and security. On the other hand, he talks about the basic conditions of any social and economic order (*Sozial- und Wirtschaftordnung*) in the title of an essay of 1953 (2003: 324). As he puts it in the first of his corollaries on *nomos*, he views law as the unity of orientation (*Ortung*) and order (*Ordnung*) (p. 42). In his Nazi-period *On the Three Types of Juristic Thought* (2004b), he distinguished jurisprudential 'normativism' characteristic of legal positivism his own earlier 'decisionism', and 'concrete-order thinking' (*Konkrete Ordnungsdenken*). His language becomes littered with ref-erences to 'concrete orders' and to 'spatial orders'. In fact, his theory of the *Grossraum* (literally 'large space') is presented in a wartime essay as the 'Grossraum order of international law' (*Grossraumordnung*) (2011: 75–124) These terms are all closely related to his concept of *nomos* and it would be possible to translate the term 'economy' (*oiko-nomos*) as the order and ordering of the house. In that sense it is redundant to speak of an economic order.

Yet there is another, no doubt related, use of the term, which is closely associated with problems of economy. Adam Ferguson (1819) is famous for introducing 'spontaneous order' thinking, and indeed his notion of civil society, so central to Foucault's understanding of liberalism, is an example of one such spontaneous order. This notion was transmitted to Austrian neoliberalism and is a key term in Hayek's evolutionary thinking of 'spontaneous social orders' (1979; Hill, 2006: 4, n. 18). The term order is crucial to the political economy in Quesnay and the Physiocrats, which appears as the 'science of order' in Le Trosne's *De l'ordre social* (Agamben, 2011: 281). Finally, the term gives itself to the very name of the German neoliberals, the *Ordoliberalen*, who describe their principles as an *Ordnungspolitik* (Ptak, 2009: 120).

The founder of this intellectual collective, Walter Eucken, would define *Ordo* as 'an order, which accords with the essence of humans; this means an order in which proportion (measure) and balance exist' (in Ptak, 2009: 105). As Ralf Ptak notes, the notion of a 'natural order' in Eucken, Böhm and Röpke, 'became a quasi-religious Ordo talisman'. But perhaps it was more than this. We have already seen that Rüstow viewed the classical liberal economy as derived from pagan and pantheistic 'economic theology'. Eucken goes to medieval scholasticism itself for the source of a project that reaches beyond such a pantheistic liberalism: 'The Ordo-thought took shape in the middle ages. It had a determining impact on the composition of the whole of medieval culture. It means the *meaningful* junction of the variety to the whole' (in Ptak, 2009: 128, n. 8). The Anglo-American understanding of the role of *Ordnung* in Ordoliberalism is not made easier by the English translator's persistent preference for 'system' over 'order' in Eucken's *The Foundation of Economics* (1950), but the dual sense of the term, as a universal natural order and particular social forms is clear in the sentence: 'A single order of Nature exists and has existed, but there is an unlimited and constantly changing variety of economic "orders" (*Wirtschaftordnungen*)' (1950: 42).

It is noteworthy that the concept of order, which is so central to his genealogy of liberal governing, receives little attention from Foucault. For the Ordoliberals sought to link the order of the competitive market to a vision of the ordering of the whole of society, through what Rüstow called a *Vitalpolitik* – a politics of life. As Lemke notes, vital politics 'relates the economy back to a comprehensive order that is external to it and ethically grounded' (2010: 106–7). In other words, a politics of life – a biopolitics – interweaves the comprehensive natural order with the actuality of existing economic orders. Yet the Ordoliberal project is perhaps only one example of an even more astonishing phenomenon: that in many cases, liberal and conservative economic and political thought traces its own central concepts, such as order, economy and government, to the most significant theologians of medieval Europe.

7.9 The concept of order in medieval scholastic thought and its relevance to modern discussions of politics and power is addressed by Agamben in a chapter of his book on economic theology entitled, in Italian, 'Il regno e il governo'. Let us persevere with the Italian title for it brings us to the heart of our problematic of power, on reign and government, and again to the maxim we have been pursuing throughout – 'the king reigns, but he does not govern'. At the heart of this problematic, and of this chapter, is the medieval notion of order.

The text to which medieval Christian scholars refer when addressing the 'most decisive question' of the relationship between God and the world is Aristotle's *Metaphysics*, Chapter X. Agamben analyses the passage in question where Aristotle first juxtaposes two interpretations of the 'highest good', as separate and autonomous, that is, transcendent, or of the order of the parts, that is, immanent (2011: 80). Immediately, however, Aristotle uses the metaphor of the army to argue that 'the good is found both in the order and the leader' and then switches to paradigms of the natural world and the household (p. 81). In the latter, 'freemen are least at liberty to act at random, but all things or most things are already ordained for them, while the slaves and beasts do little for the common good, and for the most part live at random'. The implication is that free men conduct themselves according to a unitary principle, whereas slaves and other creatures follow their nature but nonetheless act toward a common goal. Agamben concludes that Aristotle bequeaths the 'immovable mover' as transcendent foundation (*archē*) and the immanent order (*physis*) as a 'form of a single bipolar system' governed by a single principle. 'Power – every power, both human and divine – must hold these poles together, that is, it must be, at the same time, reign and government, transcendent norm and immanent order' (2011: 82, translation altered). What is useful here, for our discussion of power, is the idea of transcendence as entailing separation and autonomy (the links to sovereignty become clear immediately) and the inscription of the notion of order, or *taxis*, within the category of relation not substance.

Agamben argues that not only is 'order' the central and pervasive principle of St Thomas Aquinas's thought, but also the bearer of its 'dissymmetries and conflicts' (2011: 85). But it immediately splits into two: the relation that creatures have with God (*ordo ad unum principium* or *ordo ad deum*) and the relations they have among themselves (*ordo ad invicem*). Moreover, he continues, Aquinas, following Aristotle, thinks through the relationship between these two orders in terms of the economic management of the household (p. 86). 'The aporia that marks like a thin crack the wonderful order of the medieval cosmos now begins to become more visible', remarks Agamben (p. 87). Thus, the order of things among themselves is nothing but an expression of their relation to a divine order, and the order of things in relation to God is only expressed through their reciprocal relations among themselves.

Considered singly, the ideas that the order of the world is found in God and that the unity of God is found in the order of his creatures, are contradictions, expressing nothing but the ontological fracture of transcendence and immanence. Agamben observes that if we push the limits of this paradigm too far we have the Gnostic God totally foreign to the world in one direction and pantheism in the other. Perhaps this is exactly what Rüstow was trying to avoid in his identification of laissez faire with paganism and pantheism. It is only through the concept of order, with all its duality, that liberalism will overcome its pantheistic inheritance and achieve measure and proportion, balance and harmony in accord with human nature. It is only through this notion of *Ordo* that power will be able to be conceived as something that embraces the life of all creatures, and through which power will take the form of a vital politics or a bio-power, that can encompass both the spiritual and material wants of humanity.

7.10 It is beyond the scope of the present book, and the researches of its author, to be certain whether Walter Eucken was familiar with Hermann Krings's dissertation on 'Ordo: the historical-philosophical foundations of the Western idea', published in 1941, and his earlier paper on time and order, 'Das Sein und die Ordnung', of 1940 (see Agamben, 2011: 297). However, Eucken's view that Ordo-thinking took shape in the Middle Ages and his placing of 'measure' as a feature of order, concur with Krings's work. We do know that Eucken cites his own father, Rudolf Christoph Eucken, a philosopher of theology and Nobel Prize winner for literature, on Aristotelian method and on ideas of development, and continues, by other means, what the elder Eucken called an 'aspiration for the spiritual content of life' (R.C. Eucken, 1909; Eucken, 1950: 325, 347).

What is interesting here is the way Krings helps Agamben read Augustine on the paradoxical relationship between God and order, especially between God and measure, number and weight (Agamben, 2011: 88–9). Measure, number and weight are the order by which God arranges his creatures but themselves are not created things. They are present in things but are outside of them. Further, they coincide with God in his own being or *ordo* but are not of him. God in his being is *ordo*, order, but he is not measure, weight and number, and he is order only in the sense of ordering or arranging, that is, in an 'economic' sense. Krings thus argues: 'He is not measure, number, and weight in an absolute way, but *ille ista est* in a completely new way ... in the sense that *ordo* is no longer given as *mensura, numerus, pondus*, but as *praefigere, prabere, trahere*; as *finishing, forming, ordering*' (in Agamben, 2011: 89, original emphasis). The being of God, as order, is thus the praxis or activity that arranges things according to measure, number and weight. It is only by this economic-governmental activity that the transcendent and immanent orders, and being and praxis, can be made to refer back to one another.

Some fifteen centuries after Augustine, when Eucken founds the Ordoliberals, order will correspond both to the essence of human beings and the activity required to establish such an order. Foucault was no doubt correct when he noted, firstly, that Ordoliberalism rejected the 'naïve naturalism' of classical liberalism and thus regarded the market not as a natural phenomenon but as characterized by a 'game of competition', itself an essence, or *eidos*. He was also correct when he detected the influence of Edmund Husserl here and argued that Eucken and the Freiburg School were familiar with phenomenology and that they derived their theory by analogy to it. 'Just as for Husserl a formal structure is only given to intuition under certain conditions, in the same way competition as an essential economic logic will appear and produce its effects under certain conditions which have to be carefully and artificially constructed' (Foucault, 2008: 120). What is missing from this account, however, is the notion of order itself. According to Eucken, the idea of an order that can only be realized under a particular praxis of government is already present in the thought of the Christian theologians of the Middle Ages. It would seem a likely conclusion that Eucken had grasped that the very same theologians already had envisaged the *ordo* in relation to an *oikono-mia*, order as an economic order, and its relation to the government of the world, in their case a divine one.

This idea of a being or essence that can only be revealed by a carefully and artificially constructed set of actions is exactly what Krings found in the Middle Ages: 'being is *ordo* and the *ordo* is being; the *ordo* does not presuppose any being, but being has the *ordo* as its condition of possibility' (in Agamben, 2011: 88). Via the medieval Christian notion of the order, the Ordoliberals sought to move the market from nature to an economic and governmental order, one that is not derived from the market but which precisely is its condition of possibility. They sought to defeat the pantheistic economic theology which Rüstow had found in classical liberalism without resorting to the monotheism of the state implied in a 'protected economy, state socialism, economic planning, and Keynesian interventionism' (Foucault, 2008: 109). But in doing so, they did not seek to escape economic theology. Rather they consciously attempted to retrace the path between a monotheistic political theology and a pantheistic economic theology, which had already been taken by medieval Christian theology and its key concepts.

At about the same time that Krings was excavating the notion of order in philosophy and Eucken would make it the basis of his economics, Carl Schmitt would distinguish between three types of juridical thinking: normativism, associated with the positivism of Hans Kelsen; decisionism, his own previously preferred position; and concrete-order thinking (2004b). Schmitt too traces his notion of order to the Aristotlean-Thomist tradition of the Middle Ages (pp. 43, 73). Just as the Ordoliberals would move the market from the order of nature to the economic-governmental domain, so too did Schmitt move law from its normative order to what he called the concrete order in which law is interpreted and implemented. Against normativism which starts with the superiority of the norm and the system of norms over their application, Schmitt argues that 'the norm or rule does not create the order; on the contrary, only on the basis and in the framework of a given order does it have a certain regulating function with a relatively small degree of validity, independent of the facts of the case' (pp. 48–9). Just as the Ordoliberals gave priority to the actuality of a specific economic order over the supposed naturalness of the market, so Schmitt gives priority to the historically specific concrete juridical order over the abstractness of law in a system of norms. In this sense, there is an almost perfect concordance between Krings's assertion of *ordo* as a condition of being, Eucken's view of the economic order as realizing the essence of competition, and Schmitt's view of the juridical order as the basis of legal norms. In all cases, order-thinking seeks to stitch together the transcendent and immanent orders, and their respective powers, from the side of the immanent, that is, from the side not of being but of praxis.

Agamben will thus put this: 'Trinitarian *oikonomia*, *ordo*, and *gubernatio* constitute an inseparable triad, whose terms interpenetrate, insofar as they name the new figure of ontology that Christian theology bequeaths to modernity' (2011: 91). If this statement is open to the criticism of being an overly hasty generalization, let us just say that there has been a demonstrable conscious appropriation of these theological concepts by many 'modern', secular, and liberal, political, economic and social thinkers and thought-collectives.

7.11 We have started with the hypothesis that the concept of power is marked by a signature, which is the reversible movement between two shifting poles: power to and power over, power as capacity and power as right, facilitative power and repressive power and so on. Foucault and Schmitt are major thinkers in relation to this concept because they have identified multiple instances of this signature but, ultimately, have tried to stabilize the concept of power by locating its essence or truth at one or other of the juridical-sovereign or economic-governmental poles. But a signature exceeds the concept and keeps referring it back to a determinate field of interpretation. In both cases, as we have shown, they fail to abolish the other pole of this field: in Foucault's case, the shadow of the sovereign falls over the entirety of his work and disables his understanding of law. In Schmitt's case, he cannot think the governmental-economic character of power: he is opposed to the weak, quantitatively total state, the welfare or administrative state, and views economic rationality as a depoliticization. However, at least at one crucial moment, after the collapse of constitutional sovereignty in Germany, he is led towards, however briefly and opportunistically, accenting the immanence of power in the racial model of the relation between *Führer* and impolitical *Volk* and in a concrete-order thinking that 'will measure up to the numerous new tasks of the governmental, *völkish*, economic, and ideological condition and to the new form of community' (Schmitt, 2004b: 98).

Agamben now offers us the view that 'order' is not so much a concept as a signature (2011: 87). For him, order is a signature in the sense that it allows a displacement across domains without altering the fundamental semiotic relations. The notion of order thereby helps the bipolar model of power shift from a theological to a secular domain. It takes a set of semiotic relations and places them within another interpretative and pragmatic field; thus he claims it moves power from the theological to the secular. From our perspective, to what extent the secular notion of order borrows or transfers from theological sources in any given case is a matter of empirical and contextual intellectual history. We do not have to follow Agamben in attributing a general transference mechanism to the signature.

However, Agamben demonstrates that 'order' is also a signature in another and more fundamental sense: it is, as we have seen, a term that permits the articulation of the field of relations that constitute power, defined by the transcendent, onto-theological pole and the economic-governmental or immanent one. In this respect, Agamben makes a basic contribution to our understanding of power.

Perhaps the easiest way to understand this second work of 'order' is to view power in its legal-constitutional theorization and the distinction between constituent and constituted power and to compare it to its work in the divine government of the world. For Thomas Aquinas, the work of God is twofold: 'the first is creation; the second, God's government of the things created' (in Agamben, 2011: 92). For Thomas, this is precisely mirrored in the worldly kingdom in which 'if there was no one to establish the city or the kingdom, there would be no question of governing the kingdom'. It thus follows, 'if one does not know how a kingdom is established, one cannot fully understand the task of its government'. Thomas uses the words order and ordering to grasp this dual relation of the creation of an order and the executive government of it: *ordinatio* and *ordinis executio*. He does so in respect of both secular and divine government. In this context, as Agamben notes (p. 93), it would be interesting to trace the sources of the distinction of Abbé Sieyès between *pouvoir constituant* and *pouvoir constitué* – constituent power and constituted power – with the difference that God is replaced by the people as constituent subject. The notion of order thus bridges the constitution (or 'ordination') of a political order and the subsequent executive ordering or government of it.

Nevertheless, we have not quite finished the elaboration of the paradigm of economic theology. There is one more key term – providence.

Providence

7.12 We have noted a misstep in Foucault's genealogy of liberalism in his discussion of Adam Smith's metaphor of the 'invisible hand' (see §4.7). Foucault rejected a theological interpretation of the metaphor as being something like Malebranche's 'providential god' and subsequently concluded that economics is an atheistic discipline (2008: 278, 282). We have also observed that once the proper place is restored to Malthus's principle of population it becomes clear that its author regarded the principle as a form of divine providence and sought to resolve the consequent theodicy. Given that the principle is a presupposition of the formation of classical political economy, and its paradigmatic demonstration in David Ricardo's differential theory of rent, we were compelled to depart from the characterization of economics as an 'atheistic' discipline.

One possible reason for this misstep is Foucault's neglect of the medieval discussion of the divine government of the world, which, as Agamben notes (2011: 142), precedes the 'late' emergence of a doctrine of government and public administration. For while Foucault draws upon Thomas Aquinas's *De Regno*, he ignores his exemplary discussion, *De gubernatione mundi*, in his *Summa Theologiae* (p. 111). It is Agamben's contention that a work such as this had already elaborated the canon of concepts for what would become a science of government in the doctrine of the providential government of the world.

The doctrine addresses precisely the question that animated the principle of population: God's government of the world (the principle) and the problem of theodicy, reconciling the concomitant evil with the existence of a benign all-powerful deity. On the basis of Agamben's exegesis, we can say that the intersection of these two problems is already present in the work of the third century Stoic philosopher, Chrysippus, *On Providence*, later taken up in the 'hair-splitting' debate between Bayle and Leibniz (Agamben, 2011: 117). Yet it is Alexander of Aphrodisias who puts his finger on the basic problem, that of the particular consequences or effects of the 'divine power we call "nature"' (in Agamben, 2011: 117). The example of someone killed by a lightning strike is one not foreseen by providence 'since it did not fall for that purpose [of killing] nor was there any awareness on the part of the demiurge that created the lightning' (p. 118). Yet, given that it is possible to observe that lightning occurs in a thunderstorm, and that it strikes near to particular objects, such as trees, we have a third category between the general law of providence and its accidental effect which Agamben calls a 'collateral effect that is calculated'. By not going into the open or near trees, or by staying indoors, we have, in our example, sought to avoid the detrimental effects of lightning strikes, that is, we have sought to govern our conduct. By such a discovery, the theory of providence, without intention, founds a notion of government. 'The god that reigns, yet does not govern, thus makes possible the government. In other words, the government is the epiphenomenon of providence (or kingdom)' (p. 118).

This, we should note in passing, is exactly what the principle of population does. The tendency of the rate of growth of the population to outstrip that of the means of its subsistence produces the collateral effects of famines, diseases and wars. Yet, because it is possible to calculate these collateral effects of the providential government of the world, we can act to prevent them first, by the 'preventive check', that is by restricting procreation, and second, by the reformation of the poor laws and the establishment of colonial administration. In other words, we establish a particular form of government.

After reviewing the providence-fate distinction in a number of authors (including Plutarch and Proclus), Agamben finds that it enters Christian theology with Boethius (2011: 126–7) and his imagined discussion with Lady Philosophy. She tells Boethius that God governs things in a twofold manner. The first is providence, in the manner of 'the purity of God's understanding' (in Agamben, 2011: 127). The second is fate, governing 'with reference to all things, whose motion and order [i.e. God's understanding] it controls'. It is worth quoting a few lines for the 'peremptory clarity' with which Boethius states the twofold character of the government of the world:

Providence is the divine reason itself. It is set at the head of all things and disposes of things. Fate, on the other hand, is the planned order inherent in things subject to change through which Providence binds everything in its own allotted place ... So the unfolding of the plan in time when brought together as a unified whole in the foresight of God's mind is Providence; and the same unified whole when dissolved and unfolded in the course of time is Fate. They are different, but the one depends on the other. The order of Fate is derived from the simplicity of Providence. (Boethius, 1969: 104)

Here, then, is the paradigm of the relationship between God's sovereignty and His government of the world. When we realize that the word for 'order' in the above quote is *dispositio*, we see once again the interaction between the divine monarchy and the divine economy, the being of God and His praxis, His intelligence and His *oikonomia*. The activity of government is at once providential, in that it seeks to provide for the good of all, and fateful, in that it distributes the good to individuals, according to the chain of secondary causes and effects. 'In other words, the governmental machine functions like an incessant theodicy, in which the Kingdom [i.e. *Regno* or Reign] of providence legitimates and founds the Government of fate, and the latter guarantees the order that the former had established and renders it operative' (Agamben, 2011: 129).

   Yet there is still another aspect of this providential government to understand. For, as we saw in Malthus, humans are endowed with (or led by providence to possess) a reason and intellect and thus able to adapt their behaviour to the providential order and prudently calculate their future capacity to provide for their children. Indeed it is only by 'grace' of the principle, that 'chaotic matter' will lead to an 'awakened Mind', that humans will learn to place order on the world, and they will be led to industry and rationality. In this respect, Agamben's treatment of Thomas Aquinas is illuminating (2011: 131–9). For Thomas, divine government guides creatures toward their end. But it is not violent, in the sense of 'against nature', and must act by means of the very nature of the things governed (Agamben, 2011: 132). But God endows humans with a particular nature, characterized by reason and intellect that lead them to the truth and by language with which they form themselves into societies (p. 136). Moreover their ultimate aim exceeds their natural faculty. Humans through their freedom, that is, their own self-government, are responsible for their own salvation. But how is it possible to reconcile divine government with this self-government of creatures? (p. 133)

God cannot intervene in the necessary space of first causes, that is, having established the world according to general laws, he cannot revoke them and begin again. However, he can intervene in the contingent space of secondary causes and the pre-eminent form in which he does this is the miracle (Agamben, 2011: 134). Further, Thomas proposes a theory of grace as a kind of gratuitous help from God, not as a divine compulsion upon self-governing creatures but as a little help to exercise their freedom towards their proper end, a kind of concurrence between grace and freedom (ibid.: 137).

Just as the miracle in Thomist theology does not undo the general providence established by God, so the event (in the form of the collateral effects of the principle of population, famine, epidemic, or war) does not undo the principle of population, but, like the miracle, helps humans conduct themselves to achieve their proper end, e.g. by refraining from excessive procreation, saving for bad times, and exercising proper prudence and forethought. Just as humans receive the little help in governing themselves by God's grace, so they will by the proper form of government. That government, like that grace, must be in concurrence with humans' freedom. This, we must note, is exactly the form the liberal art of government will assume in Foucault's genealogy.

7.13 Agamben notes approvingly that the ninth-century Arabic author, Jabir ibn Hayyan, interpreted Alexander of Aphrodisias's second-century work *La provvidenza* in a manner that 'turns it into a kind of original paradigm of liberalism' (2011: 119). Again, we might wish to be a bit more cautious in the links we make. Let us simply say that the Scholastic rendering of divine government in terms of the distinctions between providence and fate and primary and secondary causes, together with its notions of grace and miracle, provides an illuminating perspective on aspects of liberal and neoliberal approaches to governing.

There is a little story that seems to sum up precisely the connection between liberalism, the catastrophe event, the miracle, and the grace of liberal government. Less than a year before his death at the age of 94, the most famous of the American Chicago School economists, Milton Friedman, wrote an opinion piece for the *Wall Street Journal* entitled 'The promise of vouchers' (2005). It was written in the immediate aftermath of Hurricane Katrina, which had devastated New Orleans and much of the surrounding area. In it he argued that rather than rebuilding its public school system, the state of Louisiana should provide parents with sizeable vouchers so they could choose the schools they considered best for their children, including privately run, publicly funded 'charter schools'. The idea had already been proposed by the Heritage Foundation, a free-market think-tank, less than two weeks after the breaching of the levees (Klein, 2008: 410), but we should also note that there was already state legislation in place to facilitate such schools (Frazier-Anderson, 2008). Friedman's piece is revealing for its final paragraph:

> If, by a political miracle, Louisiana could overcome the opposition of the unions and enact universal vouchers, it would not only serve itself, it would also render a service to the rest of the country by providing a large scale example of what the market can do for education when permitted to operate. (2005: no pagination)

It is beyond the scope of the present study to judge whether the outcome of this agitation indeed created a political miracle. Naomi Klein testifies that with the federal administration of George W. Bush backing a plan to divert funds from rebuilding public schools to vouchers for charter schools, the policy plan proved spectacularly successful, and that within 19 months, the old public school system had been almost obliterated, and the union's contract terminated (2008: 5–6). There is certainly independent evidence that the students eventually returning to school after Katrina found a very different school system, which was now tilted heavily towards the charter schools (Frazier-Anderson, 2008: 410–11). If this is the case, the evil of the loss of life and the destruction of housing neighbourhoods were the collateral damage of a providential order that gave the state of Louisiana, together with its federal backers, the miraculous opportunity to reorganize its public education system by reconstructing it in a manner consistent with that order, as a state-funded market. Thus like Malthus's famine and war, the catastrophic event occasions a miracle that instructs humans on the proper way to reach their true end, with the help of the grace of proper government.

There is a fundamental relationship between the providential order, the event as biocatastrophe, the collateral effect that can be calculated, and the praxis of government in both liberalism and neoliberalism. Liberalism imagines the economy as a natural order and neoliberalism as one that has a social, political and legal order as its condition. Similarly, while it was possible for liberalism to imagine it could calculate the collateral effects of this order, contemporary liberal governing often claims only that it is possible to anticipate and prepare for the radical uncertainty of catastrophe (Aradau and van Munster, 2011). Nonetheless it would seem possible to extend this framework to the analysis of the management of pandemics, natural disasters, human-induced climate change and, even, financial crises (Walker and Cooper, 2011).

While this story perhaps does not go beyond an analogy, we might recall that, in an introduction to another book, Friedman referred to himself as 'like an old-fashioned preacher delivering a Sunday sermon' (1968: 21). However, Hayek's economic-theological account of the competitive market price as originating with sixteenth-century Jesuits (see §7.2) suggests a more conscious appropriation. The broader question of religion and the renewal of liberalism was already foreshadowed in his opening remarks to the first conference at Mont Pèlerin (Hayek, 1967a: 155): 'I am convinced that unless this breach between true liberal and religious convictions can be healed there is no hope for a revival of liberal forces.' The new liberalism projected in this sermon from the Mont sought the grace of true religion to achieve nothing less than the salvation of the world.

7.14 Giorgio Agamben does not pretend to follow his theological genealogy through to the present day. In fact his methodology does not oblige him to do so, consisting of a movement backwards towards a 'moment of arising' of fundamental distinctions operative in the present (2009: 95). He even admits that 'the term *oikonomia* disappears from the language of the West in the course of the Middle Ages' (2011: 277). Yet, he does make a number of strategic links to the present in an appendix.

The focus of these links is, *pace* Foucault, Malebranche's 1680 theodicy, *Treatise on Nature and Grace*, and its relation to Rousseau's theory of the general will in *The Social Contract*. Malebranche, Agamben indicates, reduces the problem of providential government to the relation between God acting by 'general will' through 'general laws' and his acting through 'occasional causes' (as secondary causes are now called) (2011: 263–4). The latter simply give effect to the general will. If, on the other hand, we have God acting through a 'particular will' that is independent of his general laws, then we have a miracle. Even miracles, however, can be reduced to general will by making them the consequences of a general law that angels have been given the power to act contrary to other general laws. In this respect, Agamben notes, Malebranche's notion of a miracle corresponds exactly to Schmitt's exception (Agamben, 2011: 268). Both have the capacity to suspend norms or general laws but neither of them are outside the general juridical framework. In all these ways, Malebranche's 'simple and general laws' are indistinguishable from those being discovered at the same time by modern science. As one commentator put it, God coincides with the order of the world, the natural order, and could not violate that order and still be God (Agamben, 2011: 266).

Agamben traces Malebranche's language and concepts forward in two directions, one leading to the modern theory of democratic sovereignty as formulated by Rousseau, and the second to the *l'ordre naturel* of Quesnay and the Physiocrats. Agamben argues that it is not just the notions of 'general will' and 'particular will', which he suggests historians have already demonstrated beyond doubt, that link Malebranche to Rousseau, but the fact that 'the entire governmental machine of providence is transferred from the theological to the political sphere' (2011: 272). This gives Rousseau's public economy its fundamental structure and apparatus of articulated distinctions, such as sovereign power/government, general will/particular will, and legislative power/executive power (pp. 272–5). Agamben cites Rousseau's criticism of *les politiques*, who spend their time dividing sovereign authority, whose error arises 'from regarding as elements of this authority what are only emanations of it' (p. 274). He further shows that, contrary to those who associated this vexed term 'emanations' with mysticism and the Kabbalah, the term corresponds in Rousseau to the procession of the persons of the Trinitarian economy and the theory of causes in the providential paradigm (p. 275). The cost of this transposition of these theological distinctions is borne, according to Agamben, by the history of modern democracy which is 'nothing but the progressive coming to light of the substantial untruth of the primacy of legislative power' and which today means we have 'the government and the economy's overwhelming domination of a popular sovereignty emptied of all meaning' (p. 276).

For Agamben, the influence of Malebranche and the providential paradigm on Quesnay and the Physiocrats does not require further proof (2011: 280). He follows the use of the term 'economy' in relation to *l'économie animale* from Quesnay's earlier medical writings, where it means all that is conducive to a 'state of health', to its later application to society and its government. 'Economy for Quesnay means order, and order founds government' (p. 281). Agamben argues that order acts as a signature that relates the theological order of the universe to the immanent order of human society. The political economy of the Physiocrats therefore emerges as a 'science of order', and as Le Trosne puts it in his *De L'ordre social:* 'There exists a *natural, immutable and essential order* instituted by God in order to govern civil societies in the way most advantageous to sovereigns and subjects: men have by necessity partly conformed to it; otherwise any association between them would be impossible' (in Agamben, 2011: 282). Societies must, continues Le Trosne, grasp the general principles of this order as a whole because, having a physical basis, they 'are the only means of growth of sustenance, riches, and populations and, consequently, for the prosperity of empires and for the measure of happiness that the social state entails' (ibid.)

In the same way that Weber concludes that modern capitalist behaviour is an economic rationalization of the Protestant ethic, that Schmitt views modern law as political rationalization of Catholic canon law, and that Foucault regards modern expertise as a secularization of the Catholic pastorate, Agamben proposes that political economy is a 'social rationalization of the providential *oikonomia*' (2011: 282). While it would be prudent to restrict this hypothesis to particular intellectual movements or 'thought collectives', such as the Physiocrats and Rousseau, we have indicated that economic theology can be found in both the providential paradigm and theodicy that classical political economy would receive from Malthus, in the role of 'order' in the Ordoliberals, and in the views of key neoliberal figures such as Hayek, Eucken and Rüstow.

Three theses on 'the King reigns...'

7.15 We are now close to resolving, as far as possible when addressing the *arcana* of power, the mystery of this astonishing maxim: 'The king reigns, but he does not govern'. In earlier sections we noted how it had mislead Foucault (§4.8), Schmitt (§5.9) and Peterson (§7.4). Foucault read it as meaning much the same as his own injunction concerning the displacement of the pre-eminence of sovereignty, to 'cut off the king's head in political theory'. Schmitt read it in an almost converse way as a version of political theology that asserts the foundation of sovereign authority. For Peterson it became the hallmark of the illegitimate pagan and Jewish political theology.

For our own part, we are now in a position to propose that the phrase encapsulates three main claims about conceptions of power and the operation of power relations:

1 Both the concept and practice of power are caught between two poles, which might be expressed in terms of one or more of the following apparent antinomies: the ontological and the pragmatic; being and praxis; the sovereign and the governmental; the juridical and the economic; the theological and the secular; providence and fate; political theology and economic theology; reign and government, and so on.

2 It is necessary to address the way that theological, political and governmental rationalities, and academic cultures and discourses, seek to address the opposition between these poles. Following Agamben, theological discourses on the *oikonomia* of the Trinity, on divine, natural and worldly orders, and on providential government, have contributed notions of economy, order and providence, so that the caesura between these poles can be sutured, and power made operable. With Rousseau, Quesnay and the Physiocrats, with Adam Smith and Malthus, and with the Ordoliberals and other neoliberals, we have given examples of the transposition of these concepts into secular political, governmental and economic discourses.

3 This maxim, then, metaphorically expresses the very signature of power we have been following and establishes that any analysis of the exercise of power must go beyond the fruitful, but incomplete, questions of the 'how' of power posed by Foucault. We need also to ask: what transcendent and sovereign space of 'reign' is constituted or referred back to it in acts of governing? In the public governance of liberal-democratic societies, for instance, we might examine how professional expertise and institutions are rendered accountable and efficient, through what technologies, for which reasons and to what ends. But we need also to ask in whose name are they to be reformed, their performance enhanced and their quality ensured? The position of reign might be occupied in 'economic terms' by the global economy, or even the 'essence' of competition; it might be personified as 'the taxpayer'; it might be the

demands of international organizations and central banks; or it might be given in 'democratic terms' as 'the public', 'public opinion', the 'norms and values of the community', and so on. This kind of analysis also keeps in play the key questions of 'who decides?' and 'who judges?' Who, for example, decides when public order is in danger? Who decides what constitutes public opinion? Who judges that professionals and bureaucrats are unaccountable? By asking such questions, it keeps in play the constitution of the position of 'reign' as transcendent order and actual fact.

We could, in fact, use Agamben's work to gain insight into Foucault's demand to cut off the king's head in political theory and analysis. Oddly, he does not mention this well-known adage of decapitation. However, he provides us with a great number of examples of the imagery of a wounded, mutilated, useless or absent king. There is the wounded King of Arthurian legend, the *roi mehaigné*, who loses neither legitimacy nor sacredness as a 'paradigm of divided and impotent sovereignty' (2011: 69). There are many examples of the idle or useless King and these are in step with the Gnostic division between a good but idle god without relation to the world and an active and evil demiurge who intervenes and governs the world (p. 77). There is the doctrine of the *rex inutilis*, initially drawn from the assertion of papal power to depose the temporal sovereign, which became in the canon law of the twelfth and thirteenth centuries a doctrine of the separation of *dignitas* and *administratio*, of the office and the activity undertaken in that office (pp. 97–8).

The abjection of sovereignty implied in cutting off the king's head is continuous with these examples. To call for the academic decapitation of the juridical-institutional form of sovereignty is not to break open the space for a new paradigm of power, but to confirm the existing paradigm that rests on an articulation of an *always limited* sovereignty with effective power or, in Foucault's terms, governmentality. Moreover, were we to drag the decapitated body off and bury it, we would still have an 'empty throne'. Agamben provides examples of the images and actuality of the 'empty throne' in the Upanishads, Mycenaean Greece at Knossos, the ancient arches and apses of palaeo-Christian and Byzantine basilicas, and in the Septuagint (2011: 241–5). While he argues these are not a symbol of regality, the void is nonetheless a 'sovereign figure of glory'. In short, attempts at the decapitation, mutilation and burial of the King are part and parcel of the very 'economy' of power across many cultures. As we shall see, the empty throne might be viewed as the privileged object of sacred glorification and political acclamation. Divine and worldly reign is constituted through these practices and they are a part of the articulation of the poles of power and ensure its operability.

Three reservations

7.16 Agamben seeks now to answer von Seydel's question, 'what then remains of the "*régner*" if one removes "*gouverner*"?'. His answer is that the Kingdom, or Reign, is:

> the remainder that poses itself as the whole that infinitely subtracts from itself. Just as, in the divine *gubernatio* of the world, transcendence and immanence, *ordo ad deum* and *ordo ad invicem*, must be unceasingly distinguished for providential action to unceasingly join them, so the Kingdom [or Reign, *il Regno*] and the Government constitute a double machine, which is the place of a continuous separation and articulation. (2011: 99)

Later, this image of a 'double machine' is replaced by a series of oppositions with a specific accent:

> *What our investigation has shown is that the real problem, the central mystery of politics is not sovereignty, but government; it is not God, but the angel; it is not the king, but ministry; it is not the law, but the police – that is to say, the governmental machine that they form and support.* (Agamben, 2011: 276, original emphasis)

Agamben's work, which shows the reversibility between two shifting poles in the development of the concept and practice of power in Occidental societies, and its legacy to now 'global' notions of representative democracy and economy, is perhaps not the first to stress the need to articulate contemporary studies of governmentality with the operation of sovereign power and authority. Yet it is the broadest and deepest genealogy of the articulation of these two poles by way of an investigation of their 'moment of arising' within the theological and philosophical sources of this architectonics of power. However, despite acknowledging the massive achievement of Agamben's economic theology, we must withhold endorsement of aspects of both these conclusions in a number of ways.

1 In respect to the second of these quotations, it would appear that Agamben, at least in certain formulations, falls into the Foucauldian trap when he ultimately gives precedence to the governmental-economic axis. If Foucault occasionally falls into a historical-epochal bipolarity, in this formulation, Agamben would seem open to a trans-historical bipolarity. It would be unfortunate, indeed, if such a formulation were to undermine the fundamental insight he has gained.

2 Both of these quotations evidence the widespread tendency to describe the dual dimensional aspect of power relations as a 'machine'. We must assume that the choice of the terms 'providential machine' and 'governmental machine' is a deliberate one. However, as Agamben would be the first to point out, words and concepts carry their own excess and this one carries a particularly heavy load, not least its use in Hobbes's description of the Artificial Man, the Leviathan at the beginning of his great text (1996: 9). The metaphor of the machine moves what is an analytical observation about concepts and operations of power into a normative opposition to or awe at the machinery of power. It does this by a process of totalization and mythization as Schmitt, following Peterson, noted in his 1937 essay, 'The State as Mechanism in Hobbes and Descartes' (2008b: 91–103). For Schmitt, the image of the mortal god as machine is one 'whose "mortality" is based on the fact that one day it may be shattered by civil war or rebellion' (2008b: 100). Agamben's image of the alternative to the bipolar governmental machine is less dramatic, but no less resting on a complete de-totalization: that of the 'political operation' that 'deactivates and renders inoperative the technological-ontological apparatus' (2011: 253). It is possible to accept and use Agamben's historical and genealogical analysis of the relations of power, without accepting the normative-political project, at this stage relatively inchoate, that he attaches to it. Agamben's political radicality is thus in danger of distorting the contribution he has made to our understanding of power.

3 The answer to von Seydel's question is compelling but only in terms of the self-presentation of the reign or sovereign dimension of power. As Max Weber might have said about the modern state, it claims a monopoly of legitimate force within a domain while it divides and delegates that force onto multiple agents. Liberal critiques of state reason could equally be viewed as representing

sovereignty as comprehensive and transcendent. For our part, however, we are also concerned with the actuality of sovereign power and its concrete capacity or, better still, competence, and not simply its part within a conceptual apparatus. In this sense, sovereignty, at least in very important part, rests upon a singular competence to decide on the exception, that is, to decide when and where a threat to 'public order and security' is made and to act to overcome that threat, including when it is threatened by an external enemy.

If Foucault imagines his concepts and analyses as a 'tool box', and thus opened the possibility of different avenues of empirical study, it is not hard to imagine that Agamben offers us something like a 'jewel box' containing the most perfect, attentive analyses and the most lapidary of theses. One can admire and display these gems, but only in their uniqueness. They are very hard, if not impossible, to apply and use, and to reproduce.

8

GLORIOUS ACCLAIM

8.1 In an earlier section (§5.3) we noted Michel Foucault's observation that certain early modern texts advised that police 'must ensure the state's splendor', which is the 'visible beauty of the order and the beautiful radiating manifestation of a force' (2007: 313–14). He offered no explanation as to why the exercise of power in the state should be conceived in such terms. Perhaps he assumed that the splendour of the state, like the spectacle of the scaffold, belongs to an archaic form of power and that its remnants are today mere survivals in the face of a liberal governmental rationality. But such a view depends on the historical bipolar account of power Foucault attempted to reject in his lectures on governmentality. If we concur with the need to reject that account, then we cannot assume that what he calls here the splendour of the state is an insignificant component of the exercise of power. After all, among the liberal democracies, it is not only constitutional monarchies, such as the United Kingdom and the Scandinavian countries, but also republican governments, like the United States and France, that preserve rituals and symbols of state at formal occasions, receptions, the administering of oaths and so forth. And beyond the pomp and ceremonies of the grand occasions, there is the ever-present sombre ritual and dress of the court of law and the punctuation of the mundane existence of these societies by great spectaculars, sporting and media events. These festivals continue to organize the calendar within states and symbolize the relations between nations.

While the key finding of our engagement with Agamben's work *The Kingdom and the Glory* (2011) is its presentation of the architectonics of power as an articulation of sovereign reign and economic government, Agamben himself locates his central question elsewhere in the problem of the doxologies of sovereignty itself. He asks: 'Why does power need glory? If it is essentially force and capacity for action and government, why does it assume the rigid cumbersome and "glorious" form of ceremonies, acclamations, and protocols? What is the relation between economy and Glory?' (2011: xii).

The raising of such a 'why' question is anathema to a Foucauldian analytics with its emphasis on the 'how' question in the sense of 'what happens in the exercise of power?' The answer that Agamben gives at the very end of his book is not an analytical one but a kind of philosophical and political anthropology:

> What is at stake is the capture and inscription in a separate sphere of the inoperativity that is central to human life. The *oikonomia* of power places firmly at its heart, in the form of festival and glory, what appears to its eyes as the inoperativity of man and God, which cannot be looked at. (2011: 245)

If we are to understand what is at stake in Agamben's question and its answer, we clearly need to understand this 'inoperativity', which is 'the political substance of the Occident, the glorious nutrient of all power' and makes the human the 'Sabbatical animal par excellence' (2011: 246). The answer to his own central question will provide us with the key to the way in which Agamben will handle the signature of power.

Whatever we come to think of this particular answer, however, the question itself of the glorious form taken by power is one that should continue to be asked. It will help us formulate the constitution of the 'reign' axis of power. It will also illuminate what Schmitt (2008a: 272) called the 'rather obscure' but 'essential' aspect of political life: that of the public, and of publicity or public-ness.

Glory, acclamation and the public

8.2 Agamben has an extraordinary capacity for unearthing arcane but pertinent texts and his discussion of glory and acclamation uncovers yet another secret dossier between Erik Peterson and Carl Schmitt. Rather bizarrely, it is Peterson, notwithstanding his apparently anti-Semitic apocalyptics, who emerges as something of an unlikely hero, not only for his act of slaying Schmitt's political theology in a brief conclusion and a footnote but, by a strange twist, asserting the 'religio-political' character of both the celestial kingdom and the earthly Church which will participate in heavenly worship through its liturgy and acclamations (Peterson, 2011: 123). From this latter work, Agamben will not only derive a perspective on bureaucracy and its key concepts, such as hierarchy, office and ministry. He will also, starting with Peterson's earlier work on religious acclamations, modulated through Schmitt's theses on aspects of constitutional law, gain a point of reflection on democratic sovereignty and the study of political acclamations and public opinion.

At stake is a small book Peterson published almost simultaneously with his more famous *Monotheism as Political Problem*, entitled *The Book on the Angels* (2011: 106–42). For him, while the Christian-theological postulate of a triune God does not derive from a monarchical political order, the organization of the Church itself has an eminently political and public character, and the presence and worship of the angels are central to that publicity. Thus just as 'the emperor demonstrates the public character of his public authority when he appears in the company of his bodyguard, so Christ demonstrates the public character [*Öffentlichkeit*] of his religio-political authority when he is accompanied by the bodyguard of his angels at holy Mass' (p. 134). Moreover, Peterson argues, this public or political character has not been bestowed by the State on the Church but 'belongs intrinsically to the Church as such, whose Lord, as heavenly king, also possesses a heavenly public nature' (pp. 134–5).

For a text written by a theologian who had just rejected Christian political theology, *The Book on the Angels* indeed employs a remarkable amount of political imagery. It begins: 'The Church leads from the earthly to the heavenly Jerusalem, from the city of the Jews to the city of angels and saints' (Peterson, 2011: 107). It speaks of angels and saints as those 'who are enrolled in heaven as citizens' and cites Paul to the effect that 'we have our commonwealth in heaven' (ibid.). Agamben notices this and isolates a number of propositions (2011: 145–6). Firstly, that the cult of the heavenly Church and the liturgy of the earthly Church have an 'originary relationship' with politics. Secondly, that Peterson affirms the political-religious character of the celestial city and the Church. Thirdly, that while he denies the political-theological interpretation of the Church, he affirms its politico-religious character. Thus 'if politics, from the Christian standpoint, is solely an angelological-cultural relation between the Church and the celestial kingdom, all extrapolation of this "politico-religious" character from the worldly sphere is illegitimate' (Agamben, 2011: 146). Finally, this is consistent because the apostles have abandoned every earthly city 'to turn to the celestial Jerusalem, as a city and regal court, but also as a temple and place of worship' (p. 146). This move has 'the final consequence that the entire universe is borne along by the song of praise'.

Several further points should be noted here from Peterson. Firstly, the politicality of the Church consists in its public-ness or publicity and it is the work of the angels and of the humans who join them in hymns of praise such as 'Holy, Holy, Holy' (*Sanctus, sanctus, sanctus*) to give voice to this publicity. As Peterson put its, '[a]ll cultic acts of the Church would thus either be a participation of the angels in the earthly cult, or, to put it the other way around, all earthly worship by the Church would be understood as participation in the worship that the angels offer to God in heaven' (2011: 108). Or, as Agamben interprets: '[t]he political vocation of man is an angelic vocation, and the angelic vocation is the song of glory' (2011: 147). The other point is the division of the functions of angels between 'ministering', which is the bringing of divine announcements and particular grace to human beings, and 'assisting', the basking in the intimate relationship with the divine, that is in the glorification of God (Agamben, 2011: 148).

We might also want to note the presence of the concept of order, or *ordo*, in Peterson only one year (1935) before the Ordoliberals (Böhm, Eucken and Grossmann-Doerth, 1989) were issuing their manifesto:

> The cultus of the Church thus culminates in the religio-political dimension or, to put it differently, in the *ordo* concept of a heavenly hierarchy. So the thesis that the Christian cultus has an original relationship to the political sphere is confirmed once again. (Peterson, 2011: 123)

As we have already noted in §7.10, the notion of order was circulating widely in both German theological writings and in writings on economic policy before and during the 1930s and before that in the sociology and jurisprudence of Schmitt and Weber. In Peterson's case it is a way of thinking the relationship between the political organization of the heavenly sphere and the actual political form of the earthly Church and its liturgy, that is, the earthly government of human spiritual life. In the case of Eucken and his colleagues, it is a way of thinking the relationship between the order of the human essence and the requirements of economic and social policy, or the government of human material life. In fact, one might argue that the relationship is even closer. In both cases, the concept of order makes possible the fulfilment of the spiritual-sensual telos of humankind.

We can further observe that what Peterson studied is very much akin to a version of Schmitt's juridical rationalization of political form in the Catholic Church. In this sense, Peterson examines the medieval rationalities of Church government not simply of the earthly Church but also the celestial one it invokes.

Under Peterson's authority, then, Agamben sets his task as the investigation of glory and glorification and the parallels, overlaps and grey zones between liturgical acclamation of God and popular acclamations of Kings and Emperors. This leads him to examine the medieval discussion of angels and their dual roles and identities around the higher-status contemplation, or 'assisting' in the worship of God, and the lower-status 'administering' or efficacious fulfilment of His will in human matters. The analogies between hierarchy, ministry and orders of angels and bureaucracy can be drawn, so that Agamben concludes that long before the terminology of civil administration was developed, '[n]ot only the concept of hierarchy but also that of ministry and mission are ... first systematized in a highly articulated way precisely in relation to angelic activities' (2011: 158).

8.3 Peterson's influence on Schmitt helps push Agamben's thesis even further. Agamben argues that Schmitt's first encounter with Peterson is precisely on the problem of acclamation, when Schmitt cites Peterson's dissertation on the expression *Heis theos kai Christos* [one God in Christ], which examines its obscure, political foundations (2011: 168). This formula was not a profession of faith, argues Peterson, but an acclamation with links to those of the pagan Emperors, the cries of Orphic rituals, exorcisms, and the formulae of mysteric cults (Agamben, 2011: 160). An acclamation is 'an exclamation of praise, of triumph ... of laudation or of disapproval ... yelled by a crowd in determinate circumstances', sometimes accompanied by applause and gestures such as the raising of the right hand or waving of handkerchiefs (p. 169). It could assume the form of expression of the desire for victory, of life and fertility, of long life, strength and salvation, and approval and praise. Peterson argues that the expression acquires a juridical value when it acts not as a shortened electoral procedure but 'expresses, in the form of acclamation, the people's *consensus*' (p. 170).

In a 1927 paper on referenda, Schmitt cites this work to characterize a 'pure' or direct democracy in which 'the acclamation is the pure and immediate expression of the people as constituent democratic power' (Agamben, 2011: 171). Schmitt thus shifts Peterson's thesis to the profane and pushes it to an extreme. Drawing on Peterson's juridical and public character of the Christian people (the *laos*), Schmitt concludes that acclamations are present in all political communities; there is 'no state without the people and no people without acclamations' (in

Agamben, 2011: 172). He thus distinguishes between the constituent power of acclamation in contrast to the mere constituted or administrative form of power exercised through elections and referenda.

Schmitt's appropriation of Peterson on acclamation continues and provides another perspective on his critique of the privacy and secrecy of the electoral procedures of representative democracies. In *The Crisis of Parliamentary Democracy* he argues in a manner that is consistent with Peterson's work not only on acclamation but also on glorification and publicity:

> The people exist only in the sphere of publicity. The unanimous opinion of one hundred million private persons is neither the will of the people nor public opinion. The will of the people can be expressed just as well and perhaps better through acclamation, through something taken for granted, an obvious and unchallenged presence, than through the statistical apparatus that has been constructed with such meticulousness in the last fifty years. (Schmitt, 1985: 16)

Schmitt compares the vital sense of direct democracy to the artificial machinery of parliament. The acclamation is not a quick and efficient way to form a majority but a fundamental expression of democratic sovereignty. The acclamation, derived from pagan religious and political ritual, via the liturgy of the Church, thus indicates 'the inescapable contradiction of liberal individualism and democratic homogeneity' (1985: 17).

Nevertheless, in his *Constitutional Theory*, Schmitt will also find a proxy for political acclamations in contemporary liberal democracy: that of public opinion, which 'arises and exists in an "unorganized" form' (2008a: 275). While a privatized 'secret individual ballot' and the mere 'adding up of the opinions of isolated private people' do not fully encompass the sociological and legally diffuse notion of public opinion or of 'the people' on which it rests, these 'registration methods are only a means of assistance, and as such they are useful and valuable'. Schmitt also concedes the role of parties and demagogues in the formation of public opinion and, in his own time, 'the press, film and other methods of psycho-technical handling of great masses of people'. Schmitt thus adds the practices of the formation of modern public opinion to political and religious acclamation as rites of glorification of sovereignty and political power. Indeed public opinion becomes the modern type of political acclamation.

In a remarkable passage from 1928, which foreshadows the critique of social media, blogging, and the Internet, Schmitt suggests:

It is fully conceivable that one day through ingenious discoveries, every single person, without leaving his apartment, could continuously express his opinions on political questions though an apparatus and that all these opinions would be automatically registered by a central office, where one would only need to read them off. That would not be an especially intensive democracy, but it would provide proof that the state and the public were fully privatized. It would not be public opinion, for even the shared opinion of millions of private people produces no public opinion. The result is only a sum of private opinions. In this way, no common will arises, no volonté générale; only the sum of all individual wills, a volonté de tous, does. (2008a: 274)

The central office is of course the Internet where the shared opinions, which are likely to be on anything but politics, but are also on politics, can be more or less read by anyone (and the reader, like the writer, does not have to leave her apartment). But for Schmitt all the opinions found on the Internet remain apolitical until they become those of a people, for there is 'no people without public and no public without people' (2008a: 272). The people, he later suggests, are those who share enough so that 'the people can have the political consciousness that can distinguish between friend and enemy (p. 275), thus returning us to his view of the essence of the political.

Another way of thinking about the threshold at which this 'privatized public' can become 'public opinion' is when it enters the sphere of publicity and visibility, and to where it becomes 'taken for granted' and an 'obvious and unchallenged presence'. Public opinion, as the modern kind of political acclamation, will lead to the study of the media and the spectacle, to the various ways in which something becomes unchallengeable and absolutely present, and therefore to what might be called an analytics of publicity.

8.4 Agamben is led by Peterson's work, and Schmitt's appropriation of it, to analyse religious and political acclamation through multiple empirical illustrations. These include: primitive Church liturgy, derived from *leitourgia* (from *laos*) or 'public service', and the term Amen by which the faithful constitute themselves as the people (2011: 174–5); Andreas Adöldi's work on imperial Roman ceremonies and their 'technico-juridical' significance (pp. 176–7); E.P. Schramm's research on *Staatssymbolik* including on monograms, seals and flags (pp. 178–9); von Amira's 'archaeology of right' and on hand gestures and oaths (p. 180); the Roman republic's *fasces lictoriae*, the rods and axe assemblage borne by a special and deadly corporation, the *lictores*, who always accompanied the consul (pp. 182–4); the intricacies of Byzantine imperial ceremony and acclamation (pp. 186–8); and the work of Ernst Kantorowicz, particularly his *Laudes Regiae*, which deals with particular acclamations that developed fully in what he called 'Carolingian political theology' and began with the phrase *Christus vincit, Christus regnat, Christus imperat* [Christ conquers, Christ reigns, Christ commands] (pp. 188–93). All this is exacting material. Some of it is by those who developed strong ties to National Socialism (Schramm and von Amira). In a wider sense, the academic discussion of political acclamation, myths and symbols reached its heights during the period when the squares, *piazze* and *Plätzen* of Europe heard the acclamations of fascism. Agamben calls for an 'archaeology of glory', which would be a science dedicated to the history of the ceremonial aspects of power and right (p. 168). Let us, however, simply concentrate on one of these sources.

The most interesting chapter of Kantorowicz's book *Laudes Regiae* (1946) is perhaps the final one. For just as J.G.A Pocock gave his 'Machiavellian moment' a contemporary actuality by commenting on postmodern and post-industrial America and the Watergate scandal in 1975, so in 1941, when Kantorowicz submitted the manuscript, he finished his work by comparing the revival of the *laudes* in the Church by the Liturgical Movement with the political revival of the *laudes* as an acclamation in authoritarian and fascist regimes. He finds the *Führer* cult of the dictators, if not the new festivals of Christ the King, 'caricatures of life' which are nonetheless instructive (1946: 180).

Of concern for Kantorowicz are the overlaps between the religious and political revival of the acclamation. The beginnings of the Christian movement lie with the revival of the *laudes* by musicologists in the final decades of the nineteenth century in a drive for the reform of the Gregorian chant. This was promoted by the Benedictine scholarly battle cry of a return to the sources. The *laudes*, Kantorowicz notes, were reintroduced in Rome with the coronation of Pope Pius X in 1903 and eventually the musical reformers merged with other ecclesiastical activists to form a Liturgical Movement, in which 'the truly vital forces within the Roman Church have gathered' (1946: 183). While neither Kantorowicz nor Agamben make a point of it, it is reasonable to conclude that as the work of a Catholic convert, Peterson's *The Book on the Angels* is a kind of manifesto for this movement.

During this same period, the *laudes* reappeared on the political stage 'along with what was believed the new lodestar of political life: totalitarianism and dictatorship' (Kantorowicz, 1946: 184). In fact, Kantorowicz shows how one fed off the other. In a context of friction and counter-challenges between the Holy See and the Fascist government in Italy, Pius XI instituted a new feast of Christ the King in 1925. The familiarity and popularity of the *laudes* was manifest when, on the announcement of the election of Pius XII in 1939, 'the throng crowding the square in front of St Peter's saluted the new pontiff, as he gave his benediction from the balcony, by bursting spontaneously into the old, and yet new, chant of *Christus vincit, Christus regnat, Christus imperat*' (pp. 184–5).

Fascist movements, often with explicit Catholic and clerical components, in Spain during the Civil War, and in Mexico and Belgium, drew upon the rallying cry of Christ the King, and, Kantorowicz observes, political acclamations were 'indispensable to the emotionalism of a Fascist regime' (1946: 185). Kantorowicz finishes his book by recalling hearing a *laudes* taken from a Fascist hymnbook in Italian basilicas, which in Latin bestowed 'perpetual peace, life and health' on not only the Pope and the King but also on 'Duce Benito Mussolini, the glory of the Italian nation' (p. 186). In a footnote he notes the 'strangely egocentric' character of Nazi acclamations and links the acclamation of March 1938, *Ein Reich, Ein Volk, Ein Führer* to those 'brilliantly discussed by Peterson' in his dissertation (p. 185, n. 22).

Basing himself on Kantorowicz and the other authors we have mentioned, Agamben argues that glory is the place where the relationship between theology and politics merges and he cites Thomas Mann to the effect that religion and politics 'exchange clothes', but without there necessarily being a body underneath (2011: 194). The 'garment of glory' is for Agamben a signature that marks bodies politically and theologically, and is the place where the boundaries between politics and theology become indistinct.

A little later in his text, Agamben appears to remove the very conceptual ladder which has allowed him to follow this debate when he argues that it is not necessary to share Schmitt's thesis on secularization in order to affirm that political problems become more intelligible if they are related to theological exemplars. 'On the contrary we have tried to show that this comes about because doxologies and acclamations in some sense constitute a threshold of indifference between politics and theology' (2011: 229–30). Rather than an analogical relationship between theological and political concepts, Agamben claims to have discovered, or returned to, their indifference or the point prior to which they would be separated, the precious 'moment of arising' of his philosophical archaeology.

Agamben's conclusion dazzles us with glory. If, he asks, the governmental machine works along the two poles then what function does glory play in it? His answer is that it allows us 'to bridge the fracture between theology and economy that the doctrine of the trinity has never been able to completely resolve and for which the dazzling figure of glory is able to provide a possible conciliation' (2011: 230).

While there is no doubt an important political function of glorification in the constitution of sovereign powers, perhaps Agamben has forgotten his own earlier conclusions about the providential apparatus and the role of the miracle (or event), and the collateral effect that can be calculated, in the generation of the economic-governmental dimension of power.

8.5 Agamben's evidentiary apparatus is extremely rich and it is not our intention to do justice to all of it. However, one final key piece of evidence starts with Marcel Mauss's unfinished doctoral study of prayer (2003; Agamben, 2011: 224). In his initial definition of prayer, Mauss makes two important distinctions. One is between manual and oral rites, 'the first consists in movements of the body and objects, the second in ritual locutions' (2003: 56). Prayer is an oral rite. But within oral rites, there are magical spells and incantations, and 'the oath, the verbal contract in a religious wedding, the religiously-founded wish, the blessing or curse, the vow, the oral dedication, etc.'. All of these have the essential aim of 'modifying the state of a profane thing'. Prayer is by contrast the means of acting on sacred beings; if there is a benefit expected in the earthly realm 'this is only a byproduct and does not dominate the actual mechanism of the rite'. Mauss concludes: '*prayer is a religious rite which is oral and bears directly on the sacred*' (p. 57, original emphasis).

Mauss proceeds to explore the notion of prayer by asking, in a question which amuses the current author (as a native of its predicate) if only for its outstanding, if apparently benign, Eurocentrism, 'Do prayers exist in Australia?' (2003: chapter title, p. 69). He then draws upon research such as that reported in Sir Baldwin Spencer and F.J. Gillen's book *The Native Tribes of Central Australia* (1899), and in particular the ceremonies of the Arunta people (more commonly known today as the Aranda people). The two authors, Mauss tells us in an extended footnote, claimed to have been 'completely initiated' among the Arunta, although he gives a long list of the deficiencies of their research, which he, nevertheless, admired for the 'marvellous sense of facts' (pp. 110–12). In fact, while Spencer was an Oxford educated British biologist and ethnologist who settled in Australia, Francis James Gillen was the Australian-born Post and Telegraph Station Master at Alice Springs and, collaterally, Special Magistrate and Sub-Protector of Aborigines. He had distinguished himself by trying to ameliorate the 'dispersal' policy, a euphemism for the murder of Aborigines, and charged (without ultimate success) a notorious police constable with 'aboriginal homicide' (Mulvaney, 1983: 6–7). In these positions, then, Gillen was responsible for both the administration of the juridical order of sovereignty in the interior of the antipodean continent and the mundane governmentalization of the Indigenous population. It was through the latter that he would lead Mauss to the conclusion that despite 'its simplicity, even its crudeness', 'Australian prayer nevertheless contains all the essential elements of the more complex and refined rites to which idealist elements give the name prayer' (2003: 67).

Perhaps even more extraordinary is that the Arunta people and the colonial Gillen, via Spencer and Mauss, and his uncle and close colleague, Emile Durkheim, will lead Agamben to what he regards as the central mystery of the very power Gillen himself was in charge of establishing in the British colony of South Australia, itself soon to be a constituent state of the new Commonwealth of Australia. We should note, however, that the area of the Arunta people would soon be placed outside that new state, and they would become British subjects in a Northern Territory, administered by this Commonwealth.

Drawing on his dissertation, and on his review of Sylvain Levi's work on Brahmin religion, Agamben shows that for Mauss, using prayer as an example, the rites of glorification produce the glory which is the very substance of God, thus confirming Durkheim's thesis that the gods would die if they were not were worshipped (Agamben, 2011: 227). This point, confirmed by rabbinical literature and the Kabbalah (p. 227), and Mauss's unpublished work on nourishment (*anna*) in Brahmana (pp. 232–4), is that worship is central to the working of divine government. By extension, Agamben concludes, profane acclamations are not just an ornament of the political but found and justify it (p. 230).

Agamben thus manages to show that as far as the study of glory and practices of glorification and acclamation are concerned, theology and politics become increasingly difficult to distinguish. Following another indication by Schmitt (in his *Constitutional Theory*) on the nexus between public opinion, acclamation and public law (Schmitt, 2008a: 272; see §8.3), Agamben views public opinion as the contemporary equivalent of acclamation and argues that the media takes on a doxological function in the will-formation of the contemporary citizenry (2011: 255–6). With reference to Guy Debord's 'society of the spectacle', the media become the force of the acclamatory constitution of sovereign political power, of reign, that makes the liberal-democratic and capitalist power system operative. 'Contemporary democracy', Agamben concludes, 'is a democracy that is entirely founded on glory, that is, on the efficacy of acclamation, multiplied and disseminated by the media beyond all imagination' (2011: 256). In a parting shot, perhaps Agamben's own Parthian arrow, he argues (pp. 258–9) that theorists of communicative action such as Jürgen Habermas, seeking to liquefy popular sovereignty into communicative forms of will-formation, hand political power over to the media and its experts, and that the acclamations of the immediate presence of people in authoritarian-national regimes and the mediated communicative forms of liberal-democracies are but two sides of the same coin, that of glory.

All of this then allows Agamben to suggest, as he foreshadows in his preface, that 'the empty throne, the *hetoimasia tou thronou*, that appears on the arches and apses of the Paleochristian and Byzantine basilicas is perhaps, in this sense, the most significant symbol of power' (2011: xii). Why? The answer is that the empty throne, rather than a symbol of regality, is one of glory. 'Glory precedes the creation of the world and survives its end. The throne is empty not only because glory, though coinciding with the divine essence is not identified with it, but also because it is in its innermost self-inoperativity and sabbatism. The void is the sovereign figure of glory' (p. 245). Just as the rites of glorification actually constitute the glory that allows God to exist, political acclamations, in the broadest sense of public opinion, constitute the very sovereign power imagined in all its separateness and autonomy. By asserting that the sovereign pole of power is ultimately empty, Agamben seeks to find his way out of the signature of power. But as we foreshadowed in §7.15, has he not mistaken the *arcana* of sovereignty for its actuality, its competencies, and its materiality? Has he, in this respect, no longer in a bipolar epochal-historical sense but a bipolar transhistorical sense, fallen prey to the signature just as Schmitt and Foucault did, in their own ways, before him? Has he not sought to escape the signature of power by imagining the deactivation of a unitary Occidental bipolar power machine?

Inoperativity

8.6 This concept of 'inoperativity' (or *inoperosità* in Italian), which we have so far passed over without attention, is central to Agamben's project and fulfils several roles in respect to his approach to power. It is, first of all, a kind of political anthropogenesis. Thus in announcing his thesis, Agamben rejects the humanist-Marxist view of human species being as labour or production so that he might return politics to 'its central inoperativity, that is, to that operation that amounts to rendering inoperative all human and divine work' (2011: xiii).

Humans are thus not *homo faber* but beings whose contemplation of themselves and their own power of activity (what Spinoza calls 'self-contentment' or *acquiescentia in se ipso* (Agamben, 2011: 250)) make possible their entry into the political. 'Contemplation and inoperativity are in this sense the metaphysical operators of anthropogenesis, which, by liberating the living man from his biological or social destiny, assign him to that indefinable dimension that we are accustomed to call "politics"' (p. 251). Humans thus become human in this manner. Drawing on Judaism and Christianity, Paul (whose equivalent term is *katapausis*) and John of Chrysostom, Agamben finds this mystery hidden in the Jewish celebration of the Sabbath as a sacred day on which all work ceases and which prefigures that which is awaited in eschatology, itself a kind of eternal 'sabbatism' (pp. 239–40). The human is the 'Sabbatical animal par excellence' (p. 246).

Inoperativity is also what has been caught in the *oikonomia*, the governmental machine. It is therefore, secondly, fundamental to Agamben's political diagnostics. At the centre of the governmental machine, whether divine or earthly, is, as we have just seen, a void. In Agamben's diagnostics, glory covers divine inoperativity with its splendour (2011: 163). In both theology and politics, glory 'takes the place of that unthinkable emptiness' that is the 'inoperativity of power' (p. 242). The centre of the governmental machine is in reality empty and only the Sabbath and *katapausis*; yet inoperativity is necessary for the machine 'that it must at all costs be adopted and maintained at its center in the form of glory' (p. 242). Again, inoperativity is 'the political substance of the Occident, the glorious nutrient of all power' (p. 246).

Finally inoperativity becomes part of what might be called Agamben's political teleology. In an important essay, 'In Praise of Profanation', Agamben seeks to profane the divine inoperativity, that is, 'if "to consecrate" (*sacrare*) was the term that indicated the removal of things from the sphere of human law, "to profane" means, conversely, to return them to the free use of men' (2007: 73). Agamben aims to 'liberate' inoperativity from the glorious machine of *oikonomia* in which it now resides and return it to the use of humanity. It is this machine which must be 'deactivated and made inoperative' (2011: 166). The political goal is to wrest this inoperativity from the machine in which it has been captured, and in which it has become a material to be worked on through the production of glory. Festival and idleness have an eternal but futile return in the dreams of political utopias but only appear nostalgically as belonging to the human essence. This is in vain because they are nothing but 'the waste products of the immaterial and glorious fuel burnt by the motor of the machine as it turns, and that cannot be stopped' (p. 246).

Inoperativity allows Agamben to return to his theme of life, no longer through the opposition of *bios* and *zōē* but through an examination of *zōē aiōnios* – eternal life. He points out that in Judaism and in the New Testament the latter is not merely temporal but refers to a special quality of life and the transformation of human life in the world to come. There are alternative renderings as 'true life', 'incorruptible life' and 'carefree life' (2011: 247). Agamben himself speaks of a 'messianic life', what Paul calls a 'life in Jesus' (*zōē tou Iesou*), which anticipates the Sabbatism of the Kingdom in the present. Paul describes this by the 'as not' (*hōs mē*) as an indicator of inoperativity, such as I Corinthians 7: 29–31 which enjoins the brethren 'that both they that have wives be as though they had none; and they that weep, as though they wept not; and they that rejoice, as though they rejoiced not; and they that buy, as though they possessed not; and they that use the world, as not abusing it: for the fashion of this world passeth away' (p. 248). To live in the Messiah means to revoke every concrete aspect that we live and to make the life for which we live appear in it.

Aristotle, according to Agamben, simply got it wrong and led philosophy and politics astray when he opposed as two '*bioi*', contemplative life and political life (2011: 251). 'The political is neither a *bios* nor a *zōē*, but the dimension that the inoperativity of contemplation, by deactivating linguistic and corporeal, material and human praxes, ceaselessly opens and assigns to the living.' Eternal life is the political substance 'the machine and glory ceaselessly attempts to capture within itself'. The aim of Agamben's project then is thinking politics beyond economy and glory, giving due consideration to the hitherto hidden 'particular praxis of man as living being (*vivente uomo*) that we have defined as inoperativity' (p. 259).

8.7 This question of inoperativity might be clarified by two further examples. In a few pages in his seminars on Paul, Agamben follows the disputed etymology of the term *klesis*, which, via Luther's *Beruf*, becomes vocation or calling in Max Weber's English translation (Agamben, 2005a: 29–33). Using Weber's footnote on the Latin translation by Dionysius of Halicarnassus of *klesis* as *classis* rather than *status* (1985: 209), Agamben refers to the similarities between Paul and the 'young' Marx on the redemptive function of the proletariat. Unlike *status* in Latin, the English 'estate', or *Stand* in German, which subsume the individual in her or his place in the division of labour (the nobleman remains a nobleman, a commoner a commoner and, we might add, the wife remains a wife), class reveals the split between the individual and his or her social figure, and thus lays bare 'the contingency of each and every social figure' (Agamben, 2005a: 30). Moreover, he continues, in Marx's rendering of Stirner in *The German Ideology* we find an opposition between the revolutionary political act and mere revolt, the former respecting the creation of new institutions, the latter paying no heed to them. Agamben views Stirner as indicating an 'ethical-anarchic' interpretation of the Pauline *as not*, while Marx's interpretation portends the aporia of the role of the Party as the locus of 'right theory', just as the Church, as the institutional form of the *ekklesia*, the messianic community of those with vocations, raises the question of the true dogma (pp. 32–3). Marxism appears caught in the reduction of proletarian revolution and the proletariat to the working class, 'the worst misunderstanding of Marxian thought' (p. 31). Agamben does not directly adopt either Stirner's (via Marx) 'ethical-anarchic' interpretation against Marx, nor Jacob Taubes's 'anarchic-nihilistic' interpretation of the 'absolute indiscernability' between revolt and revolution, and worldly *klesis* and messianic *klesis*. Nevertheless, for him the aim of politics is not primarily about institutions, or redistribution to or even expropriation by a specific class, but the deactivation of the entire economic-governmental system, and of a kind of radical indifference to all specific kinds of work and concrete vocations.

In the 'Profanation' essay, one form of the deactivation is play, when sacred things are returned to common use and the 'powers of economics, law and politics, deactivated in play, can become gateways to a new happiness' (Agamben, 2007: 76). Whereas secularization represses by moving from the sacred to the profane, profanation neutralizes what it profanes. 'Both are political operations: the first guarantees the exercise of power by carrying it back to a sacred model; the second deactivates the apparatuses of power and returns to common use the spaces that power had seized' (p. 77).

A broader account of Agamben's thought would also consider his relationship to the philosopher Martin Heidegger, whom Foucault had already called, in the very last interview of his life, the 'essential philosopher' (1988b: 250). There is a note at the end of *The Kingdom and the Glory* which purportedly criticizes Heidegger for not being able to resolve the question of technology because he neglects its political locus in the *oikonomia* of being, that is in 'power's entering into the figure of Government' (Agamben, 2011: 253). But more interesting for us are the parallels Agamben draws with Heidegger's posing of the question of technology as the ultimate problem of metaphysics. The *Gestell*, or 'enframing' in its English translation (Heidegger, 1993: 325), is the 'complete orderability of all that is present' and which sets upon, gathers together, arranges and accumulates everything, human and things, as *Bestand*, rendered in English as 'standing reserve' or more simply, 'resources' (p. 323). But the decisive move here is that Agamben identifies the *Gestell* with the *oikonomia*, and 'orderability' as 'nothing other than governmentality' (Agamben, 2011: 252).

Agamben is not the first one to notice similarities between Foucault's work on governmentality, with its technologies of government and technologies of the self, and Heidegger on the question of technology (Dean, 1995; 1996). One could compare Foucault's analytics of governmental and ethical practices, that is, those that concern technologies of the self, with Heidegger's rendering of Aristotle's four forms of causality in his essay 'The Question Concerning Technology'. Thus what we seek to work on, the 'substance' of ethics or governing, the 'work' we do to govern it, the kind of 'subject' we become through such work, and the end or 'telos' we seek are the four dimensions of both governmental and ethical practices in Foucault. These four axes of ontology, ascetics, deontology and teleology, correspond to the Aristotelian material, efficient, formal and final causes. These are what Heidegger calls

four modes of occasioning within a 'bringing-forth', the propriative movement bringing the concealed into un-concealment, and through which
technology is a mode of revealing (Heidegger, 1993: 317–8).

If we use 'governmentality' in the broadest 'relational' sense that
Foucault did in *The Hermeneneutics of the Subject* (2005; see §3.7),
then it is concerned with the modes of revealing of human beings and
through them of Being, and could thus be made equivalent to 'orderability'. There are thus clear parallels with Heidegger's concept of
technē. There are further similarities to be drawn between Foucault's
concept of 'problematizations' and Heidegger's view that the 'question
of Being must be *formulated*'. In other words, the nature of Being cannot be divorced from its questioning and interrogation (1993: 45). But
where Foucault offers a genealogy of forms of veridiction based on
such problematizations, and would thus allow prima facie, counter-
problematizations, Heidegger is concerned with the 'destruction' or
the end of Western metaphysics. Governmentality is thus not simply
orderability itself but the forms of making human beings and things
orderable, which would be a different project; one which always allows
multiplicity, polyvalence and resistance, for problematization and
counter-problematization, conduct and counter-conduct.

What these notes on Heidegger and Marx reveal is that Agamben
is less interested in the analysis of power through the two poles he
has identified and examined and more with the overcoming or suspension of all governmentality or all economic and governmental
ordering or organization of society. We could say he is thus closer to a
Heideggerian interest in the 'destruction' of the metaphysical revealing and veiling of Being by the bipolar apparatus of power than with
a Foucauldian empirical analysis of the '*problematizations* through
which being offers itself to be, necessarily, thought – and the *practices*
on the basis of which these problematizations are formed' (Foucault,
1985: 11). Agamben is further concerned with the rendering inoperative of the entire system of the economic management of society
rather than with making inoperative its system of class exploitation,
after Marx, or even its system of inequality. The political aim can
thus be stated:

> The classless society is not a society that has abolished and lost
> all memory of class differences but a society that has learned to
> deactivate the apparatuses of those differences in order to make
> a new use possible, in order to transform them into pure means.
> (Agamben, 2007: 87)

Agamben's political aim thus appears as a ludic one, a profanation through play, a praxis of pure means without ends.

8.8 Of all those whose work we have considered here, Agamben has come closest to understanding the signature of power. It is in his work that the two poles of the concept are kept in play the longest, are most clearly identified, and are most broadly examined through their various sources and formulations, pagan, Christian and secular.

Yet he seeks to escape this signature just as much as, in their own ways, did Schmitt and Foucault. In his urgency to bring the 'bipolar machine', as he calls it, to a completion or finality, he forsakes the analytical intelligibility he establishes along the way. He takes the position of a commentator on our contemporary condition rather than an analyser of it. For all the brilliance of his archaeology of glory, he does not establish a science of the ceremonial and liturgical aspects of sovereignty and power, despite his assertion of its necessity, but shows how glory in fact covers over the void of sovereign power and the governmental machine. Similarly for all his understanding of publicity and public opinion in contemporary democracy, the present is but a continuing symptom of the metaphysical problems that have plagued 'Occidental' politics since Aristotle. He proves perspicacious at showing the hidden convergence, or indifference, between national-authoritarian sovereignty based on direct acclamation, and deliberative liberal-democratic sovereignty formed through a highly mediatized public sphere. However, he is not particularly useful for analysing either of them in their singularity.

Agamben's study of economic theology does support the central historical-theoretical claim that power relations must be approached along two axes of its signature, whether these are constituted as transcendent and eternal and immanent and temporal, or what we have called sovereign-reign and economic-governmental. This eluded both Foucault and Schmitt, and is thus a major achievement. However, Agamben appears driven by his own political teleology to reveal or establish 'the essential inoperativity' of power so that we might return its contents to a playful and common use. Whatever potential for resistance is offered is based on the eternal sabbatism of the human, and the possibility of an imagined point outside hitherto existing systems of the exercise of power. While this sanguine vision of human potentiality, or 'impotentiality' as Agamben puts it elsewhere (1999: 182), is not without appeal, we might ask whether it makes sense for all 'profane powers', including those of public bureaucracy and states, to be deactivated and made inoperative when, at least historically, they have formed an important limit to the glorification of the economy and the civil havoc this wreaks. Was it not, after all, the collapse of state authority and a 'transcendent' sovereignty in the face of the anarchic spiralling of an economy in crisis that prepared the way for Nazism, as Agamben himself indicates? If there is more than one way of playing the game of orderability, or of different possibilities of the arts of government or governmentality, then should we reject in entirety the intellectual and political option of engagement with how we are governed? Agamben, like Foucault before him, falls back in his moment of attempted escape to the simplest version of the signature between power as potential or capacity and power as domination. While Foucault would seek play to games of power (as agonistic relations between potentials) with the minimum of domination, Agamben will try to wrest human (im)potentiality from the machine of domination of the Occident.

It is not the aim of this book to project a politics of the present, but it seems that Agamben offers us an entirely different potentiality to the one he seeks to realize. Rather than a radical alterity to the machinery of power, does he not show the necessity today of thinking about and contesting relations of power along both the sovereign-reign and economic-governmental axes? Today, the now globally imagined economy in crisis is both the exception to sovereignty and law, and thus the rationale for governmental action and individual conduct and self-formation, and at the same time the collectively willed providential order constantly glorified in sporting events and advertising, by celebrity and financial reporting, and by crisis intervention and catastrophe management (cf. Minca, 2009). In the face of this, Agamben shows us that the analyses of the 'immanent' side of power and economy, however valuable, are not enough. Those demonstrations that the governmental economy is constituted through material, technical and performative means can only be completed by others that analyse how economic government cross references and comes to occupy a domain that at once claims a glorious transcendence and the very concrete competencies required to maintain public peace and order (expressed by Weber as a monopoly of legitimate violence and Foucault as a right of death).

There is enough in the empirical evidence of concepts of power adduced by Agamben to begin anew the relatively modest but political task of an analytics of power and resistance while putting to one side his radical politics whatever other consolations it may offer. Nevertheless, after his work, particularly *The Kingdom and the Glory* (2011), the theoretical and empirical investigation of power relations in our societies surely cannot remain the same.

Note on finance

8.9 There is, however, one theme that has escaped Foucault, Schmitt and Agamben: that of money and what Maurizio Lazzarato, among others, has called 'financialization' (2009). Commencing with Foucault's analysis of neoliberalism and noting, *en passant*, François Ewald's role in the neoliberal restructuring of the French labour market (p. 110), Lazzarato seeks to show how the rationality embodied in 'human capital theory' is linked to a technology of 'capitalization' which 'is consistent with the view that the individual's function, as a molecular fraction of capital, is not that of ensuring the productivity of labour but the profitability of capital as a whole' (p. 121). The individual becomes a 'capital competence', a 'machine-competence'; no longer a *homo œconomicus* but, in the words of Foucault, a 'life-style' and 'way of being', a way of 'relating to oneself, to time, to one's environment, to the future, the group, the family'. Foucault, due to his nominalism, of course does not make this link between human capital theory and the augmentation and composition of capital because he neglects the 'functioning of money in the transformation in the "regime of accumulation", that is, the passage from managerial/industrial capitalism to shareholding/ postindustrial captialism' (Lazzarato, 2009: 122). Further, drawing on Deleuze's view of money as 'the capitalist appropriation of virtuality', Lazzarato charts the elements of an economy in which finance allocates to itself the power of 'stating, delimiting and circumscribing what is possible for a society at a particular time' (p. 123).

Neoliberalism, for Lazzarato, presents as a reprivatization of money and a critique of anything (such as the New Deal) that encroaches on the 'sovereignty of money'. The outcomes of the transformation in the regime of accumulation include the asymmetrical effects of financialization and new forms of inequality, the necessary and functional growth of insecurity and 'precarity' among wage earners and the monetarization of state administration (2009: 123–5). The latter has two goals: to implicate employees, via their pension funds, in the regulation of social expenditures and to prevent alliances between employees and beneficiaries of social services (p. 125).

A further extension of this kind of argument would embrace the problem of the transformation of debt. Colin Crouch (2008) has argued that the neoliberal turn in public policy corresponds to a movement from a state Keynesianism to a 'privatized Keynesianism' that emerged after the collapse of systems of demand management in the 1970s. Rather than governments taking on debt to stimulate the economy, as in state Keynesianism, it was individuals and households, including poor ones, who took on the role of incurring debt. Such a system was enabled by two innovations which became clear after the financial collapse of 2008: the extension to those on moderate and low incomes of ever longer lines of unsecured credit in the form of 100 percent housing loans and multiple credit cards, and the development of markets in derivatives and futures and new financial products by which financial institutions learned to trade in risk. If the Achilles heel of original Keynesianism was the 'inflationary ratchet' of increasing public expenditure, privatized Keynesianism, according to Crouch (2008: 483), floundered on an exponentially growing mountain of bad debt and the failure of financial institutions' capacity to calculate the risks in which they were trading. Contrary to neoliberal assumptions about markets, the financial institutions of Wall Street and the City of London proved to have 'highly defective knowledge'. The recent history of the privatization of debt onto wage-earners, households and the poor, the subsequent public responsibility to save financial institutions as 'too big to fail', and the consequences in terms of public expenditure in many economies, further this narrative of 'financialization'. Foucault, however, does not make the jump from the analysis of neoliberalism to the transformation of money, finance and debt.

A parallel criticism can be made in relation to Agamben's employment of the *oikonomia* as the exemplar of the structure of power relations eminent on our present. The attempt to establish an 'economic' order is doubtless a key part of the governmental management of contemporary life. However, while Agamben recognizes that this order is fundamentally 'anarchic' and hence its constant cross referencing to a constitutive natural or transcendent order as foundation, or *archē*, he also neglects the role of money and transformations of finance which, if they do not escape it entirely, provide significant challenges for economic management. Thus Alberto Toscano has begun via Marx to explore the implications of Aristotle's distinction between *oikonomia* and *chrematistics*, the first concerning the management of the household and the second the science of monetary accumulation, circulation and interest (Toscano, 2011: 130–2). Chrematistics presages capitalism and its limitless accumulation disconnected from need and use and which, 'in having money as both origin and end, threatens to generate an entirely *unmanageable* economy' (p. 132). Chrematistics thus introduces dislocation and world crisis into the Aristotelian cosmology, just as financialization relentlessly undermines the attempt at the economic management of modern societies.

Do such observations undermine a concept of power from the perspective of keeping in play the two axes we have identified and elaborated here? The answer appears to be to the contrary. It would be a mistake to imagine that financialization is particularly new, given Marx's analysis of the virtuality of money in the nineteenth century, and examples such as the role of hyperinflation in the Weimar Republic and speculative crashes in the Great Depression. It is precisely the effects of such 'financialization' including ongoing economic crisis and the portent of catastrophe (often invoking collective memory of earlier events), that make the economic-governmental axis operable and initiate projects and programs, through international associations (e.g. the International Monetary Fund, the European Central Bank) and national governments. These include measures of debt and public expenditure reduction, restriction and reform of welfare services and benefits, recommodification of labour power, and so on. Neoliberalism, considered both as a 'thought collective' and a form of governmental reason, was born of crisis, anticipated and gained dominance through crisis and initiated waves of economic reform and social restructuring through crisis (Mirowski and Plehwe, 2009). While some have postulated a 'zombie neoliberalism', devoid of legitimacy, others have indicated how the most recent wave of financial crises has transformed it into a kind of legitimation through the pure positivity of complex systems, and notions of resilience and catastrophe (Peck, 2010; Walker and Cooper, 2011).

Financial crises are also accompanied by intensifications and reformations of the sovereign-reign axis of power both as a set of material competencies and in the forms of glorification. In regard to the first, they trigger, as was the case in Germany in the 1920s, the problem of sovereignty as a competency to recognize a situation that threatens public order and to act to secure it. By making the responsibility for the bailouts of banks and securing the financial system a *public* one, recent financial crises have become ones of the aptly named 'sovereign debt'. At the same time, the glorification of sovereign-reign reactivates all the elements at its disposal including racist and nationalist ones, and the symbols, rituals and ceremonies of constitutional monarchies and republics.

As Lazzarato himself argues, whereas Marxism regards financial crises as demonstrating the necessary capitalist destruction of all non-economic social relations, our societies display a remarkable capacity for retroversion, reactivation and reinvention of quasi-transcendentals in the face of crisis. These include the revival of racism and nationalism in the face of global movements of refugees and towards immigrants in formerly tolerant and stable liberal democracies (2009: 130–2). But it also includes new forms of the welfare state or *L'État Providence*, in which not only are benefits cut and services retracted but also disciplinary, paternalist and coercive means are combined with the attempted reformation of conduct and production of new subjectivities (Dean, 1995, 2007). The event, including financial crises, or the event-to-come – the anticipated catastrophe – are occasions for a new round of intervention and restructuring, which nonetheless continues the providential order (cf. Aradau and van Munster, 2011). This is also why social governing and the very idea of 'society' persist, despite all announcements of their death, as modalities of attempts to stitch together the juridical-institutional and economic-governmental relations of power. This problem of the 'social' and social ways of governing will be the subject of a following study.

Concluding thoughts and domains of study

8.10 The signature of power, which all three thinkers have sought to escape, must be maintained from an analytical point of view. Today the analysis of the exercise or relations of power must seek to articulate the sovereign-reign and economic-governmental axes of power without reduction of one to the other while permitting the historical variability of both axes and their interweaving. This signature is neither a universal feature of power relations nor a merely historical instance of them. Rather, it is that which continues to mark our concepts of power and frameworks of law, constitutional government and what today is called 'public governance'. It is an analytical tool, or the key analytical tool, fashioned on multiple instances of concepts of power, which allows us to identify and examine how the universal and the singular, the eternal and the temporal, the transcendent and the immanent, the sovereign and the governmental, and so on, are sutured together and made operable in any relation of power.

So let us consider in turn key concepts of recent power discussions: sovereignty, governmentality and biopolitics, and then the themes of secularization, the event and publicity.

Sovereignty can be analysed along two axes. While it is marked as the ideal-transcendent pole of power, it also takes the form of material-immanent practice. This means studying both the *dispositif* of sovereignty *and* its glorious splendour, the practices through which public peace and order are secured, *and* the liturgies, acclamations, rituals and ceremonies of glorification. A *political archaeology of glory* thus meets an *analytics of sovereign practices*. From the perspective of the former, it is possible to assume that sovereignty has a hollow centre – Agamben's empty throne – that requires infinite sustenance in the form of the glorification manifest in ritual, ceremony and symbol, and today by the doxological character of the mass and virtual media. In more direct terms, a political archaeology of glory studies the constitution of sovereign reign in its glorious form through such practices and means.

Practices of glorification and acclamation, essential to the nourishment of sovereignty, concern different publics. Thus the songs of praise and Church liturgy constitute the public character of the Christian people, just as the Nazi and fascist acclamations constitute in its direct presence the public character of the people or the *Volk*. Today opinion polls, television ratings, box office receipts, website traffic, attendance at sporting matches and performances, numbers of followers on personal 'social media' sites, and so forth, come to constitute or rather substitute for the 'public opinion' that Schmitt said is the 'modern type of acclamation'. Perhaps we could talk, with him, of a 'fully privatized public' and imagine a study of the thresholds of how this mass of privatized opinions achieves public-ness or 'publicity', becomes an obvious, taken-for-granted and unchallenged presence and can thus present itself as 'public opinion'. In this sense the political archaeology of glory meets what might be called an *analytics of publicity*, which would also be a kind of study of how public-ness arises or the forms of public visibility.

From the perspective of the analytics of sovereign practices, however, there are at least three actions of sovereignty that are important. Firstly, it can be *delegated*. If sovereignty presents itself as a supreme power, it is only within a particular domain or order. Thus, in international law, a superior, inter-state order is presupposed that delegates sovereignty to states as formal equals, each with their own domestic order. Similarly, the sovereign decision is always delegated onto particular agents: whether these are national security agencies, the military, police officers, air marshals, doctors, health professionals, ethics committees, and even prospective parents and next of kin in biomedical decisions on life and death. Sovereignty as a practice is essentially a vicarious power (recall the Pope as the Vicar of Christ).

Secondly, sovereignty can also be *arrogated*, e.g. President George W. Bush's arrogation of Congressional powers in the United States under a state of national emergency, such as after the events of 11 September 2001, or the arrogation of security agencies' decisions of who to target in 'drone' strikes by President Obama. Thirdly, it can be *abrogated* or *derogated*, i.e., annulled or cancelled, not only in the sense that particular laws can be repealed but also that particular spaces within a sovereign territory are at least partially ones where the claimed monopoly of violence does not apply (for example, sporting contests), or where taxes and duties are not levied, such as in the free port and the special economic zone. If a political archaeology of glory examines the practices of glorification necessary to sustain and nourish the sovereign, an analytics of sovereignty takes its form from this peculiar characteristic of sovereign power and consists of the study of the spaces, moments and agents of sovereign arrogation, delegation, and derogation (Dean, 2007: 137–9). By extension, liberalism and neoliberalism could be approached through their demand for specific derogations of sovereignty within the spaces of the economy and the arrogations necessary to enforce this, as already noted by Foucault's identification of the free space of the economy with the free port, or *franc port*.

An analytics of *government* remains intact, that is, as the analysis of the problematizations, rationalities, technologies, forms of subjectivity and ends (*teloi*) involved in the 'conduct of conduct' (Dean, 2010a: 30ff.). But it is only a part of the study of power and, expressed in these terms, restricts us to its immanent axis, and a particular conception of it.

Thus, even within the immanent axis, an analytics of government must free itself from the liberal critique of sovereignty and the state. Liberal problematizations take sovereignty's doxologies at face value, thus rendering it as all-powerful and all-knowing. In other words, a power analytics should not mistake the symbols, mythologies and acclamations of sovereignty and law revealed by political archaeology for the immanent and limited set of competencies and practices of sovereignty to maintain public order, to identify and act on exception and emergency, to make a decision on the enemy and declare war, and to make and enforce laws, and the historically specific delegation of those competencies onto what we call states and other political units, their agencies and agents. Similarly, rather than a general notion of law as an expression of omnicompetent sovereignty (as found in Foucault's 'juridico-discursive' conception of power) it can be approached through its practices (of law-making, implementing and administering), technical procedures and rules (e.g. of criminal and civil proof, the adversary system, pleas, appeals and penalties), institutional spaces (the dock, the court, the bench, chambers, parliament), personages (lawyers, judges, the jury) and their forms of training. A *genealogy of the arts of government* must be complemented by a *historical sociology of sovereignty and law* both as a set of competencies and institutions and as social forms of organization and legitimation, that is, the project initiated by Weber.

If sovereignty has not only a transcendent but also an immanent dimension, the same can apply to government. While government is marked as the immanent axis of power relations, it also has a transcendent dimension: in providential forms of government it invokes a divine order; in liberal forms of government it is the order of the market or of competition; in executive government it is the constitutive power that gave rise to the constituted power of the concrete juridical order; in public policy, it could be the 'taxpayer' or indeed the 'public' and 'public opinion'. The immanent axis in each case *appears* as secondary to and an outgrowth of the transcendent order by means of the event as fate, as catastrophe (such as that resulting from or anticipated by bioeconomic struggle for existence and over-population or that of human-induced climate change), and as constitutional crisis and state of emergency. The genealogy of government can thus no longer be a narrative of the becoming-immanent of sovereignty. Forms of government not only manifest themselves as historically specific and immanent 'economies of power' but also, paradoxically, actively produce the kinds of sovereign power they claim as their foundation.

The study of *biopolitics* reached a dead end with the supposition of a kind of vital political dynamics of the Right (Schmitt) and the Left (e.g., that of Michael Hardt and Antonio Negri (2000)), on the one hand, and the tragic tonality found in Foucault's account of the historical emergence of biopolitics and in Agamben's meta-historical account of the inclusive exclusion of 'bare life'. Foucault abandoned his project and we are yet to receive Agamben's promised last word on the topic of life and its forms. It is clear that a historical analysis of the attempted forms of the power and government over and of life, and of the different conceptions of life they entail, is required. But biopolitics, rather than belonging to one axis or another, is best located among their modes of articulation, as is the case with the Ordoliberals' conception of a 'vital politics' and Malthus's conception of population so crucial to political economy. Life is neither of the order of nature nor of history; and the power of and over life is concerned with eternal life and actual life, the universal and the present, the life and fertility of the population and the different forms of life (savage, indigent, civilized), 'life itself' and how we should live or would wish to live. The concept of life is rather among the different ways of interweaving what we take to be natural, eternal and universal with the singular forms of life and actions in the present. Biopolitics is both the claim to what life is and the actions to preserve and enhance it, even where that means the disqualification of the lives of others. Perhaps the *biopolitics of the population*, situated by Foucault at the threshold of modernity, here meets something like that designated by Taubes's difficult term, a *theo-zoology of life*, the divine, providential or natural order of life we invoke in the act of governing its concrete forms and orders.

We do not pretend to have reached a final conclusion with respect to biopolitics. However, we have shown that a biopolitics of the population is extrinsic to neither sovereignty nor a liberal art of governing through the economy. The liberal economy presupposes a bio-economics of scarcity and a biospatiality of territory. In fact, the biopolitical order of life is what makes possible and indeed necessary economic management and liberal governmental interventions.

The *secularization* debates, and political and economic theology, are central to the discussion of the signature of power because they produce concepts that attempt to understand and articulate aspects of the two poles of its field. 'Secularization' articulates divine and worldly rule in Schmitt, eschatology and progress in Löwith, and the process of 'rationalization' and 'disenchantment' in Weber. 'Reoccupation' in Blumenberg seeks another kind of articulation that actually mediates their divorce. 'Neutralization' attempts to show the shift from the theological to political and later, economic, central spheres of existence. Legitimation in Blumenberg articulates domination and the juridical order with a fundamental human praxis of self-assertion. The 'signature' in Agamben is extended beyond the limits we have set it, to explain the movement from the theological to the secular, and profanation becomes a practice of the movement from the exclusivity of the sacred to the common use of the profane.

All of these figures of thought are ways of addressing the audacity of the new, with its simple claim but widespread supposition that the old disappears with the new and that therefore the new is its own legitimation. There is little point in epochal divisions and narratives of the becoming immanent of a formerly transcendent sovereign power, or simply assuming that the very 'newness' of a form of power or mode of organization has a value, positive or negative, in itself. Rather, we need to be able to think the difficult relationship between the old and the new, the mythological and the rational, the sacred and the profane, and the sovereign and the governmental. Whether the first term is preserved as the object and the motor of the reconstituted relations of power, as in Roberto Esposito's immunity paradigm, remains a further question (2008: 51–2), although put in this way, that paradigm is an exact restatement of the providential problematic.

The *event*: following Agamben on the miracle, and Schmitt on the exception, we have demonstrated that the event (as symptom of crisis and herald of catastrophe) is a particularly forceful and recurrent mode of the interlacing of the sovereign and governmental axes of power in liberal and neoliberal forms of rule. We have stressed the importance of the bio-catastrophe as the occasion for the political miracle that is liberal economic management. In this respect, the development of carbon markets and geo-engineering in response to human-induced climate change, the role of new financial products in financial crises, and the management of disasters and pandemics require a *political morphology of the event* that would address the forms of the event as exception, rupture, crisis, catastrophe, and so on. This is a crucial task for an analytics of power.

Publicity: there are no events without glory, however, that is, without their acclamation and its public presence or publicity. The question of the publicity or 'public-ness' of power reconnects our study of power with its medium, in all its types, new and old. The archaeology of glory concerns not only the analysis of words (epigraphy, philology, the study of liturgy and prayer, discourse analysis) but also the things and actions, gestures and symbols, rituals and rites that can be observed and make the public-ness of power visible. Today, we are witness and respondents to, through various media and platforms, contested election results, terrorist attacks, the rituals of parties, parliaments, leaders and courts, wars, famines, epidemics and disasters, and all manner of tragedy, drama and farce. Thus the contemporary study of the event is not simply of the speech with which it is reported but of its visible and spectacular form. The morphology of the event makes it necessary to understand how an event achieves the status of public-ness and how, through discourse and argument no doubt, but also through images, gestures, emotions and symbols, something is taken-for-granted, becomes commonsense and stands as public opinion, at least within a particular political community. This is what makes what we called an analytics of publicity central to the conceptualization and study of power. (The morphology of the event and this analytics of publicity await further elaboration as components of this emergent continent of the study of power.)

The study of power today thus promises to become something more than the study of the empirical occasions on which agents realize their will against those of others. It can encompass a genealogy of the arts of government and an archaeology of glory, an analytics of sovereign practices and a historical sociology of sovereignty, a biopolitics of the population and a theo-zoology of life, and a political morphology of the event and an analytics of publicity. It raises questions of historical narrative, and the articulation of different orders, and the current spatial orientations and forms of concrete orders. It raises the question of *nomos* as well as of governmentality, of the *where* as well as the *how* of power, of who or what occupies the empty throne, and of 'who decides' and 'who judges' as much as how conduct will be shaped. The concept of order, and its capacity for articulation, is central to the study of forms and relations of power. This is the threshold that we approach today in relation to the concept of power if we recognize, with no reduction, subordination or erasure, its signature.

CONCLUSION

When François Ewald would finally accept the Legion of Honour, France's highest award, it would not be for his great efforts in the preservation and interpretation of the legacy of Foucault, rather, it would be for his advocacy of social reconstruction, or what would be called in the English-speaking world 'welfare reform' and 'labour-market reform', as the highest profile intellectual voice of *Medef*, the peak employers and business association. The biographical contingencies of his journey from Maoism to *Medef*, and from his association with Michel Foucault to his later vocation, has raised questions for many, from different intellectual and political positions, as Michael Behrent has carefully elaborated (2010: 585–6). When Jerôme Monod, a close advisor of President Jacques Chirac, made the award, he voiced the essence of these questions: 'What happened inside of you in 1968? Why this close proximity, back then, to Maoism …? What transformation [occurred] in your mind during your close collaboration with Michel Foucault?' (ibid.)

This is undoubtedly a very interesting question, but ours is a little different. It is what happens when we detach the study and analysis of power from its signature so that the juridical domain and sovereignty and the institutional form of the state become simply the sphere of economic management and administration? In our view it is that the description of liberal rationalities and technologies of government comes to occupy a space of indeterminacy with the normative contents of those rationalities and technologies. It would seem somewhat paradoxical that this philosophically abandoned state, with revolution as its converse, appears, in all its archaism and splendour, to make Ewald a '*Chevalier*' (or knight) of the *Ordre nationale de la légion d'honneur*. Perhaps the day will arrive when the French state will come to understand Foucault's role in the immanent flattening of power onto the plane of economic management and government, and honour him as a part of its own sovereign glory.

We can invoke the rule of the necessary non-correspondence of theory and practice, and between concepts of power and political positions, to escape some of the uncomfortable implications here. And surely, in the world of moral hierarchies, the famous Foucauldian, Ewald, joining in the class struggle in France (on the side of the bourgeoisie) is far less heinous, if perhaps even more puzzling, than Carl Schmitt's joining the Nazi Party on 1 May 1933, becoming president of the Association of National-Socialist Jurists, supporting the regime with his pronouncements and making statements even he would later describe as 'unspeakable'. But nonetheless they both signal dangers, and these dangers seem to inhere in the very signature of power itself, or, at least, in the most pervasive form of that signature today and in the writings of our three principals, that of the field of sovereign-reign and economic-government.

The first danger in the signature of power is illustrated by the Foucauldian trajectory. By seeking to dissociate the powers of government from those of sovereignty, or to subordinate or re-inscribe sovereignty to or within government, and by training a laser-like focus on the immanent operations of power, the genealogy of the arts of government veers towards an uncritical acceptance of the propositions of liberalism and neoliberalism. It does this because it accepts at face-value liberalism's self-understanding as a critique of state reason and as a limitation, and a making safe, of a putatively all-powerful sovereign power. Whether viewed as a movement, a thought collective, a project or program of government, or an art of government, liberalism, in both its classical and more recent forms, operates along both axes of power to employ state power to institute what it presents as a natural or quasi-natural economic order. Liberalism as art of government however has never been laissez-faire: it has always been concerned to appropriate, use, reform and revolutionize institutions of state, to seize land and establish title, to tax earnings and property, and employ the security and disciplinary powers of the state, to govern forms of life in ways consistent with the exploitation of labour-power and the generation and accumulation of value.

To different extents, both the anti-naturalist elements of Ordoliberalism and Foucauldian genealogy recognize that this is the case, as have others, including Karl Polyani (1957). But in doing so they fail to address a further dimension of the liberal imaginary: that of sovereignty. Liberalism, in both classical and more recent forms, regards sovereignty as all-powerful and all-knowing; it thus views sovereignty through its glorious and spectacular political form rather than as a set of competencies and material practices. Liberalism presents the critique of sovereignty as leading to a notion of limited government as if limited government implied a limited sovereignty. But if sovereignty, as we have seen, entails a definite set of material competencies, then it is always in some sense limited, and it is always possible for it to act through other agencies, bodies, delegates and so on. A better understanding of contemporary or neoliberalism is as an intensification of the instruments and competencies of sovereignty, at least partially in the service of a changing capitalist economy and its modes of accumulation. What is perhaps frightening today is not the archaic imaginary of an omnipotent sovereignty but the actual extension and effectiveness of certain sovereign competencies, for example, those of extra-juridical killing, made possible by military technology, which potentially brings the life of each individual on the planet into the security calculations of the president of the United States.

What emerges from the liberal, and neoliberal, critiques of sovereign power is not a new form of power dissociated from sovereignty, discipline and domination, as Foucault had hoped for at the end of his governmentality lectures, but a rationalization and intensification of sovereignty for particular sets of ends. Neoliberalism is prepared, albeit in an ambiguous way, to forsake the naturalism of classical liberalism but not the imaginary of an omnipotent sovereignty. To present itself as a focusing and intensification of sovereignty for the resolution of economic and ecological crises in the extension of capitalist exploitation and accumulation would be too much for even neoliberalism to admit, at least in public (but see Mirowski and Plehwe, 2009).

To be sure, the focus on the immanent arts of government remains revelatory of the techniques, rationalities, modes of subjectification, and limited ends, through which this is to be achieved. The individualization of risk, the transformation of social policy (welfare reform), the form of the 'enterprise' as a mode of life, and the economic subject as a locus of choice augmenting and deriving profit and satisfaction from 'human capital', are thus elements of this immanent economic-governmental form of recent and indeed contemporary liberal rule. But the analysis of the government of risk must be complemented by the securing of the sovereign order, and so too the shaping of free individual conduct with the deployment of legitimate violence, the enterprising subject with the surveillance and discipline of the 'welfare dependent', and so forth, as the present author has argued consistently (e.g., Dean, 2007: 101ff.).

There is a temptation then to shift the analytic of power away from the economic-governmental domain back to that of sovereign-reign. Here, again, there is much to be gained concerning the singular character of sovereignty as a set of competencies, above all the capacity to act in the face of uncertainty to maintain security and public order and its correlate relationship to the *jus belli*. Liberalism, from this perspective, appears not so much as a limitation on sovereignty as a critique of the political, and as an ethical, economic or even technological neutralization of political antagonisms. In such a view, the economic-governmental domain is a kind of subterfuge to distract attention from fundamental political divisions with dire consequences for new forms of war and conflict. This sovereigntist thinking views the economy as requiring and supporting a 'strong state' and delegates to it the task of economic management and government. At its worst the governmental is projected back onto the sovereign axis of power as it was in two ways with Schmitt. The first was after the collapse of the Weimar constitutional order when the relationship between Leader and People, *Führer* and impolitical *Volk*, became a kind of post-pastoral substitute for the position of the failed sovereign. The second, perhaps more fundamental because arguably less opportunistic, was his advocacy of concrete-order thinking which would complete, if not replace, his earlier decisionism. Such a perspective provides an in-principle historical-institutional account of a legal-political order such as that established through land-appropriation, colonization, settlement and federation of former colonies in 'colonial settler societies' in North America and Australasia. The concrete order becomes the foundation (the *archē*) of the subsequent exercise of political decision, and of law-making, interpretation and application. Equality and justice are thus defined in terms of this concrete order rather than an abstract normativism, as has been the case for Indigenous populations, slaves and former slaves, immigrants and refugees, racial minorities, suspected terrorists, working-class militants and protest movements, propertyless men, women and others. But this move, as insightful as it is in relation to liberal normativism, replaces the norm or system of norms with the concrete order made into a kind of transcendental. Such a position tends to disqualify not only the art of government modulated through the constructed freedom and conduct of the governed, but also the possibilities of counter-conducts, contestations and insurrections that reshape the terms of the concrete order.

It is with these two failures in mind, instructive as they are, that we turned to Agamben's economic theology and found a paradigm of power that kept open the field constituted by the transcendent and the immanent, sovereign-reign and economic-government, and the juridical-institutional and 'productive' powers, and thus appeared the closest to the recognition of the need to keep the signature of power in play; to not reduce it to a historical movement of progressive transfer or to collapse it back onto its ontological and theological foundation. Here we found the elaboration of key operations by which the relations of the two axes were articulated: in economy, order and providence, through the miracle or more broadly the event, and through the power of and over life. For all its insights however, this project would also totalize and mythologize power by invoking the Cartesian/Hobbesian image of the State-Machine, the Leviathan as automaton. Instead of an attempt to render this machine inoperative which returns us to the elementary opposition between power as domination and human (im)potentiality, we have argued that political and social analysis and political action itself must keep the field of force, or the attraction, repulsion and interaction between sovereignty and governmentality in play. Sovereignty is not only a transcendent and glorious political form, but also itself an immanent material-institutional set of practices and competencies. The art of government not only directs conducts and seeks particular ends, and attempts to find ways to manage economic and financial crises and prevent or prepare for potential catastrophes (today, environmental ones, in particular), but also enacts a concrete juridical-political order based on appropriation, accumulation, and exploitation. In this sense, each of the axes, while being marked as one side of the binary, can be approached through their transcendent and immanent dimensions.

So our three principal characters have failed, not in their recognition of the signature of power but in their desire to go beyond it. At the moment of failure they return to the simplest model of power as domination. Foucault at the end of his life would seek an ethical solution to minimize domination. Agamben, having assembled the operations of the bipolar field of power, would seek a politics to render the 'providential machine' inoperative, thus juxtaposing an absolute domination to a messianic resistance. Schmitt, as jurist and state-law theorist, could not envisage another side of power relatively autonomous from its ongoing foundation in appropriation, the system of property and distribution thus established and the *nomos* or concrete order that secures it (and here he is very close to Locke). If Schmitt has been resurrected in recent decades (and some, with good reason, would wish him permanently buried), it has been in inverse proportion to the growth of 'immanentism' in social and political thought: the denial in turn of sovereignty (dissolved in networks of governance or washed away by globalization), of the political (reduced to ethical concerns and commercial imperatives), and now of power itself (replaced by government or governance, or considered of no explanatory value at all for socio-technical assemblages).

Thus, we can say that, by themselves, a governmental genealogy of liberalism, a political theology of sovereignty, and a theological genealogy of economy and government have contributed immensely to our understanding of power but all represent cul-de-sacs, and in this sense failures. We have summarized some conclusions in §8.10 with respect to sovereignty, governmentality and biopolitics and do not need to repeat them. But, as we saw there, biopolitics is less a particular modern form of power or axis of power relations than a multiplicity of historically singular ways of articulating sovereignty and government and making them work, or rendering them operable. Life belongs neither to the orders of nature nor history. The same can be said of a number of other formations: the very persistence of the quasi-transcendental idea of 'society', and the notion of a social way of governing is another means of attempting to patch together a sovereign order, ostensibly based on juridical and political equality, with a governmental order, managing economic crisis, inequality and poverty (see Dean, 2010b). The notion of 'order' so much used and so little reflectively analysed seems very central to this task of thinking the articulation between reign and governing. It certainly has left a lasting legacy through neoliberalism and spontaneous order thinking and theories of complex systems. In any case we have already identified a number of new fields in the emergent domain of the study of power.

A new continent is emerging in the study of power, which we can see by standing on the shoulders of the thinkers addressed in this book, while acknowledging their failures. It is already being opened up and explored, but by those who remain alert enough, and restless enough. This book is dedicated to those who, despite their own luck and success, or position of relative privilege with respect to the majority of the Earth's population, not to mention the other co-inhabitants of the biosphere, refuse to accept Leibniz's precept, in his *Theodicy* (1951: 267–8, s. 225), that, having weighed up all possible worlds, God must have given us the best of them.

REFERENCES

Agamben, G. (1998) *Homo Sacer: Sovereign Power and Bare Life*. Stanford, CA: Stanford University Press.

Agamben, G. (1999) *Potentialities: Collected Essays in Philosophy*. Stanford, CA: Stanford University Press.

Agamben, G. (2005a) *The Time that Remains: A Commentary on the Letter to the Romans*. Stanford, CA: Stanford University Press.

Agamben, G. (2005b) *State of Exception*. Chicago, IL: University of Chicago Press.

Agamben, G. (2007) *Profanations*. New York: Zone Books.

Agamben, G. (2009) *The Signature of all Things: On Method*. New York: Zone Books.

Agamben, G. (2011) *The Kingdom and the Glory: For a Theological Genealogy of Economy and Government*. Stanford, CA: Stanford University Press.

Aradau, C. and van Munster, R. (2011) *Politics of Catastrophe: Genealogies of the Unknown*. London: Routledge.

Arendt, H. (1951) *The Origins of Totalitarianism*. New York: Harcourt Brace.

Arendt, H. (1998) *The Human Condition*, 2nd edn. Chicago, IL: University of Chicago Press.

Bachrach, P. and Baratz, Morton S. (1962) 'Two faces of power', *American Political Science Review* 56 (4): 947–52.

Bashford, A. (2012) 'Malthus and colonial history', *Journal of Australian Studies* 36 (1): 99–110.

Behrent, M.C. (2010) 'Accidents happen: François Ewald, the "antirevolutionary Foucault", and the intellectual politics of the French welfare state', *Journal of Modern History* 82 (3): 585–624.

Bendersky, J.W. (2007) 'Carl Schmitt's path to Nuremberg: a sixty-year reassessment', *Telos* 139: 6–34.

Bentham, J. (1950) *The Theory of Legislation*. London: Routledge and Kegan Paul.

Best, J. (2007) 'Why the economy is so often the exception to politics as usual', *Theory, Culture and Society* 24 (4): 87–109.

Blumenberg, H. (1985) *The Legitimacy of the Modern Age*. Cambridge, MA: MIT Press.

Boethius (1969) *The Consolation of Philosophy*. Harmondsworth: Penguin.

Böhm, F., Eucken, W. and Grossmann-Doerth, H. (1989) 'The Ordo Manifesto of 1936', in A. Peacock and H. Willgerodt (eds), *Germany's Social Market Economy: Origins and Evolution*. London: Macmillan, pp. 15–26.

Braun, B. (2007) 'Biopolitics and the molecularization of life', *Cultural Geographies* 14 (1): 6–28.

Bussolini, J. (2010a) 'Review essay: Critical encounter between Giorgio Agamben and Michel Foucault', *Foucault Studies* 10: 108–43.

Bussolini, J. (2010b) 'What is a dispositive?', *Foucault Studies* 10: 85–107.

Bussolini, J. (2011) 'Ongoing founding events in Carl Schmitt and Giorgio Agamben', *Telos* 157: 60–82.

Callon, M. (2006) 'What does it mean to say that economics is performative', CSI Working Paper Series, No. 005, Centre de Sociologie de l'Innovation, Écoles des Mines des Paris.

Clegg, S.R. (1989) *Frameworks of Power*. London: Sage.

Collier, S.J. (2009) 'Topologies of power: Michel Foucault's analysis of political government beyond "governmentality"', *Theory, Culture and Society* 26 (6): 78–108.

Connery, C. (2001) 'Ideologies of land and sea: Alfred Thayer Mahan, Carl Schmitt, and the shaping of global myth elements', *boundary 2* 28 (2): 173–201.

Cristi, F. R. (1984) 'Hayek and Schmitt on the rule of law', *Canadian Journal of Political Science* 17 (3): 521–35.

Cristi, R. (1998) *Carl Schmitt and Authoritarian Liberalism: Strong State, Free Economy*. Cardiff: University of Wales Press.

Crouch, C. (2008) 'What will follow the demise of privatised Keynesianism?' *Political Quarterly* 79 (4): 476–87.

Dahl, R.A. (1957) 'The concept of power', *Behavioral Science* 2: 210–15.

Dalberg-Acton, J.E.E. (1907) *Historical Essays and Studies* (edited by J. N. Figgis and R. V. Laurence). London: Macmillan.

Dean, M. (1991) *The Constitution of Poverty: Toward a Genealogy of Liberal Governance*. London: Routledge.

Dean, M. (1995) 'Governing the unemployed self in an active society', *Economy and Society* 24 (4): 559–83.

Dean, M. (1996) 'Putting the technological into government', *History of the Human Sciences* 9 (3): 47–68.

Dean, M. (2007) *Governing Societies: Political Perspectives on Domestic and International Rule*. Maidenhead: Open University Press.

Dean, M. (2010a) *Governmentality: Power and Rule in Modern Society*, 2nd edn. London: Sage.

Dean, M. (2010b) 'What is society? Social thought and the arts of government', *British Journal of Sociology* 61 (4): 677–95.

Deleuze, G. (1988) *Foucault*. Minneapolis, MN: University of Minnesota Press.

Deleuze, G. and Guattari, F. (1981) 'Rhizome', *Ideology and Consciousness* 6: 49–71.

Deuber-Mankowsky, A. (2008) 'Nothing is political, everything can be politicized: on the concept of political in Michel Foucault and Carl Schmitt', *Telos* 142: 135–61.

Dilts, A. (2011) 'From "entrepreneur of the self" to "care of the self": neo-liberal governmentality and Foucault's ethics', *Foucault Studies* 12: 130–46.

Du Gay, P. and Scott, A. (2010) 'Against the adjectival state', *Sociologica: Italian Journal of Sociology* 2.

Dunn, J. (1969) *The Political Thought of John Locke: an Historical Account of the Argument of the 'Two Treatises of Government'*. Cambridge: Cambridge University Press.

Elias, N. (1983) *The Court Society*. Oxford: Basil Blackwell.

Esposito, R. (2008) *Bios: Biopolitics and Philosophy*. Minneapolis, MN: University of Minnesota Press.

Eucken, R.C. (1909) 'Naturalism or idealism', Nobel Lecture, 27 March. Available at: http://www.nobelprize.org/nobel_prizes/literature/laureates/1908/eucken-lecture.html (accessed 7 August 2012).

Eucken, W. (1950) *The Foundation of Economics*. London: William Hodge.

Ewald, F. (1986) *L'Etat Providence*. Paris: Grasset.

Ewald, F. (1990) 'Norms, discipline and the law', *Representations* 30: 138–61.

Ewald, F. (1991) 'Insurance and risk', in G. Burchell, C. Gordon and P. Miller (eds), *The Foucault Effect: Studies in Governmentality*. London: Harvester Wheatsheaf, pp. 197–210.

Ewald, F. (1999a) 'Foucault and the contemporary scene', *Philosophy and Social Criticism* 25 (3): 81–91.

Ewald, F. (1999b) 'The return of the crafty genius: an outline of the philosophy of precaution', *Connecticut Insurance Law Journal* 6 (1): 47–79.

Ferguson, A. (1819) *An Essay on the History of Civil Society*, 8th edn. Philadelphia, PA: A. Finley.

Fischer, K. (2009) 'The influence of neoliberals in Chile before, during and after Pinochet', in P. Mirowski and D. Plehwe (eds), *The Road from Mont Pèlerin: The Making of the Neoliberal Thought Collective*. Cambridge, MA: Harvard University Press, pp. 307–46.

Flew, A. (1982) 'Introduction' to T. Malthus, *An Essay on the Principle of Population*. Harmondsworth: Penguin, pp. 7–56.

Foley, D.K. (2006) *Adam's Fallacy: A Guide to Economic Theology*. Cambridge, MA: Harvard University Press.

Foucault, M. (1970) *The Order of Things: An Archaeology of the Human Sciences*. London: Tavistock.

Foucault, M. (1972) *The Archaeology of Knowledge*. London: Tavistock.

Foucault, M. (1977) *Discipline and Punish: The Birth of the Prison*. London: Allen Lane.

Foucault, M. (1979) *The History of Sexuality*, vol. 1. *An Introduction*. London: Allen Lane.

Foucault, M. (1980) *Power/Knowledge: Selected Interviews and Other Writings 1972–1977* (edited by C. Gordon). Brighton: Harvester.

Foucault, M. (1984) *The Foucault Reader* (edited by P. Rabinow). London: Penguin.

Foucault, M. (1985) *The Use of Pleasure*. New York: Pantheon.

Foucault, M. (1988a) 'The ethic of the care of the self as a practice of freedom', in J. Bernauer and D. Rasmussen (eds), *The Final Foucault*. Cambridge, MA: MIT Press, pp. 1–20.

Foucault, M. (1988b) 'The return of morality', *Politics, Philosophy, Culture: Interviews and Other Writings, 1977–1984* (edited by L. D. Kritzman). New York: London, pp. 242–54.

Foucault, M. (1997) *The Essential Works 1954–1984*, vol. 1. *Ethics, Subjectivity and Truth* (edited by P. Rabinow). London: Allen Lane.

Foucault, M. (2001) *The Essential Works 1954–1984*, vol. 3. *Power* (edited by James Faubion). London: Allen Lane.

Foucault, M. (2003) *"Society Must be Defended", Lectures at the Collège de France, 1975–1976*. New York: Picador.

Foucault, M. (2004a) *Naissance de la Biopolitique. Cours au Collège de France, 1978–1979*. Paris: Gallimard/Seuil.

Foucault, M. (2004b) *Sécurité, Territoire, Population. Cours au Collège de France, 1977–1978*. Paris: Gallimard/Seuil.

Foucault, M. (2005) *The Hermeneutics of the Subject, Lectures at the Collège de France, 1981–1982*. New York: Picador.

Foucault, M. (2007) *Security, Territory, Population, Lectures at the Collège de France, 1977–1978*. London: Palgrave.

Foucault, M. (2008) *The Birth of Biopolitics, Lectures at the Collège de France, 1978–1979*. London: Palgrave.

Foucault, M. (2010) *The Government of Self and Others, Lectures at the Collège de France, 1982–1983*. London: Palgrave.

Foucault, M. (2011) *The Courage of Truth: the Government of Self and Others II, Lectures at the Collège de France, 1983–1984*. London: Palgrave.

Frazier-Anderson, P.N. (2008) 'Public schooling in post-Hurricane Katrina New Orleans: are charter schools the solution or part of the problem?', *Journal of African American History* 93 (3): 410–29.

Friedman, M. (1968) *Dollars and Deficits*. Englewood Cliffs, NJ: Prentice-Hall.

Friedman, M. (2005) 'The promise of vouchers', *Wall Street Journal*, 5 December 2005. Available at http://www.edreform.com/Resources/Editorials/?The_Promise_of_Vouchers&year=2005 (accessed 15 April 2011).

Friedrich, C. (1955) 'Review: the political thought of neo-liberalism', *American Political Science Review* 49 (2): 509–25.

Gallie, W.B. (1956) 'Essentially contested concepts', *Proceedings of the Aristotelian Society* 56: 167–98.

Goldschmidt, N. and Rauchenschwandtner, H. (2007) 'The philosophy of Social Market Economy: Michel Foucault's analysis of Ordoliberalism', Freiburg Discussion Papers on Constitutional Economics, 07/4. Freiburg: Walter Eucken Institute.

Habermas, J. (1971) 'Discussion on value-freedom and objectivity', in O. Stammler (ed.), *Max Weber and Sociology Today*. Oxford: Basil Blackwell, pp. 59–66.

Hannah, M.G. (2011) 'Biopower, life and left politics', *Antipode* 4 (3): 1034–45.

Hardt, M. and Negri, A. (2000) *Empire*. Cambridge, MA: Harvard University Press.

Harvey, D. (2005) *A Short History of Neoliberalism*. Oxford: Oxford University Press.

Haugaard, M. (2010) 'Power: a "family resemblance" concept', *European Journal of Cultural Studies* 13 (4): 419–38.

Hayek, F.A. (1967a) 'Opening address to a conference at Mont Pèlerin', in *Studies in Philosophy, Politics and Economics*. London: Routledge and Kegan Paul, pp. 148–60.

Hayek, F.A. (1967b) 'The theory of complex phenomena', in *Studies in Philosophy, Politics and Economics*. London: Routledge and Kegan Paul, pp. 22–42.

Hayek, F.A. (1976) *Law, Legislation and Liberty*, vol. 2: *The Mirage of Social Justice*. London: Routledge and Kegan Paul.

Hayek, F.A. (1979) *Law, Legislation and Liberty*, vol. 3: *The Political Order of a Free People*. London: Routledge and Kegan Paul.

Hayek, F.A. (2001) *The Road to Serfdom*. London: Routledge.

Heidegger, M. (1993) *Basic Writings*, rev. edn (edited by D. F. Krell). London: Routledge.

Hennis, W. (1983) 'Max Weber's "central question"', *Economy and Society* 12 (2): 135–80.

Hexter, J.H. (1957) '*Il principe* and *lo stato*', *Studies in the Renaissance* 4: 113–38.

Hill, L. (2006) *The Passionate Society: the Social, Political and Moral Thought of Adam Ferguson*. Dordrecht: Springer.

Hindness, B. (1996) *Discourses of Power: From Hobbes to Foucault*. Oxford: Blackwell.

Hindess, B. (1997) 'Politics and governmentality', *Economy and Society* 26 (2): 257–72.

Hirst, P. (1988) 'Carl Schmitt: decisionism and politics', *Economy and Society* 17 (2): 272–82.

Hirst, P. (2004) *Space and Power: Politics, War and Architecture*. Cambridge: Polity.

Hobbes, T. (1996) *Leviathan*. Cambridge: Cambridge University Press.

Hunter, I. (1998) 'Uncivil society: liberal government and the deconfessionalisation of politics', in M. Dean and B. Hindess (eds), *Governing Australia: Studies in Contemporary Rationalities of Government*. Cambridge: Cambridge University Press, pp. 242–64.

Kantorowicz, E. H. (1946) *Laudes Regiae: A Study in Liturgical Acclamations and Mediaeval Ruler Worship*. Berkeley, CA: University of California Press.

Kempner, R. and Schmitt, C. (1987) 'Interrogation of Carl Schmitt by Robert Kempner (I–III)', *Telos* 72: 97–107.

Klein, N. (2008) *The Shock Doctrine: The Rise of Disaster Capitalism*. London: Allen Lane.

Koskenniemi, M. (2002) *The Gentle Civilizer of Nations: The Rise and Fall of International Law 1870–1960*. Cambridge: Cambridge University Press.

Koskenniemi, M. (2004) 'International law as political theology: how to read *Nomos der Erde*?', *Constellations* 11 (4): 492–511.

Langbein, J. (1977) *Torture and the Law of Proof: Europe and England in the Ancient Regime*. Chicago, IL: Chicago University Press.

Langbein, J. (2006) *Torture and the Law of Proof: Europe and England in the Ancient Regime*, 2nd edn. Chicago, IL: Chicago University Press.

Latour, B. (2005) *Reassembling the Social: An Introduction to Actor-Network Theory*. Oxford: Oxford University Press.

Lazzarato, M. (2009) 'Neoliberalism in action: inequality, insecurity and the reconstitution of the social', *Theory, Culture and Society* 29 (6): 109–33.

Leibniz, G.W. (1951) *Theodicy: Essays on the Goodness of God, the Freedom of Man, and the Origin of Evil*. London: Routledge and Kegan Paul.

Lemke, T. (2001) "The birth of bio-politics": Michel Foucault's lecture at the Collège de France on neo-liberal governmentality', *Economy and Society* 30 (2): 190–207.

Lemke, T. (2010) *Biopolitics: An Advanced Introduction*. New York: New York University Press.

Locke, J. (1960) *Two Treatises of Government*. Cambridge: Cambridge University Press.

Löwith, K. (1949) *Meaning in History*. Chicago, IL: University of Chicago Press.

Lukes, S. (1974) *Power: A Radical View*. London: Macmillan.

Macey, D. (1993) *The Lives of Michel Foucault*. London: Hutchinson.

Macfie, A. (1971) 'The invisible hand of Jupiter', *Journal of the History of Ideas* 32 (4): 595–9.

Malthus, T.R. (1982) *An Essay on the Principle of Population*, 1st edn. Harmondsworth: Penguin.

Malthus, T.R. (1804). *An Essay on the Principle of Population*, rev. edn. London: Ward, Lock and Co.

Mauss, M. (2003) *On Prayer*. New York: Durkheim Press/Berghahn Books.

McCormick, J. P. (2004) 'Identifying or exploiting the paradoxes of constitutional democracy? An introduction to Carl Schmitt's *Legality and Legitimacy*', in C. Schmitt, *Legality and Legitimacy*. Durham, NC: Duke University Press, pp. xiii–xliii.

Minca, C. (2009) 'Guest Editorial. The Reign and the Glory, or reflections on the theological foundations of the credit crunch', *Environment and Planning D: Society and Space* 27 (2): 177–82.

Minson, J. (1980) 'Strategies for socialists? Foucault's conception of power', *Economy and Society* 9 (1): 1–43.

Mirowski, P. and Plehwe, D. (eds) (2009) *The Road from Mont Pèlerin: The Making of the Neoliberal Thought Collective*. Cambridge, MA: Harvard University Press.

Mouffe, C. (1993) *The Return of the Political*. London: Verso.

Müller, J-W. (2003) *A Dangerous Mind: Carl Schmitt in Post-war European Thought*. New Haven, CT: Yale University Press.

Mulvaney, D.J. (1983) 'Gillen, Francis James (1855–1912)', *Australian Dictionary of Biography*, vol. 9. Melbourne: Melbourne University Press, pp. 6–7.

Nelson, R.H. (2004) 'What is economic theology?', *Princeton Seminary Bulletin* (New Series) 25 (1): 58–79.

Ojakangas, M. (2005) 'Impossible dialogue on bio-power: Agamben and Foucault', *Foucault Studies* 2: 5–28.

Ong, A. (2006) *Neoliberalism as Exception: Mutations in Citizenship and Sovereignty*. Durham, NC: Duke University Press.

Palaver, W. (2007) 'Challenging capitalism as religion: Hans G. Ulrich's theological and ethical reflections on the economy', *Studies in Christian Ethics* 20 (2): 215–30.

Pasquino, P. (1993) 'The political theory of war and peace: Foucault and the history of modern political theory', *Economy and Society* 22 (1): 77–88.

Peck, J. (2010) 'Zombie neoliberalism and the ambidextrous state', *Theoretical Criminology* 14 (1): 104–10.

Peterson, E. (2011) *Theological Tractates*. Stanford, CA: Stanford University Press.

Plato (1952) *The Statesman*. Loeb Classic Library. London: Heinemann.

Pocock, J.G.A. (1975) *The Machiavellian Moment: Florentine Political Thought and the Atlantic Republican Tradition*. Princeton, NJ: Princeton University Press.

Polanyi, K. (1957) *The Great Transformation*. Boston, MA: Beacon Press.

Poynter, J.R. (1969) *Society and Pauperism: English Ideas on Poor Relief 1795–1834*. London: Routledge and Kegan Paul.

Procacci, G. (1978) 'Social economy and the government of poverty', *Ideology and Consciousness* 4: 55–72.

Procacci, G. (1993) *Gouverner la misère: la question sociale en France (1789–1848)*. Paris: Seuil.

Ptak, R. (2009) 'Neoliberalism in Germany: revisiting the Ordoliberal foundations of the social market economy', in P. Mirowski and D. Plehwe (eds), *The Road from Mont Pèlerin: The Making of the Neoliberal Thought Collective*. Cambridge, MA: Harvard University Press, pp. 98–138.

Rabinow, P. and Rose, N. (2006) 'Biopower today', *BioSocieties* 1 (2): 197–217.

Raulff, U (2005) 'An interview with Giorgio Agamben', *German Law Journal* 5 (5): 609–14.

Ricardo, D. (1951) 'Essay on the influence of a low price of corn on the profits of stock', in *The Works and Correspondence of David Ricardo* (edited by P. Sraffa with M. Dobb), vol. 4. Cambridge: Cambridge University Press, pp. 9–41.

Röpke, W. (1996) *The Moral Foundations of Civil Society* [Civitas Humana]. New Brunswick, NJ: Transaction Publishers.

Rose, N. (1999) *Powers of Freedom: Reframing Political Thought*. Cambridge: Cambridge University Press.

Rose, N. (2001) 'The politics of life itself', *Theory, Culture and Society* 18 (6): 1–30.

Rüstow, A. (1942) 'Appendix: general sociological causes of the economic disintegration and possibilities of reconstruction', in W. Röpke, *International Economic Disintegration*. London: William Hodge, pp. 267–83.

Saar, M. (2010) 'Power and critique', *Journal of Power* 3 (1): 7–20.

Scheuerman, W. E. (1997) 'The unholy alliance of Carl Schmitt and Friedrich A. Hayek', *Constellations* 4 (2): 172–88.

Schmitt, C. (1985) *The Crisis of Parliamentary Democracy*. Cambridge, MA: MIT Press.

Schmitt, C. (1986) *Political Romanticism*. Cambridge, MA: MIT Press.

Schmitt, C. (1987) '*Ex captivitate salus*: a poem', *Telos* 72: 130.

Schmitt, C. (1996a) *The Concept of the Political*. Chicago, IL: University of Chicago Press.

Schmitt, C. (1996b) *Roman Catholicism and Political Form*. Westport, CT: Greenwood Press.

Schmitt, C. (1997) *Land and Sea*. Corvallis, OR: Plutarch Press.

Schmitt, C. (1998) 'Strong state and sound economy', in R. Cristi, *Carl Schmitt and Authoritarian Liberalism*. Cardiff: University of Wales Press, pp. 212–32.

Schmitt, C. (2001) *State, Movement, People*. Corvallis, OR: Plutarch Press.

Schmitt, C. (2003) *The Nomos of the Earth in the International Law of Jus Publicum Europaeum*. New York: Telos Press.

Schmitt, C. (2004a) *Legality and Legitimacy*. Durham, NC: Duke University Press.

Schmitt, C. (2004b) *On the Three Types of Juristic Thought*. Westport, CT: Praeger Publishers.

Schmitt, C. (2005) *Political Theology: Four Chapters on the Concept of Sovereignty*. Chicago, IL: University of Chicago Press.

Schmitt, C. (2007) *Theory of the Partisan: Intermediate Commentary on the Concept of the Political*. New York: Telos Press.

Schmitt, C. (2008a) *Constitutional Theory*. Durham, NC: Duke University Press.

Schmitt, C. (2008b) *The Leviathan in the State Theory of Thomas Hobbes: Meaning and Failure of a Political Symbol*. Chicago, IL: University of Chicago Press.

Schmitt, C. (2008c) *Political Theology II: The Myth of the Closure of Any Political Theology*. Cambridge: Polity.

Schmitt, C. (2009) 'Three possibilities for a Christian conception of history', *Telos* 147: 167–70.

Schmitt, C. (2010) 'The age of neutralizations and depoliticizations', in *The Concept of the Political*, expanded edition. Chicago IL: Chicago University Press.

Schmitt, C. (2011) *Writings on War* (translated and edited by T. Nunan). Cambridge: Polity.

Sennelart, M. (2007) 'Course context', in M. Foucault, *Security, Territory, Population*. London: Palgrave, pp. 369–401.

Skinner, Q. (1978a) *The Foundations of Modern Political Thought*, vol. 1: *The Renaissance*. Cambridge: Cambridge University Press.

Skinner, Q. (1978b) *The Foundations of Modern Political Thought*, vol. 2: *The Age of Reformation*. Cambridge: Cambridge University Press.

Skinner, Q. (1989) 'The state', in T. Ball, J. Farr and R.L. Hanson (eds), *Political Innovation and Conceptual Change*. Cambridge: Cambridge University Press, pp. 90–131.

Skinner, Q. (1998) *Liberty before Liberalism*. Cambridge: Cambridge University Press.

Smith, A. (1976) *An Inquiry into the Nature and Causes of the Wealth of Nations* (2 vols). London: Oxford University Press.

Smith, A. (2002) *The Theory of Moral Sentiments*. Cambridge: Cambridge University Press.

Snoek, A. (2010) 'Agamben's Foucault: an overview', *Foucault Studies* 10: 44–67.

Spencer, B. and Gillen, F.J. (1899) *The Native Tribes of Central Australia*. London: Macmillan.

Strauss, L. (1996) 'Notes on Carl Schmitt, *The Concept of the Political*', in C. Schmitt, *The Concept of the Political*. Chicago, IL: University of Chicago Press, pp. 81–107.

Strong, T. B. (2005) 'Foreword', in C. Schmitt, *Political Theology: Four Chapters on the Concept of Sovereignty*. Chicago, IL: University of Chicago Press, pp. xvi–xxxv.

Taubes, J. (2004) *The Political Theology of Paul*. Stanford, CA: Stanford University Press.

Tellmann, U. (2013) 'Catastrophic populations and the fear of the future – Malthus and the genealogy of liberal economy', *Theory, Culture and Society* 30 (2): 135–55.

Toscano, A. (2011) 'Divine management: critical remarks on Giorgio Agamben's *The Kingdom and the Glory*', *Angelaki: Journal of the Theoretical Humanities* 16 (3): 125–36.

Tribe, K. (1978) *Land, Labour and Economic Discourse*. London: Routledge and Kegan Paul.

Tribe, K. (2009) 'The political economy of modernity: Foucault's Collège de France lectures of 1978 and 1979', *Economy and Society* 38 (4): 679–98.

Tuck, R. (1999) *The Rights of War and Peace: Political Thought and the International Order from Grotius to Kant*. Oxford: Oxford University Press.

Ulmen, G.L. (1985) 'The sociology of the state: Carl Schmitt and Max Weber', *State, Culture, and Society* 1 (2): 3–57.

Vasoli, C. (1977) 'The Machiavellian Moment: a grand ideological synthesis', *The Journal of Modern History* 49 (4): 661–70.

Waldby, C. and Cooper, M. (2008) 'The biopolitics of reproduction: post–Fordist biotechnology and women's clinical labour', *Australian Feminist Studies* 23 (55): 57–73.

Walker, J. and Cooper, M. (2011) 'Genealogies of resilience: from systems ecology to the political economy of crisis adaptation', *Security Dialogue* 14 (2): 143–60.

Wallace, R.M. (1985) 'Translator's introduction', in H. Blumenberg, *The Legitimacy of the Modern Age*. Cambridge, MA: MIT Press, pp. xi–xxxi.

Walters, W. and Haahr, J.H. (2005) *Governing Europe: Discourse, Governmentality and European Integration*. London: Routledge.

Weber, M. (1968) *Economy and Society: An Outline of Interpretive Sociology* (2 vols) (edited by G. Roth and C. Wittich). New York: Bedminster Press.

Weber, M. (1972) *From Max Weber: Essays in Sociology* (edited and translated by H.H. Gerth and C.W. Mills). London: Routledge and Kegan Paul.

Weber, M. (1985) *The Protestant Ethic and the Spirit of Capitalism*. London: Unwin.

Whitfield, J.H. (1978) 'Review article: The Machiavellian Moment', *European Studies Review* 8: 365–72.

Wolfe, A. (2004) 'A fascist philosopher helps us understand contemporary politics', *Chronicle of Higher Education* 50 (30): B16.

Zartaloudis, T. (2010) *Giorgio Agamben: Power, Law and the Uses of Criticism*. London: Routledge.

INDEX